The Ultimate *Walking Dead* and Philosophy

Popular Culture and Philosophy® Series Editor: George A. Reisch

For full details of all Popular Culture and Philosophy® books, visit www.opencourtbooks.com.

Popular Culture and Philosophy®

The Ultimate Walking Dead and Philosophy

Hungry for More

Edited by
WAYNE YUEN

OPEN COURT
Chicago, Illinois

Volume 97 in the series, Popular Culture and Philosophy®, edited by George A. Reisch

To find out more about Open Court books, call toll-free 1-800-815-2280, or visit our website at www.opencourtbooks.com.

Open Court Publishing Company is a division of Carus Publishing Company, dba Cricket Media.

Copyright © 2016 by Carus Publishing Company, dba Cricket Media

First printing 2016

Printed and bound in the United States of America.

ISBN: 978-0-8126-9905-0

Library of Congress Control Number: 2015956485

To my wife, thanks for fighting off the relentless tide of the dead with me.

And to Harley and Zim, welcome to the club!

Contents

Thanks

There are a lot of people to thank for helping me with this book. First and foremost, thanks to David Ramsay Steele and George Reisch for letting me do another one of these! Also thanks to all the writers, but particular thanks to Richard Greene for helping me out at short notice. Thanks to my wife who has been helpful and tolerant despite my fascination with my gut microbiome, blood sugar, and rotting corpses. Thanks to Chris Hardwick for making *The Walking Dead* fun to think about. And finally, thanks to Robert Kirkman whose work inspired everything that you are reading in this book. I can't wait to give you this at SDCC!

To the Reader

Episodes cited in this book have a season and episode number before them to help you find the episode if you want to watch it again, and to give you an idea of where the episode fits in the larger timeline of the series. For example: 5.2 "Strangers" would refer to Season Five, episode 2.

As well as the numbered chapters, there are some short contributions called "Walker Bites," which scratch the surface of a topic just enough to infect you with an idea. Whether you agree or disagree, I hope that these sharp little nips will leave you hungry for more.

Some of the chapters deal with both the comic book series and the television series (and one with the videogame). Although the TV series has been mostly faithful to the comics, there are some stark differences between the two. For example Andrea and Sophia are still alive in the comics. And because the TV show sometimes introduces events from the comics out of order, and much later than they occur in the comics, some chapters may contain spoilers even for those who are fully up to date on the TV show.

Hungry for More

Philosophy often deals with extremes. Philosophers don't set out to consider extreme situations, but we begin with normal everyday situations, like "Is it wrong to kill another human being?" Then we form a working theory or hypothesis about why we might think it is wrong to kill other human beings. Then we test and stretch it, to the point where we're asking ourselves if it's wrong to eat other human beings. We find the most extreme examples to really test our theories, intuitions, and explanations. Good theories should stand up to the most extreme scenarios.

The Walking Dead presents us with two extreme scenarios: a world where dead people are re-animated and walk around, and a world whose social, political, and economic systems have fallen apart. Both of these are extreme scenarios that are fantastically good for testing our moral, political, and religious beliefs against. It's not that we expect a zombie apocalypse to happen, but rather, if our theories about the world are good theories, then they should be able to deal with the hardest of situations. Philosophers are just dying to know that their ideas are consistent with the world, despite all the changes that could happen in the world. Non-philosophers are just hungry for answers to these questions that don't seem to have very good answers.

The most overtly dealt with question in *The Walking Dead*, in the comics, in the TV show, and in the videogames, is morality. Why should we be moral? Rick clearly isn't moral all the time, and struggles with balancing morality with survival. Why should this be a struggle at all? Should we stop everything to look for a missing girl, or should we just write her off as having looked at the flowers?

But other questions are raised like how we should treat religion in this new world, and what it says about our understanding of religion in our world. Does it give us meaning, or can we find that meaning somewhere else? Maybe in how we structure our society? We've seen plenty of attempts at a society in the TV series, such as the Prison, Woodbury, Terminus, Grady Memorial Hospital, Alexandria, and those are just the ones that have concrete locations. How these societies interact, conflict, and dissolve can help us understand the world that we live in, where nations are failing, wars are fought over resources, and people protest unjust political rule.

Yes, it's fiction. Yes, there are zombies in it. Yes, if Daryl dies, we riot. But the issues, characters, and world that *The Walking Dead* presents us are mirrors that we see our own values in. This isn't just a hypothetical scenario, because we're tested every day as to what values we're willing to give up, as against which values we refuse to compromise on.

We might not turn into zombies, but we can become the Walking Dead without them. Philosophy helps us understand our values and assumptions about the world; it clarifies them and justifies them. By reading these essays, I hope that you get a better sense of what you believe, even if you don't agree with the authors (You won't agree with all of them!), and maybe you'll know why you don't agree too.

That makes you one of us, a living philosopher hungry for more, not the Walking Dead.

I

Afraid of Being Alive?

1
Reading the Signs

SABATINO DIBERNARDO

Besides, you never were very religious.

—"LORI" (RICK) GRIMES

For those of us bitten by *The Walking Dead* in its television or graphic novel versions, an infection of sorts courses through our veins causing us to consume and be consumed by all things undead. Unlike the infectious disease in *The Walking Dead*, however, this infectious desire desires no cure; only a philosophical therapy—a *Philosophizing Dead*. Why?

If you find yourself asking "why?" a lot, it may be symptomatic of a philosophical virus already present in your cognitive system—just like the "secret" whispered into Rick's ear by the CDC's Dr. Edwin Jenner (1.6 "TS-19")—you're already infected.

What are we to make of Robert Kirkman's post-apocalyptic world in which the fulfillment of religion's most prophetic tendency has come to pass in an oddly religious apocalypse and resurrection of the dead? What is being communicated in the comics by the ironic second coming of Jesus (Paul Monroe) as a kick-ass, machine-gun-toting, ninja warrior looking to gather people into his fold while sermonizing about the "mount" (the Hilltop) and the oppressive rule of Negan? How are we to understand the pervasive religious language of salvation, sanctuary, sacrifice, sin, redemption, martyrs, and saviors, among many other religious terms?

Put simply, why do we find so much religion in *The Walking Dead*? We'll see. But in order to help us "see," a common reli-

3

gious metaphor, we'll have to read the religious signs and symptoms of *The Walking Dead*'s post-apocalyptic times. The lens through which we'll read the signs is one used by philosophers as diverse as Socrates, Søren Kierkegaard, and Friedrich Nietzsche, among others—irony. Although in its basic form irony is a literary device in which you say the opposite of what you mean, we'll emphasize the ways in which Kirkman and the writers of the AMC series use irony as "a doubleness of sense or meaning" (as Claire Colebrook puts it in her book, *Irony*) in dialogue or situational contexts to communicate something about religion. We'll have to pay close attention to the dialogues, signs, and visual imagery through which irony accomplishes its philosophical commentary.

Religion Lost and Found

We're *surrounded* by proof that the Bible was *wrong.*

—Maggie Greene

Being lost and found is a very common religious conversion theme as seen in the parables of the lost sheep and the prodigal son, for example, and the lyrics of "Amazing Grace." So, too, is a related religious theme that turns on the living-yet-dead as physically alive and spiritually dead; or, like Lazarus, biologically dead then alive.

When opposites or multiple meanings are maintained simultaneously, we encounter the philosophical concept of irony in a broad sense. This style of indirect communication appears throughout *The Walking Dead*. While the religious language, themes, and imagery found in *The Walking Dead* may be overlooked or written off as simply a nod by Kirkman to yet another pre-apocalyptic remnant of "Days Gone Bye," there may be more than a simple nod at work here; more like an ironic *wink* and a nod.

In one sense, *The Walking Dead* series finds religion by its inclusion of traditionally recognized religious texts (the Bible), religious places (churches, the kingdom, the Hilltop), religious imagery (crucifixes, crosses, the last supper), religious names (Jesus, Gabriel, Ezekiel, Aaron, Abraham, Samuel, Ethan, Shiva, Judith), and religious dispositions (faith, trust, belief, spirituality). In another sense, the *Walking Dead* characters find religion ironically. In the second season's premiere (2.1 "What Lies Ahead"), religion is found in a small church in rural Georgia.

In their desperation to find Sophia, which means wisdom—in their *loving* search for *wisdom* (*philo-sophia*), they find religion instead. The group hears the ringing of church bells in the distance. Alarmed by this walker dinner bell, they race off to discover its source. Spotting the church, they traverse a graveyard (the dead dead) as the camera pans to the marquee: Southern Baptist Church of Holy Light. Beneath the name of the church remains the final ironic Bible verse prior to the apocalypse: Revelation 16:17. This verse is from the Book of Revelation in the Christian scriptures; it is also known as the Apocalypse, which means uncovering or unveiling.

Sadly, the only revelation disclosed by the ringing bells is that they're on an automatic timer. As Rick, Shane, Daryl, and Glenn enter the house of worship, they're shocked to find a walking or, rather, a "sitting" dead congregation of three transfixed in a seemingly reverential demeanor in the pews with soulless (Jesus, in the comics, calls them "empties") eyes gazing on one of the first resurrected living dead on an enormous crucifix. Although the crucifix, icons, and candelabras that adorn the church are quite out of place for a Southern Baptist church, the ironic implications of these symbols will come to light in Season Five of the television show.

Given the unanticipated apocalypse and the resurrection of the walking dead, you might think that this would result in the loss of religion or faith rather than its perpetuation. If we recall Maggie's epigraph above in response to Hershel's Bible-thumping in the comics, which is softened a bit in the television series, we find that she's lost her religion (cue REM song) due to her reading of the bizarre signs of the times. Since religion has always been a matter of interpretation (hermeneutics in philosophy-speak) and faith (Latin, *fides*: trust), it's no wonder that Hershel has a different reading of these signs: "Proof? Depending on your interpretation this could be proof of the Bible being *right*. It's all about faith, honey" (Volume 7, "The Calm Before"). Hershel doesn't see an ironic resurrection of the dead that calls his religious beliefs into question but, rather, one that points to a rapture and seven years' tribulation. This is all chalked up to a test of faith, which is a common, if philosophically problematic, "justification" for the existence of evil despite God's absolute goodness and power; in philosophy of religion this is known as a theodicy.

In the most explicit and extended religious dialogue in the comics, Father Gabriel Stokes points to the walking dead as a sign of the confirmation of his beliefs; but not Eugene Porter: "But the living dead doesn't make me believe in the existence of a God" (Volume 11: "Fear the Hunters"). A parallel exchange is found in 5.2 "Strangers," when Father Gabriel, sitting on a rock, another biblical metaphor, surrounded by walkers, is rescued by Rick's group. In response to their questioning, he states that "The word of God is the only protection I need." Since you can always count on Daryl for irreverent sarcasm, he suggests, "It sure didn't look like it." To which Gabriel responds, "I called for help; help came."

If we focus our attention on the development of the church scenes from the comics to the AMC series, we'll notice that the comics stick to a pretty traditional treatment of the churches without naming them or using them as sites for dramatic effect or ironic commentary, sticking mainly to religious dialogue for its irony:

Comics:

Volume 11, "Fear the Hunters": The group encounters Father Gabriel Stokes; they go to his unnamed church; there's a large crucifix next to the altar; Andrea prays; Dale gets cannibalized; Rick and the group kill the cannibals at their camp.

Volume 13, "Too Far Gone": Alexandria Safe-Zone community; traditional church service led by Father Gabriel in an unnamed church.

Volume 17, "Something to Fear": Hilltop community; traditional church service led by Father Gabriel in an unnamed church.

In the AMC series, however, the explicit development of the church scenes amps up the situational and contextual irony:

AMC Series:

2.1 "What Lies Ahead": Southern Baptist Church; "sitting dead" walkers in the church; slaughter of the walkers in the church; no priest; no traditional church service; oversized crucified Jesus takes center stage; prayers, ironic or otherwise, offered to Jesus by multiple characters; use of scriptural verses on the marquee produces ironic effect.

5.3 "Four Walls and a Roof": Saint Sarah's Episcopal Church; Father Gabriel is present; no traditional church service; religious iconography emphasized; use of multiple scriptural verses in the church and a change of religious denomination produce an increased ironic effect for theological reasons; the group has its own "last supper" in the church; themes of forgiveness in the dialogue; slaughter of the cannibals in the church.

One pivotal church scene sums up the ironic commentary regarding religion toward which *The Walking Dead* has been moving steadily. We're invited to think about the slaughter of the walkers in the church as somehow "sacrilegious"; the "sacrilege" is compounded, and made explicit, by the slaughter of the cannibals from Terminus. In response to what Gabriel calls a "sacrilege" in "the Lord's house," Maggie provides the critical commentary toward which the irony throughout *The Walking Dead* has been pointing: "No. It's just four walls and a roof." There is nothing sacred about these sanctuaries and, consequently, there is nothing sacrilegious about these acts.

And one pivotal scriptural verse sums up the ironic treatment of religion as the human consumption of flesh and blood revered as a sacred act with eternal consequences:

He who eats My Flesh and drinks My Blood has eternal life . . .

This verse (John 6:54) uttered by Jesus turns on the metaphysical belief in the real flesh and blood of Jesus located in the consecrated bread (flesh) and wine (blood), its consumption by the believer, and its relation to the resurrection of the dead for certain sacramental Christian traditions other than Southern Baptists; so much so that early Christians were accused of being cannibals. The AMC series emphasizes this irony as it relates to consuming flesh and blood by the walkers and the cannibals from Terminus in order to sustain their "lives." Clues related to the resurrection of the dead are provided in the scriptural readings that flank either side of the quotation above signaling the irony:

- **Romans 6:4: Therefore we have been buried with Him through baptism into death, so that as Christ was raised from the dead through the glory of the Father, so we too might walk in newness of life.**

- **Ezekiel 37:7: So I prophesied as I was commanded; and as I prophesied, there was a noise, and behold, a rattling; and the bones came together, bone to its bone.**

- **Matthew 27:52: The tombs were opened, and many bodies of the saints who had fallen asleep were raised . . .**

- **Revelation 6:9: When the Lamb broke the fifth seal, I saw underneath the altar the souls of those who had been slain because of the word of God, and because of the testimony which they had maintained . . .**

- **Luke 24:5: And as the women were terrified and bowed their faces to the ground, the men said to them, "Why do you seek the living One among the dead?"**

Since parallels of John 6:54 in other gospels were uttered by Jesus at the Last Supper, the wood carving of the Last Supper in Gabriel's church and the "reenactment" of the communal meal and wine shared by the group during this episode highlight the situational ironies.

So, what philosophical takeaway may be gleaned by the ironic treatment of these church scenes? In AMC's first church episode (2.1 "What Lies Ahead"), it's tempting to speculate that while religion may turn us into unquestioning "walkers" sitting unthinkingly in the pews, the "walkers" may turn us toward unquestioning pleas for a sign from "religion." However, when we add the second set of church sequences from Season Five, this critical commentary draws out a further ironic layer. The "eternal life" that results from the consumption of flesh and blood is an ironically resurrected walker "life" or the living dead. And in the absence of any recognized moral authority or civility, walkers and non-walkers are free to feed on or slaughter each other: "butcher or cattle."

Signs of the Times

The signs are all there, but you gotta know how to read 'em.

—DARYL DIXON

You're probably familiar with street-corner evangelists displaying cardboard warnings of their discernment or interpretation of the "signs of the times" (Matthew 16:3): "The end is near . . . Repent." Similarly, the book of Revelation is all about signs and judgments and the all-too-familiar violence, blood, and plagues.

If religion, especially apocalyptic religion, is all about reading the signs of the (end) times and belief, so, too, in *The Walking Dead* quite a lot turns on signs and knowing "how to read 'em." When Daryl provides sage advice to Beth Greene while teaching her how to track (4.13 "Alone"), we find a hint of the doubleness or duplicity of signs at work again. Even Rick, who claims he's "not much of a believer" while offering up a desperate prayer, is looking for a sign from Jesus to keep them going: "Some kinda acknowledgement, some indication I'm doing the right thing . . . a nudge, a sign; any sign will do" (2.1 "What Lies Ahead"). A similar biblical interaction occurs when the disciples ask Jesus, "What then do You do for a sign, so that we may see, and believe You?" (John 6:30)

One of the first signs encountered by Rick in the television series (1.1 "Days Gone Bye") is a spray-painted warning frantically written—no time to include the apostrophe—across chained double doors in the hospital after Rick awakens from a coma:

DONT   DEAD

OPEN   INSIDE

It's evident that this sign points to the walkers behind the doors. But for fans, it's hard not to read this as foreshadowing Rick's psychological difficulties that await him in future episodes as well as signifying all those walkers and non-walkers who are existentially dead inside. The next sign is encountered after an attack on the prison by the governor that scatters Rick's group:

SANCTUARY
FOR ALL
COMMUNITY
FOR ALL
THOSE WHO ARRIVE
SURVIVE

Sanctuary is a religious term derived from the Latin *sanctus* (holy), which came to mean a sacred place of refuge, safety, and, ultimately, survival from external threats. In both the comics and the television series, we encounter this term when the group meets Father Gabriel, who offers his church as a sanctuary in exchange for some food. Later, Gabriel confesses his not-so-priestly sins against his own congregation: "They wanted a safe place to stay—a sanctuary. I turned them all away . . ." (Volume 11: "Fear the Hunters"; similarly, 5.3 "Four Walls and a Roof"). While arrival should equal survival, the unknown variable is the trustworthiness of those offering sanctuary. When this sign is coupled with the next sign, the group arrives at the ambiguous end of their quest.

LOWER YOUR
WEAPONS
YOU WILL BE MET
YOU HAVE ARRIVED AT
TERMINUS

If you Google "terminus," you'll find that it's a Latin term meaning end, boundary, final goal, or endpoint, and that Terminus was the Roman god of boundaries and ends—more religion. The last episode of Season Four left us wondering how to read this final term at the end of the road—Terminus—through which the group's end will be determined: will these characters live to full term or will their lives be terminated in a dead end at "the end of the line?" Is it an end *in* or *of* sanctuary? Quite a bit hangs in the balance depending on how they read this sign and how much they trust their reading. In the premiere episode of Season Five, the end is resolved when Rick smears mud across the sign leading to Terminus and adds a muddy gloss:

NO
SANCTUARY

Investing Trust

I was testing you—and you *passed.* I *trusted* you.

—JESUS

In 2.1 "What Lies Ahead," Rick's crisis of faith opens the scene as he tries to contact Morgan. His existential anxiety over his loss of faith and its implications are revisited during the church scene when three "prayers" are offered up. From Carol's piously reverential prayer to Rick's prayer of the "unbeliever" requesting some "sign" (whose "faith" is in his family, friends, and job) to the ironic "prayer" by Daryl ("Hey, J.C., you taking requests?"), the double-dealing signification of "faith" and "prayer" are on display.

In another ironic exchange in the comics between Rick and Jesus (the samurai bad-ass, not the Christians' savior), Jesus tries to explain his understanding of Rick's disbelief: "You got a guy telling you about a better place, a new way of life . . . Why would you believe him?" But Rick continues with more questions and concludes: "I'm sorry . . . but I just don't believe you" (Volume 16: "A Larger World"). What's at stake in these various sequences? Faith, trust, and belief communicated through ironic interactions with "Jesus."

Another possible clue related to the ironic treatment of faith, trust, and belief may be found in the conspicuous display of Jesus's night-time reading material: *Gulliver's Travels*, by Jonathan Swift. Not coincidentally, in this panel Jesus's partner states: "The ever-wily Paul Monroe . . . You'll never get one over on him" (Alex, Volume 21: "All Out War," Part II). *Gulliver's Travels* is described by Colebrook as an "ironic travelogue of the gullible Gulliver who moves through a series of fantastic lands all of which provide material for him to "reflect upon, criticise, and celebrate his original home of England."

Swift's book narrates the fictional adventures of Lemuel Gulliver and his encounters with different cultures populated by miniature people, gigantic people, academics on a floating island, rational horses that can speak, and beastly, human-like Yahoos that cannot speak, among others. Swift satirizes the different cultures' self-righteous trust in their moral or rational superiority based on their respective philosophical, religious, and political beliefs. Similarly, Kirkman's tale of post-apocalyptic communities and their respective philosophical, religious, and political beliefs functions as an ironic critique of faith and trust in these beliefs by raising existential questions regarding moral or rational superiority by foregrounding the ever-present tension between trust and doubt. Kirkman's inclusion of *Gulliver's Travels* signals an ironic commentary on the fictional travels of Rick and other survivors in a post-apocalyptic world that repays gullibility with death or undeath.

Finally, in a panel drawn like a religious painting in the comics, Jesus provides his own ironic profession of faith: "You're a leader we can *follow*" (Volume 19: "March to War"). The ironic reversal is complete: Jesus—the follower—believes, trusts, and confesses faith in Rick—the leader. Rick's "savior" role is solidified by Maggie's passionate profession of faith in Rick: "If there's *one* thing in this world that I'm certain of . . . I know *this* . . . *I believe in Rick Grimes*" (Volume 20: "All Out War," Part I). And in Volume 22 of the comics ("A New Beginning"), Rick's "religious" status as worshipped by the community foretold by Jesus comes to pass.

What's at stake philosophically is the difficult existential necessity of a this-worldly faith, trust, and belief based on ambiguous signs rather than on unconditional faith. There's nothing unconditional or free here (show me the ~~money~~ . . . trust). Investing trust with an expectation of a return is the name of the "economic" game that plays itself out in *The Walking Dead*. But, as with investments in general, there's no guarantee of a return on your investment of faith, trust, or belief in another person, God, or even yourself, if Rick's any example. And, perhaps, the critical commentary is that this not-so-unconditional exchange is also found in religion.

Notions of sacrifice, redemption, which means to buy back or reclaim, and debt are central to Christianity and require faith, trust, and belief just like monetary or credit systems. Take the redemptive sacrifice of Jesus for the sins of humanity through which he pays a debt that could never be repaid otherwise. Only through an exchange of faith, trust, and belief in this act can one be redeemed. If you're also a *South Park* fan, check out 13.3 "Margaritaville" and the ironic treatment of this religious exchange: Kyle, fittingly, a Jewish character, sacrifices himself and his credit (Latin, *credere*: to believe) in Jesus-like fashion to pay the debt of the consumerist South Park residents for their sins against "the Economy" with his American Express card. So, what's the point?

- **Because "secular language" is used in religious contexts, a secular reading of religion may be possible.**

- **Because "religious language" is used in secular contexts, a religious reading of the secular may be possible.**

- **Because terms such as faith, trust, belief, debt and credit, among others, signify in both contexts, we have the possibility of ironic doubling and critical commentary.**

- **Because irony calls into question the supposedly mutually exclusive contexts or "language games" of both, each discourse may be viewed as "infecting" the other.**

Trust in signs, often yielding potential double meanings, is common to both religious and secular contexts: If you want me to have faith in you, trust you, and believe in you toward whatever religious or secular end, you'll have to show me some signs that you're faithful, trustworthy, or believable; but since I can never be certain that I'm not mistaken or being deceived, there's always a risk. That's the ongoing secular-religious dilemma and ironic commentary in *The Walking Dead*, where faith, trust, and belief become the most valuable of "currencies" in a post-apocalyptic world with pre-apocalyptic existential implications as well.

NEVER AGAIN NEVER TRUST WE FIRST, ALWAYS.

So ends the finale of Season Four—our terminal sign—with this enigmatic "writing on the walls" of an inner room in Terminus ceremoniously lit by candles like some religious or cultic ritual. What type of sign could this be? Is it a cynical negative imperative or a quasi-religious commandment? Or, is it just some well-intentioned word-to-the-wise from those in the post-apocalyptic know?

The premiere of Season Five provides the backstory for this sign and its changing significance from non-ironic to ironic based on the circumstances that turned a trusting, idealistic bunch into a fine-tuned machine of butchery for their acquired cannibalistic appetites. But this contextual change only underscores the paradoxical nature of the sign by generating a double bind: If you trust the sign, you transgress it; if you distrust the sign, you transgress it. Either way, philosophically speaking, you're S.O.L. How do you invest trust in a sign that requires trust in not trusting? And if the intention of the sign could change based on a change of context ("The signs . . . they were real. It was a sanctuary." Terminus Mary, 5.1 "No Sanctuary"), couldn't it change again in an endless game of intentionality?

(Trust Me) Never Trust. This paradoxical predicament is the ironic double bind that confronts the characters in *The Walking Dead* and us in our daily interpersonal interactions as an implicit "trust me" or "believe me" structure to our statements. This is the necessary yet uncertain nature of trust given the ever-present possibility of being deceived or mistaken. As with any investment, the absence of certainty or absolute knowledge highlights the risks involved with any investment in trust—religious or otherwise. So, in order to minimize, while not eliminating, this existential risk, Rick's group develops its own secular-religious ritual of inclusion—a confessional questioning:

How many walkers have you killed?
How many humans have you killed?
Why?

And at the end of the pre- *or* post-apocalyptic day, what's reinforced is the necessity and uncertainty of faith, trust, and belief yielding another "confessional" questioning:

In whom do you trust?
To what end?
Why?

Dead Reckoning

Today's the day of reckoning, sir.

—JOE (THE CLAIMER)

In one of the most visceral scenes in the television series, Rick, pushed to his psychological breaking point in order to protect Carl, turns "biter" as he gnashes his teeth deep into Joe's throat. In this bloody scene, television Rick makes good on comic book Rick's statement: "We *are* the walking dead!" (Volume 4: "The Heart's Desire") and the ironic day of reckoning has arrived.

If apocalyptic religion has always been about a day of reckoning, existence itself reveals our individual reckoning with death through our own unique apocalypse or terminus—our own "dead reckoning." The Greek philosopher Epicurus argued in his *Letter to Menoeceus*, "Death, the most dreaded of evils, is therefore of no concern to us; for while we exist death is not present, and when death is present we no longer exist." While this may have soothed those for whom Hades offered only a fearful, shadowy afterlife, it's unlikely to provide much relief when reckoning with the irony of death *and* not death *both* being present in the shadowy afterlife of the undead.

Similarly, as a naval metaphor indicating true north, a dead reckoning may be as necessary as it is impossible; unless what one reckons is the death of all such absolute reckoning in the aftermath of the annihilation of all "true" cultural and religious direction. Nietzsche's prophetic parable "In the horizon of the infinite" also uses a naval analogy to explain the uncertain or foundationless place of existence after the death of God and absolute metaphysical values or standards: "We have left the land and have embarked . . . and there is no longer any 'land!'" (*The Gay Science*, Section 124).

In Nietzsche's parable "The madman" (Section 125), this recognition of the absence of all absolute direction, meaning, and value takes on biblical proportions. Nietzsche asks if we've not heard of the madman who was looking for God with a lantern during one morning in the market place, only to be met with derisive laughter and sarcastic questioning from those who had ceased believing in God: "Has he got lost? asked one. Did he lose his way like a child? asked another. Or is he hiding? Is he afraid of us? Has he gone on a voyage? emigrated?" To which the madman with piercing glances responds: "*We have killed him*—you and I." He then proceeds to ask how this is possible: "How could we drink up the sea? Who gave us the sponge to wipe away the entire horizon? What were we doing when we unchained this earth from its sun? Whither is it moving now? Whither are we moving? Away from all suns? Are we not plunging continually? Backward, sideward, forward, in all directions? Is there still any up or down? Are we not straying as through an infinite nothing?"

The madman continues along this line of questioning noting the infinite darkness that descends upon the world, requiring lanterns in the morning, with the death of God and all absolute metaphysical meaning and value. Given the immensity of this act of deicide, the madman asks, "Must we ourselves not become gods simply to appear worthy of it?" After this proclamation, the madman looks at the silent and astonished crowd, throws down his lantern, and states ironically: "I have come too early . . . my time is not yet" and thereby echoes and opposes a similar proclamation by Jesus as one who has come too early (John 7: 6–8).

Even though his listeners included those who did not believe in God, they did not have ears to hear the madman's all-too-early pronouncement; they were not yet ready to understand the full implications of the death of God, whose influence continues "living" long after he is "dead." The same morals and values were still influencing Western thought and culture, even though in the place of God some other humanly constructed absolute had filled the void. Afterward, the madman was said to have gone into various churches asking, "What after all are these churches now if they are not the tombs and sepulchers of God?" As we saw in the AMC series church scenes, echoes of Nietzsche's questions resonate as the death of God, murder, madness, and religion take place not within a church but, rather, four walls and a roof. The obliteration of all absolute metaphysical standards, limits, boundaries, or ends sets us adrift without the possibility of any absolute sense of direction, true north, or a dead reckoning.

Finally, Kirkman and company's secular-religious parable of walkers in their ironic apocalyptic book of revelation, perhaps inadvertently, provides us with a new secular-sacred narrative; even if, like Nietzsche's madman, it has "come too early." For those unfortunates without eyes to see, all they see is a "zombie" tale rather than a critical commentary on religious and metaphysical desires and the all-too-human tendencies that threaten existence once the thin layer of civility is gone. In the end, the religion that *The Walking Dead* finds is symptomatic of an infectious desire that continues to plague a post-apocalyptic world contaminated by another infection. Its ironic revelation of an undead "resurrection" mimics apocalyptic religion while standing it on its head by calling into question the religious and metaphysical desires for signs of absolute truth, meaning, and value in a world "without appeal"—for some sign that "everything works out the way it's supposed to" (Mika, 4.14 "The Grove") or that "God has a plan for everyone" (Father Gabriel, Volume 11: "Fear the Hunters").

The Walking Dead serves as an ironic warning sign, warning us against putting absolute faith, trust, and belief in signs—religious or otherwise. Why? Because they may not turn out to be how we "read 'em." The reason we find so much religion in *The Walking Dead* may be related to the strategic deployment suggested by Eugene: "fight fire with fire" (5.1 "No Sanctuary")—religion with religion. And for those of us afflicted with our own infectious desire for the undead, perhaps thinking more about *The Walking Dead* performs a similar therapeutic function—a philosophizing dead.

2
Maybe Jenner Was Right

Steven B. Cowan

In the final episode of Season One of *The Walking Dead* (1.6 "TS-19"), we meet the CDC scientist, Jenner, who has been working tirelessly to find a cure for the plague that has turned most people on earth into "walkers."

All of his experiments have failed. And now he doesn't even have the comfort of his beloved wife, another CDC scientist who became the unfortunate Test Subject 19. What's more, the CDC facility has almost run out of fuel to operate the generators. The loss of power means that not only is there no way to continue his work, but also that the facility will self-destruct in a fiery explosion to prevent all the deadly diseases stored there from getting out. When Rick Grimes and his group of survivors arrive at the CDC facility to seek shelter, they soon discover that Jenner has decided to end his life by staying in the CDC facility when it self-destructs.

Apparently, Jenner has reached the conclusion that out there in the "real world," the apocalyptic world populated by flesh-eating undead walkers, there is no meaning or purpose to human life—no reason to go on living. Two members of Rick's group, Jacqui and Andrea, reach the same conclusion and decide to join him in suicide, though Dale manages to talk Andrea out of it before the building explodes.

Did Jenner and Jacqui make the right choice? Or did Dale, Rick, and the rest of the group? The question of the meaning and purpose of life in a zombie apocalypse is a frequent theme in *The Walking Dead,* with the question raised as to whether or not suicide is the better option. In Season Two, when Carl has been shot and is thought to be dying, Lori, his mother, tells Rick, "Maybe Jenner was right. . . . If he dies tonight, this ends for him" (2.3 "Save the Last One"). Later in the same season (2.6 "Secrets"), Lori takes some morning-after pills to abort her pregnancy (though she changes her mind and throws them up just in the nick of time). She did this because she struggled to find a reason to bring a new life into the horrific walker-infested world.

Is there a reason? Can human life have meaning and purpose—can we find significance and happiness—in such a world?

Camus's Only Question

Though living in *this* world and not a zombie apocalypse, the existentialist philosopher, Albert Camus, wrestled with the same questions. He lived through World War II, particularly Nazi-occupied France, and was well-acquainted with man's inhumanity to man. What's more, he was an atheist. He did not believe, therefore, in any grand divine purpose or meaning bestowed upon the universe and humanity by an all-powerful, all-knowing and benevolent deity.

Faced with a world filled with apparently meaningless pain and suffering, then, Camus concluded that life is absurd and that the only meaningful philosophical questions is, "Why should I not commit suicide?" All other philosophical issues had to take a back seat to this one. For if there is not even a reason to live another day, if continued existence in this world is quite literally meaningless, then all the other intellectual endeavors of philosophers—indeed all the other endeavors of any human beings—are even more meaningless.

This is precisely the question that occupied the mind of Dr. Jenner in the days leading up to his fateful decision to check out when the CDC facility blew up. He perfectly represents the existential angst that Camus faced in the face of an impersonal, uncaring, and even hostile universe. Jenner thought hard about the question, "Why should I not commit suicide?" And his answer was, "No reason at all." So, he said goodbye to the cruel world of the walkers.

Jenner's answer to the question is certainly a legitimate answer if one is convinced, like Camus, that life is absurd. Jacqui acknowledged its legitimacy when she joined Jenner in his suicide pact. Andrea acknowledged it too, at least for a moment. Even Lori Grimes takes this answer to the question seriously when she wonders whether or not Jenner was right. But she, perhaps like Andrea, eventually thought better of it. So did Camus.

Michonne's Moxie

Camus believed that life is absurd. We want life to have meaning. We want our lives to be significant. We want our suffering to have a purpose. We want the good to be rewarded and the bad punished. But the universe we live in doesn't so much as know we exist. It cannot care about us or sympathize with our plight. Nature brings us into existence unknowingly and uncaringly, and then erases us from the scene and eventually from memory. Life simply has no objective meaning or purpose. Yet Camus would not agree with Jenner's decision to commit suicide. Despite life's absurdity, there is reason to go on.

Camus draws a lesson from the ancient Myth of Sisyphus. For various offenses against the gods, Sisyphus, the King of Corinth, was forced to roll a huge boulder up a high hill. After grueling toil he would succeed in reaching the summit only to see the rock roll back down to the bottom. He was condemned to repeat this absurd exercise for all eternity. Camus likens life in an impersonal universe to Sisyphus's meaningless toil. There appears to be no rhyme or reason to continue pushing the boulder up the hill. It is a pointless labor. Likewise, human existence is a pointless labor. As Camus sees it, it serves no apparent purpose. All the works of mankind, for good or bad, seem not to matter at all in the grand scheme of things, given that there is no God to give us a purpose for being here.

Should we just give up, then? Should Sisyphus? Shouldn't he just sit down beside the rock at the bottom of the hill in despair? Shouldn't we all simply check out of this world like Jenner did? No, said Camus. There is a reason for Sisyphus (and us) to push that rock up the hill one more time . . . and again . . . and again. What reason? In a word: *revolt*. Camus believed that meaning can be found in the stubborn refusal to cave in to the pressure of life's absurdity. Thumbing his nose at the gods, Sisyphus can find significance in strutting proudly back down the hill and pushing the boulder once more with dogged determination to not be daunted by his fate. And we, like him, can lead meaningful lives by spitting in the face of the uncaring universe and getting up each morning to live life as long and as fully as we can, absurdity be damned.

The Walking Dead character who comes closest to representing Camus's Sisyphus is Michonne. When the walker plague broke out Michonne fled with her boyfriend and their son to a refugee camp. While she was away on a supply run, the camp was overrun by walkers and her boyfriend and son were killed. Refusing to be overcome with the emotion of her loss, she picked herself up and stubbornly resolved to survive. Removing the jaws and arms of her boyfriend and another family friend (both now turned walkers), she put leashes around their necks, and using them for camouflage, she became a Nubian samurai warrior.

By the time we get acquainted with Michonne at the beginning of the TV show's fourth season, though, she had softened a bit. That is, until the Governor destroyed the prison Rick Grimes's group was living in. Then the group was scattered and Michonne was forced to survive on her own once more. In the episode, 4.9 "After," we see Michonne walking through a forest surrounded by a herd of walkers, her presence camouflaged by two newly leashed walker "pets." She doesn't seem to care. It appears that she is giving in to despair. But when she sees a walker who looks a lot like her, she comes to her senses. In facing her own likeness, and perhaps realizing her own mortality, and the apparent hopelessness of her situation, she realizes that she *is* the Walking Dead, and yet she's done nothing to deserve that lot. She feels compelled to reject that plan of the world. So, she draws her sword and slays all the walkers including her two "pets." After letting out a blood-curdling wail, she marches off to find her lost friends, standing tall in what may be described as a Camusian state of revolt.

Revolting Against Camus

Not everyone is satisfied with Camus's answer. Camus writes that as Sisyphus marches proudly down the hill to take up his task once more, "One must imagine Sisyphus happy." Perhaps. But why? One likely reason we may imagine Sisyphus happy is that his "revolt" means that he is shaking his fist at the gods, refusing to be tamed by them. And that may appear to many of us as meaningful and significant. But who is Camus shaking his fist at? Who is Michonne revolting against? Who would we be defying if we followed Camus's lead? According to Camus, no one. Again, the universe doesn't so much as know we exist, much less care whether we wallow in despair or thumb our noses at it. If there were no gods to defy, then, we may doubt that we can truly imagine Sisyphus happy. Even if we can, we may wonder if that's only because he is living a lie, pretending that the impersonal universe cares whether or not he lives or dies.

Aware of this problem, Camus appeals to human dignity. Yes, the revolt, in order to be meaningful, must be a revolt *for* something that is true and worthwhile. And it is true that we cannot literally thumb our noses at non-existent gods. But, by revolting against the absurdity that the impersonal universe prescribes for us, we uphold the intrinsic dignity of human life. Every person has value and dignity. Every person deserves to be treated with compassion and respect.

For example, Gareth, the leader of the cannibals at Terminus, might seem at first blush to be a Camusian revolter. After all, he has stood up, like Michonne, and shaken his first at the absurd world of the walkers and determined to live. But the difference between Gareth and Michonne is that Michonne sees and respects the intrinsic dignity of other people, while Gareth butchers and eats them with cold callousness. Camus would approve of Michonne's revolt but not Gareth's, for Gareth's "revolt" is not grounded in the recognition of universal human dignity. And this is why, according to Camus, we may imagine Sisyphus (and Michonne) happy.

Questions remain, however. The most serious one is this: Why, in an absurd, atheistic universe, should we think that human life has intrinsic value and dignity? Camus believes that it does, but offers no reason to think so. He just thinks that it's obvious that humans have dignity. Other philosophers, including existentialists, have doubted that human beings can have intrinsic value within an atheist worldview. The existentialist Jean-Paul Sartre is a case in point. He held that human life does *not* have intrinsic dignity and value. And this implies, of course, that there is no objective morality. What counts as right and wrong are more or less matters of personal preference.

For Sartre, human beings are thrust into an absurd world without rhyme or reason. Since there is no God, there is no divine plan, no divine purpose for our lives, and no morality imposed on us from any external source. Each person has absolute freedom to forge his own purpose and meaning defined by no one but himself. All that matters to give life significance is that you assert yourself by choosing to live "authentically"—that is, in accordance with your own freely chosen path. But, of course, an authentic life can be one in which you slay walkers and help others survive (as Michonne helped Andrea), or one in which you take the role of tyrant in Woodbury and perform experiments on walkers *and non-walkers*, as did the Governor, or one in which you lead a group of cold, compassionless cannibals like Gareth did. For Sartre, there is no moral difference between these choices. After all, who's to judge?

If human life has dignity and value, then Camus's answer to our question can be an attractive one. But, as we have seen, it's a debated question whether there is a basis for human dignity in a world without God.

Hershel's Hope

A different response to the question, "Why shouldn't I commit suicide?," is to deny the assumption that prompts the question in the first place. The assumption is that God does not exist. But what if he does? Then maybe life is not absurd and meaningless even if it sometimes seems so.

Hershel Greene is the man of faith who exemplifies the religious answer to the philosophical question of life's meaning. Hershel believes in a personal God who works providentially in the course of history to guide the world and the individuals who inhabit it to the fulfillment of his good purposes. It is this belief that gives Hershel hope that the terrible events that have befallen the world have meaning. God has a purpose in allowing the walker apocalypse, a good purpose.

Hershel's hope in divine providence is made clear in numerous ways in the TV series. Once, while the group is living on Hershel's farm in Season Two, he and Rick admire a beautiful landscape. Hershel remarks that such experiences often lead him to reflect upon God. When Rick suggests that recent tragic events haven't given him much reason to think well of the Almighty, Hershel attempts to persuade him otherwise:

HERSHEL: Lori told me your story—how you were shot, the coma. Yet you came out of it somehow. You did not feel God's hand in yours?

RICK: At that moment? No, I did not.

HERSHEL: In all the chaos you found your wife and boy. Then he was shot and he survived. That tells you nothing?

RICK: It tells me God's got a strange sense of humor. (2.4 "Cherokee Rose")

Though Rick struggles with faith (and often seems to lean in the direction of a Camusian-like revolt), Hershel clearly views life's events as infused with divine purpose. We see his hope expressed in other ways as well such as those occasions when we see him reading his Bible. When things are going badly, it's not surprising to see Hershel look for meaning in the only place he believes it can be found, namely in Scripture. His hope also propels him to sacrificial action in the face of serious danger. During the deadly flu epidemic in Season Four, Hershel's determined to enter the cell block where the sickest patients are quarantined and care for them as best he can. Though Rick and Hershel's daughter, Maggie, plead with him not to go, he refuses to be deterred.

> You step outside, you risk your life. You take a drink of water, you risk your life. And nowadays you breathe, and you risk your life. Every moment now. . . you don't have a choice. The only thing you can choose is what you are risking it for. Now, I can make these people feel better and hang on a little bit longer. I can save lives. And that's enough reason to risk mine. (4.3 "Isolation")

It's certainly possible to interpret Hershel's determination to help the sick as a Camusian revolt. Perhaps he thinks that it's absurd that people have to die even though they have done nothing to deserve it. So, he tries to impose some order on the situation by saving their lives—lives that he believes have intrinsic value. However, given his religious faith, this interpretation would not be the most plausible one. More plausible is the view that not only do we see here that Hershel believes that his life has meaning and purpose, but also that his purpose is found in living (and dying) for a cause that is bigger than himself. And, for him, that sense of purpose is derived from his faith in God.

No Camusian "revolt" will do for him. Meaning in life can be real only if the events of life, especially the horrific events of life, play some significant and necessary role in a greater and grander story told by God. And, of course, that story must have a good ending—an ending in which good triumphs over evil, justice is eventually done, tragedy turns into blessing, and lasting peace and happiness are enjoyed by the faithful if not by all.

However, we finite humans cannot always see God's purposes. And this lack of sight can be troublesome even to those strongest in faith. On one occasion, Hershel says to Rick in exasperation, "I can't profess to understand God's plan. Christ promised the resurrection of the dead. I just thought he had something a little different in mind" (2.13 "Beside the Dying Fire"). Later, when the flu epidemic has reached its worst point, and many lives have been lost despite Hershel's and Dr. S's best efforts, Hershel tries to read his Bible again but can't. All he can do is weep (4.5 "Internment"). Does this mean that he has lost his faith; that he realizes his faith is vain? No. It simply shows that believing that life has meaning even when we cannot see that meaning is often very difficult. But continuing to hope, as Hershel does, is precisely what it means to walk by faith instead of sight.

A Larger World

No doubt, at this point you can see some similarities between the religious answer to our question and the Camusian answer. The Camusian looks at the tragedies and struggles of life and cannot see a reason for them. They seem absurd and pointless. The theist, the one who believes in God, is often in the very same position. He cannot always see the purpose or meaning in the tragic events of life. So how should we behave? That question confronts the theist and the Camusian alike. And in answer they both prescribe that we work to impose order on the absurdity; that we fight to uphold human dignity through compassionate action. So, then, how are the two positions really any different? They are both equally about revolt.

There are differences, though. First of all, theism provides a way of explaining human dignity. It tells us why human life is valuable and meaningful. It is because human beings are created in the image of a personal, benevolent God who instills human life with intrinsic value and gives objective purpose to their existence in the world. So, unlike Camus's position, theism does not leave human dignity as an unexplained brute fact—and one that runs counter to what we might actually expect in an atheistic universe. Secondly, the theist's "revolt" does not admit the absurdity of life but rejects it. Instead, it requires trust that God does in fact have good reasons for life's tragedies; that they are not meaningless despite appearances.

Critics of the religious answer to our question might claim, however, that Hershel's hope is a cop-out. It is, they might say, an irrational coping mechanism for those who are too weak to face the reality of life's absurdity. Or, less severely, the critic could claim that, however comforting the religious answer might be, it is (in Camus's words) "philosophical suicide." The religious answer requires us to embrace the existence of God, something for which we have little or no evidence.

Perhaps the critics are right. Again, it depends upon whether or not God actually exists. If he does not, then maybe the best we can do in finding a reason to live is Camusian revolt. I suppose that if you're convinced of the non-existence of God, then following Sisyphus back down the hill to push on the rock once more is better in some sense than Jenner's alternative.

On the other hand, if God does exist and we have reason to think he does, then having hope in divine providence even in a walker apocalypse, would not be a cop-out, nor would it be intellectual suicide. It would, in fact, be the sensible thing to do. But what reason might we have to believe that God exists?

Belief in God as Properly Basic

There have been many arguments that philosophers have given for believing in the existence of God. My own opinion is that several of these arguments are strong enough to make belief in God at least rational. But we need not pursue that issue here (it certainly is not pursued, at least directly, in *The*

Walking Dead). Instead, let me suggest that rational belief in God may not need any strong philosophical arguments. Maybe, that is, belief in God can be properly basic.

Philosophers distinguish two kinds of beliefs: basic beliefs and nonbasic beliefs. A *nonbasic belief* is a belief that I have because I have other beliefs. Or, more precisely, it is a belief that is based on or derived from other beliefs. An example would be the belief that *Socrates is mortal* which I logically deduce from the beliefs that *All men are mortal* and *Socrates is a man*. Another example would be the belief that there is a bird just outside my office window on the occasion of hearing (and coming to believe that I hear) a tweeting sound outside my window.

A *basic belief*, on the other hand, is a belief that is not based on other beliefs. It is a belief I hold independently of other things I believe. For example, suppose I peer out my window and *see* a tree in my front yard. I naturally form the belief, "There is a tree in my front yard." I don't infer the existence of the tree by means of any argument. I simply form the belief due to my visual experience of it. My belief that there is a tree in my front yard is a basic belief. What's more, it is a *properly* basic belief. That means that my basic belief, in this case, is appropriate or justified. It's justified in virtue of the visual experience that provides the occasion for forming the belief.

Well, why can't belief in God be properly basic in a way similar to my belief that there is a tree in my front yard? What if, following the Protestant Reformer John Calvin, human beings have been created by God with a *sensus divinitatis* (a sense of the divine)—a faculty analogous to vision that (barring some defect) produces belief in God in appropriate circumstances? In such circumstances there would be nothing irrational about believing in God. And belief in God in such circumstances would constitute a properly basic belief, as Alvin Plantinga has argued. This does not mean that belief in God would be groundless or arbitrary. Just as my belief that there is a tree outside my window is grounded in my visual experience of the tree, so my belief in God may be similarly grounded. A person may see (or at least think he sees) God's hand at work around him.

We may even have some reason to believe that we might have a "divine sense" like I'm describing. Most people believe sense perception consists of the five senses—sight, touch, hearing, taste, and smell. But there is good reason to believe that these are not the only senses available to us. People seem to be aware of where their bodies are, for example, without touching anything, or seeing their limbs. Scientists call this the "kinesthetic sense." Perception of heat is also different from the sense of touch. We can also recognize that some people have expanded sensory abilities. There are individuals who are "super-tasters" being able to perceive tastes and flavors others cannot; and others who are tetrachromats—they can perceive colors that others cannot. So it should not be a stretch to think that we may have a sense of the divine.

Consider again the episode of the TV series, 2.4 "Cherokee Rose," where Hershel says that the sight of a beautiful landscape often leads him to contemplate God. And though Rick could not seem to see it, Hershel believed that he saw God's handiwork in the events that led Rick to find his family after waking up in the hospital, and then eventually to Hershel's farm. Events like these would provide for Hershel the grounds for a properly basic belief in God.

Consider also the episode, 5.10 "Them." On the open road again and desperate for food and water, and having just lost two beloved members of the group, the remaining survivors are at their lowest. If there was ever a time at which they seemed "God-forsaken," it is now. Many of them are tempted to give up hope. Sheltering for the night in a barn, Rick suggests that their continued survival depends on their telling themselves, "We are the walking dead." Later in the night, as a terrible storm passes over, the barn is assaulted by a herd of walkers. It is all the group can do to hold the door to keep them out. The scene then changes to show a calm, sunny morning. As Maggie and Sasha leave the barn, they (and we) learn that a tornado leveled a myriad of trees and killed or disabled all of the walkers. But the barn is unscathed. (Although we don't see the tornado, the AMC episode summary indicates that it is a tornado.) Sasha says, bewildered, "It should have torn us apart." Though none of the characters explicitly acknowledge it, many viewers of the show no doubt thought that this was an act of divine providence, a sure sign that they were not "God-forsaken" even if they, for whatever reason, were unable to see it. Surely *Hershel* would have seen it had he been there. (He *wasn't* there, of course, because he was killed by the Governor in the previous season.)

From Rick and Co.'s Refusal of Despair to God

If a person has a properly basic belief in God, as we might surmise that Hershel did, then he has every reason to accept the religious answer to the question of life's meaning, and a reason to go on living even in a zombie apocalypse. But what about those who don't (or won't) have a properly basic belief in God? For those people, it may be possible to approach the issue in the opposite direction.

Though Camus did not put the matter in these terms, he might have been sympathetic to the idea that belief in the dignity of human life and its intrinsic meaningfulness is a properly basic belief. He did take it as a brute fact that human life is valuable. And it is not hard to imagine that a person might say the same thing about human life having intrinsic meaning and purpose. Indeed, many of us find it impossible to believe that life is really absurd despite the harsh realities we often have to confront. This may very well be why Dale, Lori, Rick, and others refuse to succumb to Jenner's despair even though they may find it difficult to articulate the reasons for such refusal—though it does *not* seem for most of these characters that the reason has anything to do with a Camus-like revolt.

They simply believe (*know*?) that life in their world is not ultimately absurd. It is a basic belief for them that it is worthwhile to continue the struggle and hope for better days. That's what most of us believe too. Though it might be difficult to prove that this belief is *properly* basic, I find it even more difficult to fault anyone for thinking that it is. And if it is properly basic to believe in human dignity and the meaningfulness of life, then we have reason to believe that God exists. For as we have seen, for such beliefs to be explicable, God must exist.

So, if Lori had been speaking to Hershel instead of Rick when she asked if Jenner was right, we know that Hershel would have replied, "Of course not." And he would have reasoned that life can never seem so absurd as to shake our confidence that it isn't, nor cause the person of faith to give up on the God who gives it meaning—though, certainly, we must often pause and weep.

3

I Want *You* to Survive

SETH M. WALKER

Imagine you're pushing your way through a crowd of hungry walkers as fast as you can. Your ankle is sprained and swelling fast as the guy next to you helps hold you up. Hobbling ahead of the bloodthirsty horde, you realize you're both out of rifle rounds, have only one shot left in each of your pistols, and aren't going to make it. There are just too many of them. What do you do? Put yourselves out of misery before it's too late? Keep going and hope for the best? Or, force the other guy to stay behind with a bullet to the leg so you can get away? You'd have a choice, just like Shane did. And that's the point. But, why choose one way or the other, and for what reasons?

Survival in AMC's undead-infested world of *The Walking Dead* is a theme that comes with the territory. But, what does *survival* even mean in this sort of world anyway, and why is it even worth the trouble? Is human life always meaningful and worth living, regardless of the quality and circumstances? And if so, are some lives in such a world more meaningful or valuable than others?

During the second season (2.3 "Save the Last One"), we witness one of the most obvious examples of human worth being calculated: Shane sacrifices Otis's life so he can escape an undead onslaught and get medical supplies back to Hershel in time to save Carl. It isn't hard to notice that Carl's life has more value to Shane than Otis's. But, from a pragmatic point of view, Shane's decision seems ridiculous: Otis's life should appear far more valuable to him than Carl's. In a more recent example during the fourth mid-season finale (4.8 "Too Far

Gone"), The Governor (though I guess it's technically "Brian Heriot" at this point, right?) explains to his new group why they must attack and take over the nearby prison: "I want *you* to survive" (my emphasis). He then elaborates to his new companion, Lilly, regarding her life and the life of her daughter: "I'm gonna keep you alive. I'm gonna keep Meghan alive. The only judgment on me I care about is whether you two are still breathing."

These types of examples highlight the ways characters make choices regarding the value of certain human lives on the show, but they also raise questions about the meaning of life itself. Some characters throughout the series—many, actually—preferred the taste of a bullet, dangling indefinitely from a noose, or playing an active role in the colorful display of a thermobaric explosion (ahem, Jacqui and Dr. Jenner). But, are suicide and an awkward, impractical drive to save the lives of youngsters the only possible options?

Opting Out

For now, let's assume that life is so terrible in this sort of world that we would be better off with a quick death before things get even worse. If this were the case, a relatively painless suicide would seem like a pretty nice option. It certainly did for Jacqui and Dr. Edwin Jenner at the end of the first season (1.6 "TS-19"). And it did for countless others throughout the entire series as well; from the owners of the horse Rick borrowed (and sacrificed to an inner-city group of walkers) in the first episode (1.1 "Days Gone Bye") to the family Michonne came across during a supply run with Carl in 4.11 "Claimed." Not everyone had it in them to face the cruelty of a world now set on eating them alive.

According to Jenner, the only thing waiting for those trying to survive is just "a short, brutal life and an agonizing death." "Wouldn't it be kinder," he asks Rick before the CDC in Atlanta self-destructs, "more compassionate, to just hold your loved ones and wait for the clock to run down?" This proposition might sound a bit hasty and irrational at first, but maybe Jacqui was on the right track when she explained her decision to stay behind with Jenner: "I'm not ending up like Jim and Amy" (who both suffered the horrible death Jenner described).

We can probably assume the millisecond of pain she suffered was much less agonizing.

We've All Done the Worst Kinds of Things Just to Stay Alive

Now let's assume that life is still meaningful and worth living, no matter how wretched things may be or seem, so we shouldn't start "opting out" when life gets a little bit harder (I know, "a little bit harder" is definitely an understatement for these individuals). During the same scene in "TS-19," the thought of being locked in a facility that is about to blow up sets Rick's group off in a panic. "Let us keep trying as long as we can," Lori begs Jenner, as the group struggles to find a way out. When he finally gives in and opens the door, Rick says he's grateful. Jenner then gives him that chilling response we all never forgot: "The day will come when you won't be."

But, we really haven't seen Rick seriously reflect back on that rebuttal. Sure, there have been a few instances that have had Rick and the others question how worthwhile their existence is in this world, especially when children's lives are involved. But, the drive to keep going has remained strong. And sometimes, as in the case of Shane and Otis's supply run, lives are even risked to save those who might not actually seem to be *worth* it. The fact that the two of them went in the first place indicates that even the *possibility* of saving Carl's life was worth risking their own. Nobody at Hershel's farm—Rick and Lori included—seemed to disagree. When Shane injured his ankle, he told Otis to go on without him, knowing that they both couldn't make it out alive. Otis, apparently aware of the fact that Shane *was* worth saving, refused, leaving Shane with only one option if he wanted to get the supplies back to Carl and save his life: injure Otis and sacrifice him to the walkers chasing them. Shane clearly didn't feel the same way Otis did about him.

Shane's insistence on keeping certain individuals alive—particularly Carl and an unnamed Judith—is noticeable in several instances after that night, leading up to his staged murder attempt of Rick, who he believed wasn't fit to protect his own family. And Rick has acted in nearly the same way, which *did* result in Shane's death, not his own, at the end of Season Two.

Ever since Hershel operated on Carl and saved his life, he has always been adamant about the boy's survival. At the end of Season Two, he tells Rick, "You've got to get your boy to safety . . . Please, keep your boy safe . . . You've only got one concern now—just one: keeping him alive." And Season Four ends with Rick fully embracing this position as well: "I'm gonna keep him [Carl] safe. That's all that matters," he tells Daryl after they survive an ambush by Joe and his "claimers" (4.16 "A"). But, Rick isn't alone when it comes to looking out for children. The Governor displays the same sort of tendencies with Meghan. After our villain-turned-family man (turned villain again) explains his desire to take over the prison, Lilly asks him what Meghan is going to be in this sort of world. "She's gonna be alive," he blatantly responds, as if that's all that matters.

The case of Judith is even more confusing. The fact that Lori decided to keep the pregnancy implies that she considered the possibility of a new human being and its care more important than her own safety. Her decision to not end the pregnancy created a liability for the group as they struggled to survive. Even though the majority of her pregnancy took place between the second and third seasons, we can probably assume that Lori being pregnant placed the group in a much more vulnerable position than they would have otherwise been in. And when it came time to deliver (3.4 "Killer Within"), Lori didn't hesitate to instruct Maggie to cut her open to save the baby. The thought of even losing the baby at that point was placed in direct contrast with the alternative: "*This* is right," Lori told Maggie (my emphasis).

Sophia Only Matters to the Rest of Us to the Degree She Doesn't Drag Us Down

But, the underlying question for this position is "Why?" Why is life seen as being meaningful and unconditionally worth living for these individuals, and why the strong emphasis on *just* staying alive for some of them in particular?

Are these characters worth more to the group alive than dead? Does their instrumental value—their usefulness—make them worth the risk? In the Shane-Otis-Carl example, Shane and Otis are both skilled gunmen, and Otis is presented as an experienced hunter who is familiar with medical equipment and surgical procedures. Carl, at this point in the series, is a young, inexperienced child who cannot offer the group much practical assistance—at least not in comparison to Shane or Otis. He doesn't appear to have more instrumental value than Shane or Otis, and yet, they risk their lives to save him. And even more astonishing, Shane determines that at least one of their lives (poor Otis) is worth less than Carl's. And even *more* astonishing than that, Shane's statement to Rick two episodes later (2.5 "Chupacabra") about abandoning the search for Sophia directly contradicts his own actions from before: "Alive or not, Sophia only matters to the rest of us to the degree she doesn't drag us down." Any one of the others could have easily said the same thing about Carl before Shane and Otis went out looking for supplies.

And what about Judith? Could the survivors really have believed that Lori's life was less important to the group than a newborn baby's? Judith could not (and still can't!) contribute anything to the group when she was born, and *only* placed Lori and the others in vulnerable situations during the pregnancy. Judith's birth cost Lori her life and replaced her as a new liability for the group: not only do they have to worry about keeping her alive, but they have to deal with her cries and walker-attracting newborn-baby-babble as well. Daryl, Maggie, and Glenn repeatedly risked their own lives going out on baby formula runs from the prison, and Judith's crying placed Tyreese, Carol, Lizzie, and Mika in danger on the road after the prison fell. During 5.1 "No Sanctuary," Martin (one of the so-called "Termites") tells Tyreese that saving babies in this world is "kind of like saving an anchor when you're stuck without a boat in the middle of the ocean." Quite the analogy, no? As an adult already familiar with surviving in a walker-infested world, Lori was clearly worth more to the group than a newborn baby—even if she was a rather poor driver.

The Governor's obsession with Meghan's survival resulted in him killing two strong and militant leaders in his new group. The mere thought of the camp not being safe put the Governor into a psychotic frenzy that resulted in their deaths (4.7 "Dead Weight"). Meghan's life wasn't worth the lives of Martinez and Pete—at least in terms of usefulness to the group. But it didn't stop with *just* those two lives either: The Governor placed the lives of everyone in his new camp and Rick's group at the prison in danger trying to secure a safe place for Meghan—a pre-adolescent girl who's even more inept than a Season-Two-Carl, and really only a few degrees less of a liability than Judith. So, what gives?

Little Girl Goes Missing, You Look for Her

The greater importance of certain lives over others doesn't seem to be based on instrumental value—at least not in these instances. But, if individuals were viewed as having value in themselves (inherent value), regardless of their usefulness for the group (instrumental value), then an emphasis on surviving *no matter what* might start to make sense. Both Carl and Meghan would matter just as much as Otis and Rick—or anyone, for that matter. But do the actions of those in our examples make any *more* sense from this point of view?

American philosopher and animal rights theorist Tom Regan put forth what he called the "subject-of-a-life" criterion as the basis for inherent value in *The Case for Animal Rights*. Although he explored this idea in the context of non-human animal rights, his criterion can be applied here as well. According to Regan, having inherent value means that we are not valuable based on our usefulness to others. Our value is also not calculated based on the sum total of the intrinsic value of our experiences. Carl, Meghan, Judith, The Governor, Lori, Shane, and Otis are all valuable in themselves—regardless of how good or bad their experiences are, and regardless of how useful they are to their groups.

But, determining whether or not someone is inherently valuable isn't as easy as just "merely being alive" or "merely being conscious." According to Regan, individuals like Carl are "subjects-of-a-life" if they have: "beliefs and desires; perception, memory, and a sense of the future, including their own; an emotional life together with feelings of pleasure and pain; preference- and welfare-interests; the ability to initiate action in pursuit of their desires and goals" and "a psychophysical identity over time." We can be pretty certain that Carl satisfies this list.

What about someone like Judith? Can we definitively claim that a newborn baby has the same sort of "sense of the future" or "psychophysical identity over time"? No, of course we can't

definitively make that claim. And Regan owns up to that ignorance, too. For him, the jury is still out on the matter, and
because of that, we should play it safe and give newborn babies
the benefit of the doubt, "viewing them *as if* they are subjects-
of-a-life," even though "we may be giving them more than is
their due" (p. 320). A final stipulation Regan adds is that subjects-of-a-life have "an individual welfare in the sense that
their experiential life fares well or ill for them, logically independently of their utility for others and logically independently
of their being the object of anyone else's interests" (p. 243). This
is what truly separates his understanding of inherent value
from instrumental value.

Now More than Ever, Our Most Precious Asset

But, *just* satisfying the subject-of-a-life criterion still doesn't
seem to fully solve our dilemma here. The survivors are noticeably selective towards those they wish to keep alive, with children mostly given priority. Let's not forget that the entire first
half of Season Two revolved around searching for a missing
Sophia (and what a great use of time and energy that ended up
being!). Near the middle of Season Two (2.4 "Cherokee Rose"),
Hershel stated that children are "now more than ever, our most
precious asset." Shane displayed a similar understanding a
couple episodes later (2.6 "Secrets") when he justified his sacrifice of Otis: "A little boy lived because of what went down that
night." These types of sentiments don't really line up with the
subject-of-a-life criterion.

According to Regan, inherent value is not a matter of
degree; individuals who satisfy it can't do so to a greater or
lesser degree than others. The subject-of-a-life criterion "does
not assert or imply that those who meet it have the status of
subject of a life to a greater or lesser degree. . . . One either *is*
a subject of a life, in the sense explained, or one *is* not. All of
those who are, are so equally" (pp. 244–45). So, even if we
decide that Carl is rather useless, instrumental value doesn't
matter for the subject-of-a-life criterion. And if inherent value
is what matters most, then Shane and Otis are just as valuable
as Carl, which means risking both their lives for his was
arguably a poor decision. Everyone could have reasonably

decided that Carl just wasn't worth the effort (risking two *more* lives to possibly save one).

But, here's the problem: everyone involved agreed that Carl *was* worth the effort. And everyone seemed to agree that Judith was worth it too (and by *it*, I of course mean Lori). Lilly certainly didn't put up a strong fight about what was at risk for Meghan's safety. And the preference for children being spared becomes selective itself as well. Shane clearly cared much less about Sophia's wellbeing when she went missing than he did Carl's. He even told Lori in 2.5 "Chupacabra" that he'd abandon the search if it meant keeping Carl—and by extension, her—safe. And in 4.8 "Too Far Gone," the Governor shared a similar confession with Hershel regarding their daughters. Hershel asked him, "If you understand what it's like to have a daughter, then how can you threaten to kill someone else's?" "Because they aren't mine," he replied.

So, getting back to Hershel's remark, what's going on with this seemingly illogical reverence for children throughout the series? Maybe it's the perceived innocence of children in a cruel, devastated world that has Hershel gung-ho about their status in it. Though if that's the case, we realize such innocence is hardly guaranteed in this sort of setting. Carl has grown colder and more cynical since recovering from his gunshot wound in Season Two, leading up to him gunning down a surrendering Woodbury teenager at the end of Season Three (3.16 "Welcome to the Tombs"). And let's not forget about Lizzie, a psychologist's flower-loving nightmare, whose death in season four (4.14 "The Grove") reminds us that children aren't *always* blindly saved. The fact that her death (well, execution) involved a fixation on beautiful flowers full of life ("Just look at the flowers, Lizzie . . .") is noticeably ironic. Innocence is hardly a given for children in this world, and with enough time, we can be sure Meghan would have been equally influenced by this harsh reality. Maybe Judith will prove us wrong, if she survives long enough.

These People You Need to Keep Alive, Do You Love Them?

It doesn't seem like the reason for *just* staying alive is being based purely on instrumental value, and it doesn't really seem like it's being based purely on inherent value either. The lives of children are being prioritized over more capable members of their groups, which disrupts the criteria for both inherent value (since they are being unequally elevated in worth) and instrumental value (since they are typically much less useful than the others). But, these examples might be revealing how characters on *The Walking Dead* are actually calculating their choices when it comes to survival.

The obvious rationale we can provide for most of the characters' actions is that they love the people they are trying to protect, and that's why they want them to survive. Shane loves Carl so much that he's willing to sacrifice Otis's life to make sure he survives. The Governor, presumably, feels the same way about Meghan and her safety—and by extension, Lilly's. And other adults aren't exempt from these matters of preference either; for the most part, everyone's determined to do whatever it takes to find Sophia in Season Two.

Lives are constantly risked in order to keep the groups strong. Whether or not safety in numbers is what matters most, or that the communal bond has become greater with walkers on the loose, this type of situational ethic—revolving around love and lingering cultural values of family, procreation, and community—has determined some pretty pivotal moments throughout the series.

Not Everything Has to Mean Something . . . but It Can

But, there is a third perspective we haven't discussed yet: life is not inherently meaningful, but that doesn't mean it can't be worth living or made meaningful. Near the end of Season Four (4.10 "Inmates"), while Maggie, Bob, and Sasha are searching for Glenn, Sasha tells Bob they should be searching for food and shelter instead:

BOB: Yeah, why's that?

SASHA: So we can live.

BOB: Then what?

SASHA: *What?*

BOB: Maybe we didn't survive just to keep surviving.

SASHA: Shit happens. Not everything has to mean something.

BOB: No, it doesn't have to, but it can. If you make it that way. And that's what it seems like we're doing. And I'm down with that.

If we were trying to survive after a global meltdown, surrounded by walking, flesh-hungry corpses, I'm sure we would have a hard time trying to find some sort of lasting happiness and meaning. But, that doesn't mean it wouldn't be possible. According to French philosopher Jean-Paul Sartre, "Man is nothing else but what he makes of himself." This "first principle" of his existential philosophy rests on the assumption that we are thrown into the world with the freedom to create a meaningful existence for ourselves—or not. Everything is a matter of choice, and we alone are fundamentally responsible for the choices *we* make (we are "condemned to be free," Sartre states). Bob, Sasha, and all of the others in *The Walking Dead* didn't *will* themselves into a world that would crumble within their lifetimes. But they are free to do anything they want. Following Sartre, they have this fundamental liberty, and they are definitely *condemned* to do something about it.

Hershel told Rick and Maggie at the beginning of Season Four (4.3 "Isolation"): "You step outside, you risk your life. You take a drink of water, you risk your life. And nowadays, you breathe, and you risk your life. Every moment now—you don't have a choice. The only thing you can choose is what you're risking it for." Bob and Sasha could have abandoned their search for Glenn and sought food and shelter instead, "just to keep surviving." But, they didn't. They chose to help Maggie find him and have that search mean something for all of them. The same could be said for Eugene and the agenda he hid from Abraham and Rosita to help Glenn in his search for Maggie.

Thinking about their search in this way, we can reconsider the search for Sophia during Season Two. Searching for her appeared to have meant just as much to Carol as searching for Glenn did to Maggie—regardless of how the meaning and value of their sought after objects was being calculated. But, just as Bob and Sasha (and Eugene!) had a choice to either help foster that meaning and contribute to a *better* existence beyond mere survival, Rick and company—especially Daryl—had that choice as well. They could all have scrapped the search and moved on to the next meal and shelter. I'm sure not getting pierced with his own bolt or shot in the head would have been much more pleasing to Daryl, too. But, in a world where one wrong step can mean a fate far worse than anyone but Jenner could have predicted, the *search* itself for something more might be all the survivors have.

The world may not seem as pleasant and convenient to the survivors as it once was, but their lives consist of choices. They did before, and they still do. They can view the world around them as lost and "opt out," proving Jenner right after all. They can hold on to some sort of value, meaning, or emotion and try to uphold it. Or, they can realize their freedom within a world that has been literally stripped of its constraints and *choose* what to make of it—find the "good out of the bad," our late optimist, Bob, might say.

Every choice the characters make becomes a risk—a risk that may prove fatal. But, that doesn't mean it can't *mean* something either.

WALKER BITE

Let's Just Do What's Right

WILLIAM J. DEVLIN AND ANGEL M. COOPER

One of the prominent themes in *The Walking Dead* is the struggle to be (or become) a good person in a post-apocalyptic world.

Early in the show, one character who embodies the idea of being good is Dale Horvath. Dale is the paradigm of being good and maintaining one's humanity, as well as the voice of reason for the group. He confronts Shane about his immoral behavior, telling him, "This world, what it is now, this is where you belong. And I may not have what it takes to last for long, but that's okay. 'Cause at least I can say when the world goes to shit, I didn't let it take me down with it" (2.7 "Pretty Much Dead Already").

Dale is unwilling to compromise his morals in the post-apocalypse. He recognizes that this commitment may threaten his life in the new world, but he will not sacrifice his humanity just to survive.

Dale keeps his humanity by relying on the moral theory known as *deontology*, the view that an action is morally good so long as it's motivated by the right moral principle, regardless of the consequences. This theory was made famous by Immanuel Kant. Kant maintains that our actions are good when they are in accordance with, and motivated by, our moral duties—which include such actions as being honest, not committing suicide, and helping others in need.

In order to know our moral duties, Kant introduces a universal moral principle known as the *categorical imperative.* One formulation of this principle is the *humanity formula,*

43

which states, "Act in such a way that you treat humanity, whether in your own person or in the person of another, always at the same time as an end and never merely as a means."

From Kant's point of view, characters such as Shane, the Governor, and the Termites act immorally because they treat others (Otis, Randall, the people at the prison, victims at Terminus) as means for survival and not as ends, or people to be valued and respected, in themselves. To treat people as ends is to treat them as fellow human beings who are free to choose their own values, projects, and goals. According to Kant, we should respect the freedom of others, as we would want them to respect our own freedom.

Dale treats other people as ends rather than means. That is, he treats them as human beings whose freedom of choice must be respected. To treat people as a means, on the other hand, is to treat them as an object of utility and to ignore their freedom. For example, the Termites treat their prisoners as means rather than ends by eating them. They use their prisoners as food supply (and maybe for some camp-side conversation), seeing them as objects for their own survival rather than other human beings who deserve to be free to pursue their own goals.

Dale's deontological reasoning is prominent throughout Season Two. One example of this reasoning is Dale's decision to delay telling everyone that the RV is fixed while they are searching for Sophia. He explains, "Sooner or later, if she's not found, people will start doing math. I want to hold off the needs of the many versus the needs of the few arguments as long as I can" (2.1 "What Lies Ahead"). He rejects appealing solely to consequences in his reasoning; rather, he uses deontological reasoning, as he suggests they have a duty to search for Sophia, no matter what. For Dale, it's wrong to use a consequentialist ethics to decide to give up on looking for Sophia— such an approach would treat her as a means. Or, as Rick puts it, "Little girl goes missing, you look for her."

A clearer example of Dale's use of deontology, and his plea to save the humanity of the group, concerns his attempt to save Randall from execution. Rick dictates that Randall will be put to death, on the grounds that "he's a threat." Dale objects, "You can't do this. You don't want to do this. . . . you can't just decide on your own to take someone's life. . . . there's got to be a process. . . . He's just a kid . . . you think about your son and the message you're giving him . . . shoot first, ask questions later?"

Dale suggests that we have a moral duty to not treat Randall as a means for safety; rather, we must respect Randall's right to life as a person. Moreover, as he suggests to Shane, failure to follow deontology entails a loss of humanity: "Killing him doesn't change all of that [the danger of Randall's group]. But it changes us." Dale's deontological justification for saving Randall culminates in his argument to the group in the farmhouse:

> This is a young man's life, and it is worth more than a five-minute conversation! . . .You saved him and now look at us. He's been tortured. He's gonna be executed. How are we any better than those people that we're so afraid of? You [Rick] once said that we don't kill the living. . . . But don't you see that if we do this, the people that we were, the world that we knew is dead? And this new world is ugly, it's harsh, it's the survival of the fittest, and that's a world I don't want to live in, and I don't believe it's a world that any of you want to live in, I can't . . . please let's just do what's right. ("Judge, Jury, Executioner")

Dale sees that executing Randall could produce good ends insofar as it keeps the group safe from an outside threat. But he objects on the grounds that it violates the humanity formula— it treats Randall as a means to an end. Furthermore, Dale suggests the real problem with focusing solely on mere survival: it will kill the idea of being good and, with it, the old world and humanity. Sadly, Dale—the moral voice of reasoning in the group—does not survive much longer. By the end of the day, he is killed by a walker. But unlike Shane, the Governor and the Termites, Dale chooses to live as a good person over mere survival. So he dies holding onto his humanity and keeping his morality, and dignity intact.

Dale's appeal to deontology is opposed to both the consequentialist approach of Shane, the Governor, and the Termites, and to Rick's eventual espousal of virtue ethics. This three-sided battle between deontology, consequentialism, and virtue ethics is a major theme which continues throughout the show.

II

Not the Good Guy Any More

4
Lie or Die

Gordon Hawkes

When our trusty crew of main character survivors rescues Father Gabriel Stokes from walkers, Rick is immediately suspicious of him, despite his helpless appearance and priestly attire (5.2 "Strangers"). "I don't trust this guy," Rick tells Carl. As Gabriel is supposedly leading them to his church, he tries to make a joke. "Maybe I'm lying about everything and there's no church ahead at all," he says. "Maybe I'm leading you into a trap so I can steal all your squirrels."

No one laughs. They have just escaped from Terminus, where they'd been lured by signs promising "Sanctuary for all." But, of course, the signs were lies—bold, diabolical, barefaced lies. Instead of a safe haven, Terminus was a human slaughterhouse, where new arrivals were butchered like pigs and barbecued for dinner. For the survivors, lies and deception are deadly serious.

Unsurprisingly, the characters condemn lying and condemn it harshly. Yet, at the same time, there are situations throughout *The Walking Dead* where lying seems to be the right thing to do. These two claims lead to a conundrum: How can lying be both wrong and right? And if lying is wrong, but also sometimes right, how do we know *when* it's right to lie?

Lying Is Dead Wrong

Before we can discuss the ethics of lying, we need to know what lying is. For starters, we can make a distinction between "lying" and "deceiving." All lies are acts of deception, but not all acts of

49

deception are lies. When Rick's group pretends to be absent from the prison, they *deceive* the Woodbury invaders into thinking they are gone, but they don't *lie* (3.16 "Welcome to the Tombs"). Lying requires making a statement, whether in speech, writing, sign language, or even in the form of a biter-gram. The Governor lies when he tells Tara and Lilly that his name is Brian (4.6 "Live Bait"). But, on this definition, he also lies by waving a white flag as he approaches the National Guard's camp (3.3 "Walk with Me"). A white flag in that context makes the statement "I come in peace." His real intention, of course, was to kill them all.

In addition, lying is not just stating something false. The speaker has to believe the statement is false. When Abraham tells others that Eugene knows the cure for the plague, he states something false. But he doesn't lie, because he believes the statement is true. Lastly, lying requires an intention to deceive. The Governor doesn't lie when he tells Meghan that he's a pirate, since it's a joke (4.6 "Live Bait"). He has no inten-tion whatsoever of convincing her that he's a genuine pirate. In summary, lying is stating something you believe to be false with the intention to deceive.

Now that we're clear on what lying is, we can ask: Is lying wrong? Our moral common sense tells us that, yes, lying is indeed wrong. Both the good and the bad characters share this intuition. On the one hand, Rick feels burdened with guilt after lying to Carl about the whereabouts of Sophia. "I lied to him this morning," Rick confesses to Hershel. "It wasn't a big lie, but it was enough" (2.4 "Cherokee Rose"). On the other hand, even the Claimers forbid lying, despite being a nasty, brutish gang of rapists and killers, and despite having only three rules.

Liars are judged harshly in *The Walking Dead*. They are condemned alongside the worst kind of people. For example, Carl justifies the killing of Gareth and the other cannibals to Gabriel by simply pointing out that they were "liars and mur-derers" (5.7 "Crossed"). Also, the Governor and Martinez come across three decapitated bodies, evidently executed, bearing the labels of their crimes: "Liar," "Rapist," and "Murderer" (4.7 "Dead Weight").

We can understand why the survivors condemn lying so strongly by considering its effects. Lies erode trust. People can't live together, let alone survive together, if they can't trust each other to tell the truth. Joe, the leader of the Claimers, understands this well. He explains to Daryl that he created the rules, including the rule against lying, "to keep things from going Darwin every couple hours" (4.15 "Us").

The more liars the characters meet and the more lies they uncover, the more they're tempted to become hardened towards helping and trusting outsiders. Rick's group resists the temptation to become completely hardened, and they still take in strangers, including Michonne, Bob, Tara, and Gabriel. They're not naive, though; they still ask their three questions. When the temptation to write off outsiders completely is not resisted, however, the erosion of trust, taken to its ultimate conclusion, yields a hellish society like Terminus. Their motto—"Never again. Never trust. We first, always"—turned them into soulless demons. Their leader, Gareth, so completely lost trust in outsiders that he concluded, "You're either the butcher or you're the cattle" (5.1 "No Sanctuary"). Notice, however, that the Termites still have to tell each other the truth in order for their commune to function. The complete absence of truth would mean chaos.

Not only do lies destroy trust, they also allow evil people to manipulate and gain power over others, usually in order to bring them harm. From the right lips, lies are a coercive force. Shane is able to lure Rick into the woods in order to murder him by saying that he saw Randall escape (2.12 "Better Angels"). The Governor is able to get his people to risk their lives attacking the prison by convincing them the prison is full of "thieves and murderers" (4.8 "Too Far Gone"). Most impressively, the Termites are able to get their victims to do all the hard work of transporting their sorry carcasses the many, many miles to Terminus, simply through the power of false promises. The lies that bring gullible victims to Terminus have just as much power as the physical intimidation and threats used to herd them into cattle cars once there.

Now, it seems clear that, in general, lying is morally wrong, especially lying to bring about injustice. No one praises the malicious lies of Shane, the Governor, and Gareth. But what about lies told to *prevent* injustice? Are there ever situations where it is right to lie?

When Honesty Is Not the Best Policy

In episode eight of Season Two, Rick, Hershel, and Glenn are in a bar when two armed men walk in (2.8 "Nebraska"). These men, Dave and Tony, are clearly no pair of Mormon missionaries. They have traveled from Philadelphia with a large gang and they're looking for somewhere to stay. Dave, who wants to know where Rick's group is holed up, peppers them with impertinent questions. Rick doesn't want to reveal that they're staying on a nearby farm. At a crucial moment, Dave makes an educated guess about their living arrangements and puts the question directly to Rick: "You got a farm?"

If there were ever a situation in which it would be right to lie, this is it. The Philadelphia gang is about thirty men, armed with heavy artillery. They had recently gang-raped teenage girls while forcing the girls' father to watch (2.11 "Judge, Jury, Executioner"). Clearly, these are not the sort of men you'd invite home for dinner. If Rick tells Dave the truth, he puts the lives of everyone on the farm at risk. If the gang learns the whereabouts of the farm, then, in Rick's words, the boys will end up dead and the women will wish they were. But if Rick lies, he protects his friends and family from the murderous, rapist thugs.

Furthermore, telling a lie in this situation is arguably the only way to avoid revealing the truth about the farm. Remaining silent or evading the question would have the same effect as telling the truth. In fact, when Rick, Glenn, and Herschel do stay silent in response to the question, Dave jumps to the obvious conclusion: "This farm . . . it sounds pretty sweet. . . . So, come on, let's take a nice friendly hayride to this farm and we'll get to know each other."

Admittedly, Rick has a third option aside from lying or telling the truth, namely, blasting Dave and Tony with his .357 Magnum revolver—an option he eventually chooses. For the sake of a stricter moral dilemma, we could imagine that Rick is unable to fight back or run away . . . (*Tries to imagine Rick unable to fight back, but only sees Rick in the Season Four finale, unarmed, surrounded, head butting Joe and biting his neck like a savage [4.16 "A"]) . . . Then again, maybe not.

So, should Rick lie in answer to Dave's question? Some philosophers, notably Immanuel Kant and St. Augustine have argued that lying is *always* wrong, and, therefore, Rick should tell the truth. Now, these philosophers were certainly no lamebrains, but their claim is extremely unconvincing. The same moral common sense that tells us that lying is wrong also tells us that telling the truth to a bunch of thugs, who will then use that information to murder everyone we love, is crazy.

Rick faces a moral dilemma: lying is normally wrong, but telling the truth or staying silent would also be wrong in this case. How can we sort out this seeming conflict between our moral intuitions? Assuming Rick should lie, how can we make sense of lying being wrong, and yet sometimes being right? And how can we know when it is right to lie?

Losing Our Humanity

The moral dilemma that Rick faces in the showdown scene is quintessential *Walking Dead*. Robert Kirkman explains:

> My main goal with *The Walking Dead* was to show how . . . living in a world like this twists and turns things around to where morals get twisted and peoples' actions that they would think are normally wrong end up being the right thing to do. (Season 1 DVD, "Featurette")

Lying, which Rick would normally think is wrong, becomes right.

Some people take scenarios where "morals get twisted," like Rick's lie-or-let-die dilemma, to prove that morality is not *objective*. Here, "objective" means universally true independent of what anyone thinks. The fact that Tony Moore was the original artist for *The Walking Dead* comics is an objective truth. It's true for everyone, even for those who mistakenly believe Charlie Adlard was there all along (though they'd have to be blind to think that). If lying were objectively wrong, so the argument goes, then it should be wrong for everyone, in all cases, without exception. But Rick's circumstance appears to be a clear exception to the rule, so, they conclude, lying is not objectively wrong. They further assume that any other supposedly objective moral rule could have similar exceptions.

Thus, lying can be both right in one case and wrong in another without contradiction because morality is not objective, but rather *subjective*. The truth of moral statements depends on what people believe, not on unchanging moral truths "out there" that we discover. More specifically, *moral relativism* is the view that right and wrong are determined by the moral beliefs of the individual person or by the prevailing beliefs of the culture. For example, the Claimers believe lying is wrong. Therefore, the statement "Lying is wrong!" is true *for them*. The Termites, however, believe lying is right. Therefore, the statement "Lying is wrong!" is false *for them*. There is no contradiction since right and wrong are relative to people's beliefs. As moral beliefs change, so also do right and wrong. There is no one true morality for all.

According to moral relativism, if Rick believes it is wrong to lie to his son, Carl, but right to lie to Dave and Tony—and we'll assume most people would agree with his beliefs in these cases—then lying is wrong in the first case, and right in the second, without any contradiction. In order to know when it's right to lie, we need only consult our own beliefs or the beliefs of our culture.

Unfortunately, moral relativism is a bit like Eugene's mullet: it might appear sensible at first glance . . . viewed from a certain angle . . . in dim light—but when you step back and get the whole picture, it's no longer quite as attractive. At least three reasons count strongly against this theory.

First, if moral relativism were true, then we couldn't meaningfully criticize the actions of other people or cultures. Bob could tell Gareth and the other cannibals who are eating his leg, "This is wrong!" But he would merely be saying, "This is wrong . . . *for me!*" Oddly enough, if Bob were a moral relativist, he would need to affirm that they *ought* to eat his leg, since that's what they believe is right.

Second, if moral relativism were true, there could be no moral progress or improvement, only moral change. Terminus began as a community that offered sanctuary to strangers, but after being attacked, became a community that butchered them. Neither the first nor the second policy is morally "better" or "worse" on moral relativism. Terms like "better" and "worse" imply an objective moral standard that moral beliefs can approach more or less closely.

Lastly, some acts seem to be wrong no matter what. The Claimers see nothing wrong with raping women and young boys, based on their attempt to rape Michonne and Carl ("A").

The Philadelphia gang saw nothing wrong with gang-raping teenage girls. These examples don't convince us that rape must be right for those respective gangs. Rather, they convince us that believing something is right doesn't make it right. In other words, rape would still be wrong even if walkers ate every last person who condemned rape and left only those who approved.

Arguably, the Governor champions the moral relativist enterprise. He's a man who does precisely what he believes he ought to do. He explains his moral philosophy to Mitch: "You will never have to worry about whether you were doing the right thing or the wrong thing. Because we will do the only thing" ("Dead Weight"). This thinking leads him to murder Martinez, Pete, and Hershel, lie to everyone he talks to, and lead dozens of others to their deaths in a needless battle with the Prison (4.8 "Too Far Gone"). Any moral theory that ends up with the Governor as its poster boy has something wrong with it.

Someone might want to hold on to moral relativism despite these objections. But that person should weigh the cost of accepting the theory. Suppose Rick decided to abandon his family and friends, and join Dave and Tony's gang. Suppose he told them the truth and led them straight to Hershel's farm himself. What would be wrong with Rick doing that according to moral relativism, assuming he and his new gang believed it was right? At one point Dale tells Andrea: "The world we knew is gone, but keeping our humanity . . . That's a choice" (2.11 "Judge, Jury, Executioner"). By "keeping our humanity," he means continuing to do what is objectively right—not just what we decide is right. For Dale, the circumstances have changed, but right and wrong haven't. Those characters who treat right and wrong not as something they need to discover, but as something they can decide for themselves—most notably the Governor, Gareth, and the residents of Terminus—they become less than human. As Daryl says, "They ain't people" (5.1 "No Sanctuary").

I Just Reasoned I'd Be Doin' Them a Solid, Too

If we reject subjective morality, then we're left with the alternative: morality is objective. But how can we respond to the criticism subjectivists raise? If morality is objective, how can it be right for Rick to lie if lying is objectively wrong?

One objective theory of morality in particular seems well suited to solve the dilemma. *Utilitarianism* bases the moral value of an action on its consequences. An action is more or less "right" (or "wrong") in relation to the good (or bad) it produces. "Good" is going to be defined in a number of ways, but usually "happiness" or "pleasure." We ought to do that which leads to good outcomes, and avoid those acts which lead to bad outcomes. For example, it's right for Beth and Daryl to burn down the moonshiner's cabin (4.12 "Still") because it has good consequences: it makes them happy. In contrast, it would be wrong for the script writers to kill off Daryl because that would have very bad consequences: if Daryl dies, we riot.

Weighing the consequences seems to account neatly for our common-sense view of when lying is right and when it's wrong. In order to know when it's right to lie, we need only consider the consequences of a lie in whatever circumstances we find ourselves. It's right for Rick to lie to Dave and Tony because, on balance, it's better to have two Philly boys upset that they were deceived than to have a dead family.

Only the consequences of an action are relevant in evaluating its rightness or wrongness. This means that no act, including lying, is wrong in itself. The end justifies the means. If Carol's lying to the Alexandrians leads to good consequences, such as her continued safety and the protection of her group, then lying is the right thing for her to do. Although right and wrong are relative to consequences, morality can still be objective, as we've defined it, because the goodness or badness of the consequences can be true independent of people's beliefs.

While utilitarianism deserves to be taken much more seriously than moral relativism (and Eugene's mullet), it's a little bit like Woodbury: it has a neat and tidy outward appearance, but it's a lot more complicated under the surface. Oh, and it has problems.

First, on the practical side of things, the utilitarian approach is actually difficult to apply. For any action, there can be unintended consequences, and what is meant for good can turn out badly. Eugene reasoned like a utilitarian in deciding to lie about being a scientist who knows the cure to the plague, and needing to get to Washington, DC. Once his lie is exposed, Eugene explains that he believed DC held the "strongest possibility of survival." He continues:

If I could cheat some people into taking me there, well, I just reasoned that I'd be doin' them a solid, too, considering the perilous state of the city of Houston, the state of everything. (5.5 "Self Help")

Eugene's lies created terrible consequences—many people died along the way, Abraham had a breakdown, and Eugene got himself beaten to a pulp—but whether his lies were justified or not depended on consequences he couldn't have foreseen.

Second, the notion that only the consequences are relevant to judging our actions yields counterintuitive moral judgments. Carl fails to kill a walker stuck in the creek bed, and this leads to Dale being killed by that same walker. "If I had killed it, Dale would still be here," Carl says (2.12 "Better Angels"). Based solely on the consequences, it would seem we'd have to judge Carl's action, or inaction, to be wrong. But does it make sense to say that it was *morally* wrong for Carl not to kill the walker? Intuitively, we agree with Shane's reply: "This ain't your fault." Something more than just the consequences must be relevant to judging actions.

Lastly, the utilitarian approach might work well for some moral dilemmas, but in some cases, it seems to yield conclusions that conflict with deeply held moral intuitions. For example, Rick is faced with a hard choice when Michonne first comes to the prison. The Governor threatens him with all-out war unless he gets Michonne. Rick can turn Michonne over to the Governor, who will most likely torture and kill her, or Rick can allow her to stay. "Is she worth it?" the Governor asks. "One woman . . . worth all those lives at your prison?" (3.13 "Arrow on the Doorpost"). If consequences are the only thing that matter, Rick should hand over Michonne to the Governor, but Rick decides in the end that such a betrayal of an innocent person is wrong, no matter how beneficial the consequences.

Again we are left searching for a better solution to the moral dilemma.

Morally Obligated to Lie and to Kill

After both Mika and Lizzie are dead, Carol confesses to Tyreese that she was the one who killed Karen and David and burned their bodies. She pushes a gun across the table and tells him, "You do what you have to do" (4.14 "The Grove"). Carol has every reason to believe that her act of confession will lead to bad consequences. Rick warned her: "When Tyreese finds out, he'll kill you" (4.4 "Indifference").

Why would Carol confess when she fully expects something bad to come of it? Tyreese might kill her in revenge. One explanation, and a plausible explanation, is that she confesses simply because she knows it's the right thing to do, consequences be damned. What sort of theory would capture this notion that certain acts are right or wrong by their very nature, regardless of consequences?

Deontological ethics takes a moral act to be right when it is done in accordance with a correct moral rule or duty. The focus is on the nature of the act itself, not on the outcome. For instance, Gabriel had a moral duty to give aid to his parishioners, whom he locked out of his church. Had he instead let them in, his act of protecting them would have been right, not because it saved lives, but simply because it conformed to his duty. His actual act of shutting them out was wrong, not because people died, but because it did not conform to his moral duty.

There is disagreement over how we know these true moral rules—whether it's through our reason or conscience—but it is our duty to follow them, irrespective of the results. This approach to morality can be summed up by the phrase, "Duty for duty's sake." You do what's right 'cause it's right.

When we apply this theory to Rick and the Philadelphia boys, it doesn't seem to solve the problem at all; rather it seems to make it worse. Rick has a moral duty to tell the truth. He also has a real moral duty to protect his family and friends from harm. But the only way for him to fulfill the first is to break the second, and the only way to fulfill the second is to break the first. Rather than this theory offering a solution to the dilemma, the moral dilemma seems to be an objection to the theory!

How can a deontologist solve the dilemma? Some deontologists, like Immanuel Kant, believed that moral duties are perfect obligations. Moral rules are "absolutes." They cannot be trumped or overridden by more important principles. There are no exceptions. You ought never to lie, even if the Governor were at your door asking the whereabouts of Michonne who happens to be hiding in your house. (We get the feeling that if Kant were a character in *The Walking Dead*, all his friends would be dead.)

But others understand moral rules and our corresponding moral duties to be "objective" in the sense that, while they are universally true, they can be overridden by more important principles. So even though Rick has a real moral duty to tell the truth, his duty to protect innocent people from homicidal "douchebags" is clearly a more important duty. Therefore, Rick ought to fulfill the duty to protect (which, in this specific instance, happens to require lying). We weigh the duties and act according to the more important one. The more weighty principle overrides the less weighty principle. This is a case of choosing the greater good. We are obeying the principle of the greater good. Rick is obligated to lie!

This procedure of weighing duties against each other is only necessary when there is genuine conflict between *moral* duties. For instance, Rick understands his moral duty to preserve his own life. He also understands the basic moral duty to not harm others. It's pretty obvious that going around shooting people in the chest isn't very neighborly. But when Dave moves to kill Rick in the bar, the only way for Rick to stay alive is to pump Dave and his friend full of lead (2.8 "Nebraska"). He can only fulfill his moral duty to preserve his own life by doing some severe harm to Dave and Tony's vital organs. It's clear, in that circumstance, what the more important duty is, namely, preserving his own life. Up until the point that Dave drew his gun on him, Rick could fulfill both duties without any conflict.

Seeking guidance from moral duties as a general approach has the advantage of being consistent with our common-sense understanding that special duties arise from special relationships. For instance, Lori, as Rick's wife, has a special obligation to share with him things that she's not obliged to share with others, such as Shane. For this reason, when she keeps her pregnancy a secret from Rick, he takes that as a breach of her obligations to him as her husband, and is upset that she told Glenn before him (2.6 "Secrets"). This example also illustrates that the duty to tell the truth extends beyond just the negative prohibition of lying. We have a sense that we have a duty to be forthcoming with the truth with certain people, depending on their relationship to us.

The deontological approach has one further advantage over utilitarianism: it can take into account consequences, but also other factors for evaluating actions, such as motives. When

Hershel volunteers to take care of the sick in the prison, he tells Maggie, "I can save lives. That's reason enough to risk mine" (4.3 "Isolation"). This is a noble motive for a noble action. But if his motive were instead a secret desire to stab patients in the skull after they've died because he enjoyed it, not to prevent them from being walkers, then his action would no longer rightfully be called noble. Motives certainly seem relevant in evaluating the rightness of actions.

As a solution to the moral dilemma we've been looking at and as a moral theory to guide us through either our own messed up world, or the supremely messed up world of *The Walking Dead*, deonotological ethics is the best option we've found. This theory is like Alexandria: while there are undoubtedly other options out there, this option needs to be shown to be unworkable before abandoning it.

The Walking Dead All Based on a Lie?

We can conclude, then, that there are cases where lying is morally justified, and Rick's showdown with Dave and Tony in the bar near the farm is one of them. But, we shouldn't use this conclusion as license to lie whenever it's convenient. We still need to be guided by certain principles in making moral decisions. Lying, then, may be necessary sometimes in an imperfect world like ours, and, no doubt, necessary more often in a royally messed up world like *The Walking Dead*.

But what about in the world of creating comics? In the Season 1 DVD featurette Robert Kirkman explains that when he made the initial pitch for *The Walking Dead* to Image Comics, he was shot down twice. The editors were skeptical that a straightforward zombie story would sell. On the third go round, Kirkman changed his pitch. He told them that his zombie story was really just a set up for an alien invasion. Aliens had infected the world, he suggested, as a way of softening up resistance prior to their planned takeover. After several comics were in print, one of the editors, Eric Stephenson, called Robert and said, "I'm a little curious. . . . You told me about this invasion thing and I don't see anything that is setting up the alien invasion coming." Robert laughed and said, "There's not going to be an invasion. I just told you guys that to get you to do the book. I knew it was going to be a cool book,

I knew that people were going to love it, but you guys just kept throwing roadblocks in my way, so I gave you the alien invasion."

Was it right of Kirkman to lie? I'll leave it up to you to decide. Regardless, even if Kirkman was wrong, I'm sure we can all find it in our hearts to forgive him.

5
Back from the Dead

WILLIAM J. DEVLIN AND ANGEL M. COOPER

After weeks in a coma, Rick Grimes awakens to a post-apocalyptic world. He's alone and confused in a deserted wasteland amidst piles of corpses and flesh-eating zombies. Fighting his way through the "walking dead," Rick has two goals: survival and finding his family. However, once he reunites with them, Rick questions whether survival is the only remaining goal.

Following Dale Horvath's advice, he comes to learn that even though "the world we knew is gone," we must keep "our humanity" (2.11 "Judge, Jury, and Executioner"). He realizes that he and other survivors can save their humanity by developing their moral character. The zombie apocalypse offers new moral dilemmas, such as: What should the group do with Randall? Should Rick sacrifice Michonne to the Governor? Should the group allow the Termites to live?

Throughout the series, we find that the characters justify their moral decisions through at least two moral theories: virtue-ethics and consequentialism. Furthermore, as the characters face these moral dilemmas, they run the risk of losing their humanity. Whether it's by murdering the living, leaving others behind, torturing prisoners, etc., they are forced to ask themselves if they can "come back" from "the worst kinds of things just to stay alive."

The Walking Dead suggests that human beings, in this post-apocalyptic world, fundamentally have two choices concerning how to live—to merely survive or to strive to live as morally good persons. The show suggests that those who choose to merely survive justify their moral decisions based on the consequences of their actions. However, this choice runs the risk of losing our "humanity," or moral character. Alternatively, the series proposes that those who choose to live as morally good people justify their moral decisions in terms of their character, and not simply by consequences. But by following this choice, the characters risk losing their lives.

Just Another Animal Who Understands Nothing But Survival

When Rick and the Atlanta group are stuck on top of a building, Merle beats T-Dog and asserts leadership of the group. Rick restrains him, pointing out that "we survive this by pulling together, not apart" (1.2 "Guts"). He justifies his behavior by appealing to the ends, or consequences, of his actions. With survival as one of his primary goals, he restrains Merle to prevent him from hurting members of the group.

Rick offers moral reasoning from the position known as *consequentialism*, or the view that the moral worth of an action is determined by its consequences. The platitude "the ends justify the means" applies. The most famous consequentialist school is *utilitarianism*. As John Stuart Mill explains, utilitarianism is grounded in the "Greatest Happiness Principle" whereby "actions are right in proportion as they tend to promote happiness; wrong as they tend to produce the reverse of happiness." Rick's reasoning is utilitarian in spirit. Here, Merle is wrong to think solely about his own well-being. He should focus on increasing the chances of survival for everyone; and in order to achieve that end, they should work together.

While Rick explores various moral theories (more on this later), this view of utilitarianism is slightly distorted. Like other characters, Rick is not concerned with happiness, but *survival*. As Officer Dawn Lerner explains to Beth, "Every sacrifice we make needs to be for the greater good. The second it isn't, the second we lose sight of that, it's all over." In this respect, the Greatest Happiness Principle has been replaced by the "Greatest Survival Principle," where actions are right if they promote survival for the greatest number; wrong if they produce the reverse of survival. This is summed up neatly by Enid's acronym which is also the title of episode 6.2 "JSS," "Just Survive Somehow." The Greatest Survival Principle seems to be a common-sense moral principle for a post-apocalyptic world inundated by walkers. However, as Dale and Lori suggest, using the Greatest Survival Principle as the guiding principle for all decisions in life, even a post-apocalyptic life, is a bad idea. Those who lead by survival alone risk losing their "humanity." We can see this point through three antagonists: Shane Walsh, The Governor, and the Termites.

The Right Choices Are the Ones that Keep Us Alive

Prior to the outbreak, Shane appears to be a morally good person with his humanity intact. He's a good friend to Rick, who cares for his family when he is in a coma and even attempts to save him in the hospital. He leads a group of survivors, helping them maintain a somewhat stable life. However, we gradually witness Shane's humanity unravel as he collapses into madness, paralleled with his commitment to the Greatest Survival Principle.

While Rick and the group are trapped within the city, Amy pleads with Shane to rescue them. Shane objects, stating, "We do not risk the rest of the group." (1.2 "Guts"). We see Shane's first appeal to consequentialism and the Greatest Survival Principle as a leader. While it's possible to find them, Shane reasons it is not worth it by the Greatest Survival Principle. Risking the lives of others for those who may already be dead does not maximize the chances for survival. This line of reasoning dictates Shane's behavior, and ultimately, accounts for why we, the viewers, come to see Shane as acting immorally for the remainder of the series. In 1.5 "Wildfire," when Rick challenges Shane's leadership, Shane contemplates shooting Rick. We later learn Shane's reasons. While searching for Sophia, Shane tells Rick, "You got every able body at your disposal out scourging these woods for a little girl we both know is likely dead."

To Shane, Rick has not adjusted to the post-apocalyptic world. He misses the ultimate goal: "Survival, Rick." For Shane, though Rick was a leader as Sheriff in the old world, he cannot lead anymore. Shane points out that leading, "means making hard decisions. . . . I'm trying to save lives here. . . . It's math, man. . . . Sophia, she only matters to the degree in which she don't drag the rest of us down." While Shane's concern for survival is reasonable (post-apocalyptic world or not), it is his obsessive commitment *solely* to survival that makes us question his moral character.

The clearest example of Shane's obsession with Greatest Survival is his act of sacrificing Otis to save himself and Carl. 2.3 "Save the Last One" opens with a maniacal Shane shaving his head, a metaphor for his loss of humanity and collapse into madness. Earlier, when Shane and Otis retrieve medical supplies, the two heroically risk their lives to save Carl. They find themselves overwhelmed by the number of walkers chasing them and with next to no ammunition left to defend themselves, Shane shoots Otis, leaving him as bait for the walkers so he can escape with the supplies. He later reveals the murder to Rick: "One of us wasn't gonna make it out. It had to be him. One shot to the leg, Carl lives" (2.10 "18 Miles Out"). Shane reasons that 'sacrificing' Otis maximized survival, as it allowed him to live, save Carl, and protect Lori.

Shane's 'sacrifice' of Otis marks his plummet into moral chaos and his loss of humanity. His decisions become based solely on the number of individuals surviving. He murders Randall (2.12 "Better Angels") and insists on killing the walkers in the barn, despite Hershel's protest (2.7 "Pretty Much Dead Already"). Shane's own self-reflection of his loss of humanity is encapsulated when he looks upon Dale in a truck's mirror, and yells:

> Do you got something to say, Dale? Well, go ahead, man. Mr. Moral Authority, huh? The voice of reason. Let me ask you something, man. What do you do? What do you do to keep this camp safe, huh? . . . If I was such a danger, if I was such a threat, what did you do to stop me, huh? I smashed up on there, I saved Carl. That's me. That ain't you. That ain't Rick. That's me. (2.8 "Nebraska")

The series displays an exceptional use of literal mirror-reflections to indicate philosophical reflections. When Shane and Rick fight about Randall, Shane breaks a window. We see a bloody Shane look at his reflection, where he looks like a walker himself—Shane no longer looks human, indicating the loss of his humanity.

Shane's loss of his humanity eventually reaches full fruition, and his obsession with survival leads to his demise. After killing Randall, Shane lures Rick out alone in the woods so that he can kill him. Rick, however, is aware of Shane's plan. Rick stabs Shane, killing him. As Rick later explains, he had to kill Shane because "He lost it. He lost who he was" (3.6 "Hounded"). Rick recognizes that Shane lost his humanity and, as such, had to be killed.

You Kill or You Die. Or You Die and You Kill

We're first introduced to the Governor as a character who, unlike Shane, has already lost his humanity. Though he hides under the cover of being a morally upright leader, we quickly discover that the Governor is a ruthless, immoral dictator who leads the town of Woodbury under the rule of the Greatest Survival Principle. He applies this principle to dealing with Rick's group at the prison. Seeing them as a threat to the town's survival, he advocates Merle's torture of Glenn and conducts the torture and attempted rape of Maggie (3.7 "When the Dead Come Knocking"). These acts are justifiable as means to an end—namely to locate and massacre Rick's group.

Ultimately, the Governor makes three attempts to dispose of Rick's group. First, he leads an attack on the prison, flooding it with walkers (3.10 "Home"). Second, he stages a meeting with Rick for a negotiation, where he asks for Michonne in exchange for peace (3.13 "Arrow on the Doorpost"). However, this agreement is a lie, as the Governor has planned to kill Rick and his group when they arrive with Michonne. Third, he leads a full-on assault of the prison (3.16 "Welcome to the Tombs").

In each attempt, the Governor adopts consequentialism to justify his actions. He sees Rick's group as a threat to the survival of his people and so he must eliminate them. But his failure to eliminate the threat propels him further into madness. Upon witnessing his army flee from the prison, he winds up massacring them—the same people he tried to save.

Despite this atrocious behavior, we are given a glimmer of hope that the Governor can save his humanity. He reappears in Season Four, befriending the Chambler family. Becoming a partner to Lilly and a surrogate father to her daughter Meghan, the Governor takes on a new name, Brian Heriot, and a new life. He seems to have re-discovered his humanity. Even Martinez, his former henchmen, acknowledges this: "You seem different now; changed . . . the family really brought you back." (4.7 "Dead Weight"). Despite this hope, 'Brian' fails to recapture his humanity. Realizing Caesar cannot keep them safe, 'Brian' murders him and later Pete Dolgen, so that he can become commander of the new group.

Chillingly, as the Governor drags Caesar to the pit of walkers, he screams: "I don't want it, dammit! I don't want it!" He is aware that killing Caesar is a move to become leader, live solely by the Greatest Survival Principle, and destroy any hope he had for saving his humanity. Later, while on his way to kill Pete, he simply tells Lilly that he is "surviving" (4.7 "Dead Weight").

As leader, 'Brian's' first act is to convince Pete's brother, Mitch, to join him by appealing to the Greatest Survival Principle: "if you join me, I promise you, you will never have to worry about whether you were doing the right thing or the wrong thing. Because we will do the only thing." Here, 'Brian' solidifies his loss of humanity. Justifying his actions by the Greatest Survival Principle, the Governor returns to his crusade against Rick's group. He explains that their current location is too dangerous, so they need to relocate to the prison. But he can't live with Rick and Michonne, so he must eliminate that group to help maximize the survival of his group. As he explains to his people about Rick's group:

> They got walls, fences, plots of land for farming. We could live there. . . . If we're willing to take it from 'em. Now you saw me—I tried. I tried to die. 'Cause I didn't want to accept that you couldn't live in this world without getting blood on your hands. I found you people and I don't want to die. I don't want you to die. (4.8 "Too Far Gone")

Using Hershel and Michonne as bargaining chips, the Governor leads his people to the prison to convince Rick to give it up. Rick pleads with him, but he is too far gone. He beheads Hershel and leads a final assault on the prison. This time, however, the Governor's maddening obsession with the Greatest Survival Principle comes to a tragic end. After Michonne runs him through with her sword, Lilly—the one person left whom he loves—shoots him.

You're the Butcher or You're the Cattle

Perhaps the most radical example of a group who sacrifice their humanity through the Greatest Survival Principle is the "Termites," led by Gareth. When Rick's group splinters after the fall of the prison, they each come across signs pointing towards Terminus, with the promise of: "Sanctuary for all. Community for all. Those who arrive, survive."

But once they arrive, they discover there is no sanctuary. Instead, they find themselves literally treated like cattle being prepared for the slaughter. They are herded into a train car prison and later ushered to the "slaughterhouse" to have their throats slit and become prepared as food for the Termites. Unbeknownst to Rick's group, there once was "sanctuary" at Terminus. As Gareth's mother, Mary, explains to Carol, "The signs, they were real. It was a sanctuary. People came and took this place. And they raped and they killed . . . over weeks, but we got out and we fought and we got it back. And we heard the message. You're the butcher or you're the cattle." In 5.1 "No Sanctuary," we're shown glimpses of the horrors the Termites went through. Like Rick's group, they were imprisoned in train cars by marauders. But rather than be prepared for a quick death, the Termites were beaten, raped, and killed, seemingly all for the enjoyment of the group that overtook Terminus. The horrors they endured help to unravel their humanity. While imprisoned, Gareth's brother, Alex regrets offering sanctuary to others in need: "We should never have put up the signs. What the hell did we think was gonna happen? We brought them here." Gareth tries to justify their morally admirable decision, "We were trying to do something good. We were being human beings," to which Alex cynically replies, "What are we now, Gareth?" Poetically, as if answering Alex's question later in time, when Rick, Daryl, Glen, and Bob escape the slaughter, Daryl announces, "They ain't people." Seeing their good intentions turn against them, the Termites take back their home, not by moral fortitude, but by becoming butchers and making everyone else their cattle.

The Termites survive according to the Greatest Survival Principle and by relinquishing their humanity. Treating visitors as food, they are both morally and emotionally detached from their victims. When the butchers hold Rick and others over the trough, they behave as if they are working an ordinary job. One butcher practices his swing before he bludgeons the back of Sam's head (whose throat is nonchalantly cut by the second butcher). Gareth casually walks in with a clipboard (as if he were oblivious to the frightening screams of their victims), asks the butchers about their shot counts, and gives them orders to get their cattle "to the driers." He then goes back outside putting on his "public face" to lure in future livestock. When Bob pleads with Gareth not to kill them, explaining there is a cure and imploring him to "take a chance" as they can "put the world back to how it was," Gareth apathetically replies, "Can't go back, Bob."

The Termites are indiscriminate about who they treat as means to the end of their survival. After Alex is killed, we see that he, too, is on a slab, being prepared as food for the group. When walkers enter Terminus, those Termites who fall down are not rescued by their brethren—rather, they are left for dead. Martin even explains to Tyreese, "I don't have any friends. I mean, I know people. They're just assholes I stay alive with." Like all Termites, Martin is in the group for survival. He has no moral attachment to them; rather, they all use each other for the sole purpose of staying alive. Notably, he tells Tyreese, "You're a good guy. That's why you're gonna die today. It's why the baby is going to die."

The Termites have lost their humanity since they believe being morally good entails losing one's life. Thus, they see humans as only a means to survival, depicting a madness Rick's group had yet to encounter in other followers of the Greatest Survival Principle. If someone becomes useless while alive, then there is no point in saving them. The best option is to eat them. This is how Mary justifies their cannibalism to Carol, "It's what it had to be. And why we're still here."

When Gareth and the remaining Termites kidnap Bob and eat his leg, Gareth coldly summarizes his journey to cannibalism through the Greatest Survival Principle:

> I want to explain myself a little. You see, we didn't want to hurt you before. . . . These aren't things that we want to do. They're things we got to do. You and your people took away our home. . . . Now we're out here like everybody else trying to survive. And in order to do that, we have to hunt. Didn't start that way, eating people. It *evolved* into that. We evolved. We had to. And now we've *devolved* into hunters. I told you. I said it. Can't go back, Bob. I just hope you understand that nothing happening to you now is personal . . . we would have done this to anybody. . . . But at the end of the day, no matter how much we hate all this ugly business a man's got to eat.

From Gareth's perspective, his turn to cannibalism is justified on the grounds of survival. The act of hunting and eating others evolved as a means for living, no matter how "ugly" it may be for everyone. Likewise, he turns to hurting Bob according to the Greatest Survival Principle, since he finds they must both hunt and hurt in order to survive another day. At the same time, Gareth recognizes that he has now "devolved" in terms of losing his humanity. But, like Shane and the Governor, he abides by the claim that survival is the priority. Furthermore, he claims that it is impossible to come back from what they are. While the show suggests that Shane and the Governor have hope for "coming back" from the moral dead and saving their humanity, we do not get the sense that Gareth can return. Despite his initial morally good character at Terminus, he consistently holds to the view that there is no going back.

Ultimately, however, Gareth and the Termites not only lose their humanity, but also their lives. In 5.3 "Four Walls and a Roof," Gareth's group once again becomes the cattle, while Rick's group become the butchers and hunters as they lure the Termites into Fr. Gabriel's church for a literal slaughter.

It's Time We Started Planting

As Lori is dying, she tells Carl that he is going to beat this world, listing his virtues: smart, strong, and brave. She warns him: "Don't let the world spoil you" (3.4 "Killer Within"). She doesn't tell Carl to live by the Greatest Survival Principle, but by the moral view of *virtue ethics*. Telling him to be a good person, she's not worried about Carl surviving; she's worried about who he is and the kind of life he will lead.

Virtue ethics does not focus on consequences to determine right actions; rather, it looks at the character of an individual, who we should be and what kind of life we should live. Aristotle, the founder of virtue ethics, argues that human beings are inherently concerned with living a good, or *flourishing*, life—one where we can attain happiness, achieve success, grow, and thrive. In 2.10 "18 Miles Out," Andrea criticizes Lori for focusing on putting "fresh mint leaves in the lemonade," something Andrea deems unimportant. Lori replies, "We are trying to create a life worth living." Lori wants the group to have a life that includes happiness, a life where the group can thrive. Aristotle wasn't talking about fresh mint leaves in the lemonade, but in the world of the walking dead, the characters take what little happiness they can get! In this sense, Lori relies upon virtue ethics to save her humanity by seeking, not just to survive, but to live the good life.

Aristotle thinks we have a function that is essential to our being, which is "activity of the soul in accord with reason." In order to acquire the good life, we must develop reason and act accordingly. We reason well by attaining *virtues*, which are human excellences. When we develop our reason and act with it, we act virtuously. When Lori lists Carl's qualities, she lists his moral virtues of intelligence, strength and bravery. Other Aristotelian virtues include generosity, friendliness, and wittiness. We will see all these virtues develop and deteriorate in Rick.

Aristotle calls virtues "states" because we acquire them; like Hershel's recommendation to Rick that they start planting seeds, virtues are grown from seeds that become habits. If your bravery is not a habit, then it is not a virtue you have acquired. We need to practice bravery by acting bravely in different situations until it becomes second nature, and likewise with other virtues. We accept that Rick is a brave person because we can list dozens of times when he acts bravely. But we would not call Merle "a brave person," even though we may call his last act of releasing Michonne and going after the Governor a brave act. He is rash in most other situations during his life. And although Lori practices virtue ethics, we argue that Rick becomes the model for virtue ethics in the post-apocalyptic world. We can see this through Rick's struggle to keep (or regain) his humanity in a world where morality seems to be lost.

There Are No Rules Anymore, Man, We're Lost!

Before the apocalypse, Rick is a confident leader with a clear moral code. When he's called to help with a police car chase, he immediately takes charge, putting up road spikes and getting everyone in position for the speeding car. He chastises an officer for talking about being on TV and tells him to make sure the safety of his gun is off (which it's not). Rick's leadership appears easy and natural to him.

However, when he later wakes up from his coma to discover a new world, his confidence wavers. His moral code is shaken. He is no longer the sheriff with specific rules to follow. Now he must become something new. In the first two seasons, we watch as Rick desperately tries to hold onto his good character, but flounders morally. He makes moral decisions using various ethical theories, as if he is uncertain how to live. He employs a rule-based ethics for some decisions, claiming, "We don't kill the living" (1.5 "Wildfire") and "a little girl goes missing, you look for her. Plain and simple" (2.2 "Bloodletting"). Rick also toys with the Greatest Survival Principle. He repeatedly explains that he would do anything to produce the outcome of his family's safety and survival (2.9 "Triggerfinger"; 2.10 "18 Mile Out").

At the same time, he questions his decisions and contradicts the reasons for them. He wonders if he should be more like Shane and follow the Greatest Survival Principle. He also questions his choice to look for Sophia. In "What Lies Ahead," he asks God if he is doing the right thing in looking for her and again in 2.8 "Nebraska," he questions whether looking for her was a good idea. In "18 Miles Out," Rick voices his moral disorientation, telling Shane, "there are no rules anymore, man, we're lost!" But what he really means is that *he* is morally lost. As we've seen, many of the other characters have already decided which moral framework to embrace. Rick is the one who flounders, morally.

Though Rick is morally lost, we still see him as a good person, as he is trying to carry Aristotle's virtues over from the old world. He displays bravery and Aristotelian reasoning when he decides to save Merle on the roof, explaining "*I* can't let a man die of thirst. *Me*" (1.3 "Tell it to the Frogs"). Rick must go back for Merle because of the kind of person he is. He does not have the character of someone who lets a man die of thirst (1.2 "Guts"). He is generous, giving guns to the Atlanta Nursing Home group (1.4 "Vatos"). He is friendly and compassionate, going out of his way to help people, often risking his life for others. And he is witty—well, as witty as one can be in a world where dead people eat you— joking with others (calling himself "Officer Friendly" when Merle asks him who the hell he is).

Rick also demonstrates practical wisdom. He comes up with clever ideas, such as wearing guts to get by the walkers in

Atlanta (1.2 "Guts"). He values contemplation, taking time to think about important decisions rather than just acting on them like Shane. He will not choose to kill Randall until he has had time to think about it. He tells Carl, "Think. It's a good rule of thumb for life" (2.11 "Judge, Jury, Executioner"). Rick values wisdom and thinks his moral decisions through carefully. Thus, Rick questions how to make moral decisions and, as his journey develops, he becomes more and more confused. But, he holds onto the virtuous character he cultivated from his old life—that is, until he kills Shane.

You're Cold as Ice, Officer Friendly

Once Rick kills Shane, he begins to lose himself. As he is strangling Shane, Rick yells, "You did this to us. This was you, not me. Not me!" (2.12 "Better Angels"). Rick places responsibility for this act with Shane because he can't accept it as something he would do. It's not part of who Rick is, the kind of person he is, to kill Shane. So he tries to convince himself that it was not his choice. However, when he describes the scene to Lori he admits:

> He pushed me and I let him. After a while, I knew. I knew what he was doing. What he was up to. And I kept going. I didn't stop. I could have. But I just wanted it over. . . . I wanted him dead. I killed him.

Rick knows he could have stopped himself from killing Shane, but he killed him because he wanted to. The old Rick would not have killed him. This new world has finally changed Rick and it continues to do so until he's no longer recognizable.

After Shane's death, Rick's character changes quickly and dramatically. Detached and thoughtless, he acts more like Shane, following the Greatest Survival Principle, and begins losing his humanity and collapses into madness. Slowly, Rick abandons the virtues from his old life. He's no longer friendly and witty, but cold. His coldness starts to appear after he kills Shane and tells the group that he will make the decisions. If they don't want to follow him, he declares, "Send me a postcard. Go on, there's the door. You can do better? Let's see how far you get" (2.13 "Beside the Dying Fire"). He loses his generous nature, as he will not give the prisoner group guns and refuses to help them unless they give up half of their food. He loses his compassion, not allowing any new people to join the group (3.9 "The Suicide King"). He even loses his bravery, becoming rash and vengeful. When Andrea travels to the prison to urge a deal between Rick and the Governor, he informs her that he will not compromise: "We are going to kill him" (3.11 "I Ain't a Judas"). He also gives up his prudence and simply acts. Rick kills Tomas (3.2 "Sick") and throws Andrew out of the prison, all without a thought. Once Lori dies, Rick becomes totally lost. He's erratic, temperamental, and vengeful. Moreover, he becomes delusional, having visions of Lori and talking to phantoms on the prison's dead phone. His worst moment is when he's willing to turn Michonne over to the Governor to give the group a better chance of survival (3.13 "Arrow on the Doorpost"). Similar to Shane's reasoning towards Randall's execution, Rick believes that Michonne must be sacrificed for the group.

We Get to Come Back

Ultimately, Rick does not succumb to the Greatest Survival Principle and the loss of his humanity. Two people bring him back: Lori and Carl. While Rick prepares to give up Michonne, he sees an image of Lori standing on the bridge, looking down at him, as if she's judging who he has become. Lori is the virtue ethicist of the group and lets Rick know that her family's good characters are most important. With this vision, he changes his mind, exclaiming to Hershel, "I can't. I won't" (3.15 "This Sorrowful Life"). Lori's judging gaze compels Rick to look inward at who he has become. He later explains, "I couldn't sacrifice one of us for the greater good because we are the greater good." We can see a contrast in Rick's statement here compared to Dawn's in Season Four. As Rick begins regaining his moral character, he claims that sacrificing someone in the group would be acting *against* the greater good. Dawn, on the other hand, following the Greatest Survival Principle, claims that she must sacrifice people *for* the greater good.

Later, Carl shoots a surrendering kid and explains: "I couldn't take the chance. I didn't kill the walker that killed Dale. Look what happened. You didn't kill Andrew and he came back and killed mom. You were in a room with the governor and you let him go and he came back and killed Merle. I did what I had to do" (3.16 "Welcome to the Tombs"). Carl provides reasons for killing the kid that are similar to Rick's in Season Three. He, like Rick, is starting to follow the Greatest Survival Principle. Lately, Rick is unwilling to give anyone a chance because he thinks it's too great a risk to the group. Rick doesn't let the prisoners or Tyreese join his group. He allows Michonne in but tells Carl he is only allowing her to stay with them because of what she can do for them ("Clear").

Now Carl also states that he's not willing to take the risk of giving someone outside of the group a chance. Likewise, Rick explains to the group that he killed Shane because he had no choice. Carl too argues that he killed the kid because he had to. After Rick sees Carl following the Greatest Survival Principle like Shane and himself, he lets the people of Woodbury join their group in the prison. This generous act is the second major turning point for Rick. Rick sees his son becoming the cold animal that Lori feared, and he recognizes himself in Carl. So he changes.

Rick starts to resemble the old Rick, as he is regaining his humanity. But he has not completely come back. Neither he nor Carl carries guns. He becomes a farmer and makes no decisions for the group. And he's back to doubting his moral choices. However, now Rick seems to have a clear goal—to save his own and his son's moral characters. He explains that he almost wound up like the crazy woman he meets in the woods—willing to do anything to feed the undead "Eddie." He tells Daryl, "I almost lost my boy. Who he was" (4.2 "Infected"). Rick is now concerned with saving their humanity. He starts to trust himself again and begins to regain some of his virtues. He acts bravely, helping with the walker breakout in the sick ward. He's clever, as he uses the piglets to lure the walkers away from the prison. He's generous and compassionate, as he lets the Woodbury people into the prison, and tries to help the crazy woman in the woods. His friendliness starts to reappear. He loses the coldness and anger he had in the previous season and easily converses with the others.

Rick's salvation of his humanity culminates when negotiating with the Governor. He demonstrates his moral character, pleading for peace: "Now you put down your weapons, walk through those gates you're one of us. We let go of all of it, and nobody dies. . . . We've all done the worst kinds of things just to stay alive. But we can still come back. We're not too far gone. We get to come back. I know. We all can change" (4.8 "Too Far Gone"). He realizes that, in the new world, he cannot make his decisions based on consequences. Like Lori, Rick advocates virtue ethics. He values the virtues that make him who he is and decides that he can't give up those virtues for mere survival.

This Is a Good Place to Start

Rick chooses to save his humanity and live the good life, instead of mere survival. However, his journey is not over. Rick knows how to make moral decisions, but he must still determine the virtues that make for an excellent character in the new world and cultivate those virtues to build an excellent character. Some virtues from the old world will likely transfer to this one. Yet, as Rick points out, he has changed. When he, Carl, and Michonne are threatened, he rips a man's throat out with his teeth and repeatedly stabs another man. Daryl says to Rick, "But that ain't you." Rick replies, "It ain't all of it, but that's me" (4.16 "A"). Although Rick has come back, he recognizes that the apocalyptic world has changed him. The virtues he acquires now will be different from the ones he had previously. He will need to find a way to balance an excellent character with the drive to survive and protect his son.

In Season Four, Rick struggles with the balance between virtue and survival. Although he has cultivated many virtues, he is clearly not the kind hearted sheriff as before. Rick now has a hardness to him and he is willing to do a lot more in order to keep himself, Carl, Judith, and the group safe. We see a brutality about him. In Season Five, he immediately wants to return to Terminus to kill the Termites. Later, when they finally capture them, Rick listens to Gareth's pleas with no compassion. Furthermore, before the massacring, Gareth reasons with Rick that he must have kept them alive this long for a reason and Rick chillingly responds, "We didn't want to waste the bullets." He then tells Gareth that he made him a promise and kills Gareth with the machete that he claimed he would in "No Sanctuary."

While Rick is harder and colder, he hasn't returned to the madman he was becoming earlier under the Greatest Survival Priniple. He massacres the Termites, but justifies his actions, explaining to Gareth that he can't let them live because "they will do this to anybody." He also listens to the perspectives of the others in the group and is willing to help others in need. While he doesn't trust Father Gabriel, he helps save his life and allows him into the group (though still warning him that the group is his "family" and he'll kill him if he's threatening them). Compare Rick's treatment of Father Gabriel with how those following the Greatest Survival Principle would treat him. Shane would have either not allowed him to be part of the group or killed him. The Governor would have used him to his own advantage. The Termites would have eaten him. Likewise, Rick forgives Carol for killing Karen and David and he wants to join Abraham's group in their mission to save the world (but won't do so if it means leaving Carol and Daryl behind).

Thus, Rick demonstrates that he cultivates virtues reflected in the context of the post-apocalyptic world. As Bob is dying, he thanks Rick, telling him, "Before the prison, I didn't know if there were any good people left. I didn't know if anybody was left. You took me in. 'Cause you took people in. It was you, man. . . . Nightmares end. They shouldn't end who you are. And that is just this dead man's opinion." Bob sees Rick's virtuous ways. And although he is changing and seeking to survive the post-apocalypse, he's also seeking to hold onto his humanity.

Agreeing with Bob's analysis, Rick replies, "I'll take it."

WALKER BITE
Differentiating the Dead

SABATINO DIBERNARDO

If you think that dead is dead, think again. *The Walking Dead* universe populated by "things" that are both dead and alive or neither dead nor alive causes us to rethink this truism by differentiating "the dead"—the undead from the dead dead; the living from the living dead; and the undead from each other.

By negating "dead," we get its opposite, "undead" and by qualifying "dead" with its opposite, we get "living dead." Even prior to reading one sentence of the comics or viewing one episode of the AMC series, this act of differentiation has already occurred in the title: *The Walking Dead*.

Unlike the premiere television episode in which Morgan used the term "walkers" when correcting Rick's false assumption that Morgan killed a man, the inaugural issue of the comic book series begins with Morgan's minimally differentiated catch-all term "things." Rick's immediate response is to reinterpret Morgan's classification: "Things?" You mean those monsters . . ." (Chapter 1: "Days Gone Bye").

After rescuing Rick, Glenn introduces the term "zombies" to name "those things." Later, while talking to Tyreese, Rick redescribes them as "half-rotten ghouls" then "roamers" due to the different behaviors exhibited by the "zombies" in Atlanta: "Most of the zombies just sat around, not doing anything unless *provoked*. Then our camp was attacked . . . So I gotta think there are other kinds of zombies that roam around, always on the move. I figure *roamers* is as good a name as any" (Chapter 2: "Miles Behind Us"). What's apparent here is that the world, even a fictional one, doesn't divide itself up into names and classifications based on some pre-existing essence, concept, or identity. Humans, even fictional ones, perform these differentiating acts of naming and classifying that construct their worlds. Different societies and different cultures within those societies describe and thereby divide their worlds up differently; different names for the "same things," whatever the things, in innumerable languages point to the "arbitrary" nature of terms within each "contingent" system of language.

There's an ever-growing list of supplemental names for those "things" in *The Walking Dead*: walkers, roamers, lurkers, biters, floaters, lame-brains, geeks, monsters, meat puppets, empties, deadies, creepers, swimmers, dead ones, eaters, ghouls, skin-eaters, the infected, stinkers, and rotters, as well as abominations, corpses, freaks, and other, sometimes quite colorful, variations and combinations. You can find all these at http://walkingdead.wikia.com, which also notes the different names commonly used by the various groups in the comics and the television series; even the "same" groups found in both media use different terms—walkers or roamers.

So, although the different communities in *The Walking Dead* share a common language, they don't share a common system of classification or context; although the different communities share a common interest in naming this threat to their existence, they don't name it in the same way. While these differences argue against any necessary connection between a name and the thing named, the socially and culturally constructed classifications may be divided up in terms of the following: *actions performed*, *states of (non)being*, and *(pejorative) descriptions*. Language, convention, and context precede those previously unknown things.

One example of this process of linguistic construction unfolds in the comics when Rick explains to the inmates at the prison, "Those *things* are everywhere . . . We've taken to calling them zombies, I guess though, it was a *while* before we could *say* it with a straight face" (Chapter 3: "Safety Behind Bars"). Why this slightly embarrassed justification? Well, we all know that zombies, like Rick, are just fictional constructions, but what's more important is that Rick's self-conscious reflection provides some insight into *how* naming functions. If things had some self-evident essence that corresponded necessarily between a name and the thing named, justification and its accompanying emotions would be unnecessary. But since this is precisely what we don't have, questions about naming and convention are always possible, as illustrated below:

- Rick's questioning of the title "Governor": "Governor?" The Governor responds: "I wear the title with a *smile*. It's more of a joke than anything else. But *fuck it*. Who's out there to say otherwise? I almost went with *President*— but I thought it sounded too silly" (Chapter 5: "The Best Defense").

- Rick's questioning of the naming of The Kingdom: "*The Kingdom?*" Jesus responds: "Yeah. Look man, I didn't name it" (Chapter 18: "What Comes After").

- Earl Sutton's distaste regarding Paul Monroe's allowing people to nickname him "Jesus": "It's a stupid nickname—disrespectful, frankly. You look like certain depictions of the guy, but it seems like you think pretty highly of yourself that you've let the nickname stick." Jesus responds: It's not like *I* came up with it—there are a lot of people here—it's an easy name to remember!" (Chapter 19: "March To War").

In each case, there's a disclaimer, distancing, or joking disavowal of the act of naming due to the value judgments evident in the criticism or questioning. The kneejerk reactions seem to indicate, at some level, a self-conscious awareness that naming is a process for which namers and cultures are responsible.

Naming tells us something about the namers. When Jesus classifies the undead as "empties," based on their internal state of (non)being, the nickname "Jesus" and the name "empties" say something about both the fictional namer and Kirkman as namer. Another crucial issue is raised by the Governor's remarks: naming as a conferral of power. By calling names and naming into question, we also call into question the authority to name. Without any absolute authority or standard, what appears to be "natural" may turn out to be a self-interested exercise in self-authorized power. Names, titles, classifications, and categorizations communicate all kinds of meanings and implications with existential ramifications: names and naming matter.

One particularly telling example regarding the justification of a classification is provided by Alice, the doctor's assistant in the comics' narrative of Woodbury. While taking care of Rick after his hand had been cut off, she indicates a general nonchalance about naming the undead: "the biters, zombies, whatever"; but later, she pokes fun at the construction of two subcategories of zombies as roamers and lurkers by Rick's group: "Two types? That's a little *silly*. They *all* bite. *Biters* makes a ton more sense. Just saying . . ." Rick agrees, and Glenn, using the now-familiar distancing disclaimer, states: "Wasn't me who came up with it" (Chapter 6, "The Sorrowful Life"). Although these exchanges may be viewed as inconsequential asides, they're better understood as examples of the "common-sense" belief that language is natural or transparent; that language corresponds directly with the world in itself. When different languages or classifications collide, the commonality of "common sense" may need rethinking. Alice's appeal to (common) sense wouldn't make sense to Michonne or Andrea, since they've seen to it that not *all* "biters" bite. "Common sense" and "making sense," then, indicate that sense is *made* common by convention.

Finally, differentiating the dead challenges not only common-sense notions of naming but also the dogmatic insistence on strict boundaries between related opposites. By occupying an uncertain middle space between what something is and is not, the either/or opposition between *the living* and *the dead* is called into question by the *living dead*. And if you think the linguistic issues involved in differentiating the dead are restricted only to naming those fictional things, think again. By replacing *the living* and *the dead* with another supposedly strict opposition, *us* and *them*, the social, political, and ethical implications for our own world of inclusions and exclusions become painfully evident. When Rick states, "There will always be '*us*' against '*them*,' but we need to never forget . . . we are '*us*' and the dead are '*them*'" (Chapter 21: "All Out War"), he displays a dogmatic desire to police the boundaries of these related opposites that can't stop their reversal or slippage. But even Rick comes to realize the irony that the *us* may turn out to be *them* . . . "We are the Walking Dead!" (Chapter 4: "The Heart's Desire").

6
Punishing Negan

WAYNE YUEN

Death is everywhere in *The Walking Dead*. It's personified by the walkers surrounding our survivors; an ever-looming spectator watching and waiting for our heroes to join them. The walkers are regularly featured in the television series, with every episode serving up a wonderfully macabre way for Rick and Co. to dispatch a walker. They're literally fighting off death for one more episode. But we also know that at any moment they could lose that fight. It is this fight against death that defines who they are. Do we give up the fight and surrender to the walkers? Do we band together, or go it alone? Do we condemn others to help ourselves or our group to survive? It is this last question that gets explored in a particularly intriguing way in the comic series. Rick is finding himself in a position that he hasn't seen since the apocalypse: being part of a civilization.

So let's get some spoilers out of the way first. I'm going to keep the spoilers to a bare minimum here. In order to do this, I'll need to be vague about the fate of many characters. Viewers of the television series should also keep in mind that the comic series and TV series have differed substantially in how the storylines have played out and which characters have lived and died.

If you have only watched the television series, and have not read any of the comics there are a few things that you need to know. In the comic series, after the war with the Governor, Rick and our group of survivors go to Washington, DC, because of Eugene's lie. In Washington, they discover a band of survivors who have made a "safe-zone" in Alexandria where they can live.

Walls keep walkers out and protect their society. We see this play out at the end of Season Five.

This society isn't all chocolate pudding though. Alexandria is threatened, in the comics, by another group called "The Saviors," who threaten death and destruction if they are not paid in food and supplies. Their leader, a man by the name of Negan, kills a long-time member of Rick's group to get his point across: submit to the deal or die. This kicks off a long war between Rick's group against Negan's Saviors. In the end, our heroes are victorious, and Rick decides that Negan should spend the rest of his life behind bars, to the shock of many other characters, who expected Rick to kill Negan.

If there is a list of characters in *The Walking Dead* who deserves the death penalty, Negan is most definitely on the list. He gleefully wields a bat wrapped with barbed wire that he calls "Lucille" and takes sadistic pleasure in utilizing her on others, he outright murders individuals to terrorize and intimidate groups of people to submit to a mafia-like protection scheme, he has several wives by offering women and their spouses extra food and supplies so long as the women are monogamous with him alone, and failure to maintain monogamy with Negan is punished with permanent disfigurement on the part of the husband alone (he wants his women to look pretty). All in all, Negan is a terrible human being (but strangely delightful as a villain!). Rick, however, doesn't condemn Negan to the specter of death that everyone is fighting against. So if Negan is so terrible, why doesn't Rick execute Negan?

A Justified Death

There are two broad arguments for punishments in general: Retribution and Deterrence. Retributionists believe that punishments function as either fair play or a kind of equality. Let's look at fair play first. Under this model of retributivism, what the rules or laws of our society dictate punishments should be for a given crime is what the person should get. The simplest analogy would be to think of sports; for example hockey. In Hockey, when a player hits another player with their hockey stick, it is a penalty. If the hit causes a player to bleed, it is a four-minute penalty, if not, then it is a two-minute penalty. The team will now be down one player for two or four minutes while the other team is allowed the full number of players.

That's simply what the rules state. It doesn't matter if the hit was accidental, or if the other player really deserved being hit with a hockey stick. The rules are clear: hit another player with a hockey stick, two minutes, if they bleed, four minutes. Doing anything else wouldn't be fair, because it wouldn't be playing by the established rules of the game.

Now in *The Walking Dead*, there is no clear society that is governing these people, just their own moral judgments. So this retributive model wouldn't work. There's also at least some reason to question its application to our world as well. Although the fair play model explains why certain crimes are associated with certain punishments, it gives no rationale for the connection between the punishment and the crime. It could be the case that we simply assign the death penalty to people who high stick in hockey. I'm fairly sure that if such a rule were to be instituted, hockey fans would accept it so long as they continue to allow fighting in the game. If those are the rules then those are the rules. The punishments attached to the rules could be completely arbitrary and have no relevant connection to the crime committed. That doesn't sound fair! This suggests that there needs to be a moral justification to determine the connection between crime and punishment.

The other possibility is retribution as a kind of equality. In this form, the punishment tries to equalize the harms that has been done between the victim and the criminal. If the criminal has stolen $100 worth of goods, than the criminal should not only return the stolen goods, but also be deprived of $100 worth of goods. The simplest way to characterize this form of retribution is to say that criminals are going to receive justice in the form of "An eye for an eye." In the case of Negan, he's killed many innocent people who were not threatening him or his belongings in any way. He's terrorized the lives of others and coerced others with death and disfigurement to loved ones to get his way, and has killed innocent people simply to get others to comply. To give him retributive justice in the sense of equality, Negan would also have to be deprived of his loved ones, be terrorized, and killed. It might simply be impossible for us to deprive Negan of his loved ones, because outside of Lucille, it's not clear that he loves anyone. But we certainly can execute him.

On the other side of this coin is deterrence. Under this view of punishment, we punish people because we either want to dissuade that person, or other people, from breaking the rule in the first place, or other people in the future from breaking the rules like the criminal did. There are many reasons that we follow the law, but when there is little incentive for people to follow the law and individuals can personally gain from not following the law, people tend to break the law, especially if there is no punishment attached.

So imagine a world where people didn't get fines for speeding on the highways. Such is the case in *The Walking Dead*. When Glenn gets behind the wheel of a Challenger (1.2 "Guts") I'm pretty sure he's not maintaining the speed limit. He drives as fast as he can because it's exhilarating and more importantly, at least for this point, there is no punishment to deter him from doing this. Glenn has no incentive to follow the posted speed limit, so he simply doesn't. One reason that you and I might not drive like Glenn does is because we are dissuaded or negatively-incentivized to follow the law. If we drive like Glenn, we might get caught by a highway patrol officer and be given a fine that we would rather not pay. But in the case of death as a punishment, I can't dissuade you from your future actions by killing you. So why execute people under deterrence? Let's go back to the speeding example. Clearly, not everyone gets tickets for speeding. The cost of having enough police officers to catch every speeder prevents us from doing so. But what happens when a highway patrol officer pulls over a speeder and is giving that person a ticket on the side of the highway? Everyone else slows down! The one speeder being caught, deters others from speeding as well. So, in the case of execution, the punishment is deterring others from committing similar crimes as the condemned. We might not stop Negan from terrorizing other people, but executing Negan might send a clear message to the other Saviors that such behavior in the future will not be tolerated.

A Larger World

But as I mentioned, Rick doesn't choose to execute Negan. There are at least three reasons that are given for why Negan shouldn't be executed. The first one comes from Rick: "We're better than him." This argument needs to be unpacked a bit. Rick, and many others in the real world, seem to think that in executing an individual we become equivalent to the criminal. Since we want to be better than criminals, we ought not to do what criminals do, so in this case, we ought not to kill.

Unfortunately, this line of reasoning has some problems. If we examine all of the legitimate punishments we have for criminals, we quickly see they all have criminal counterparts. If we fine criminals, then it amounts to stealing from them. We're better than criminals, so we can't fine them. If we imprison criminals, then we're doing something that criminals do as well, hold us captive against our will, and not letting us leave. The error in reasoning here is that in the case of punishments, we are inflicting it upon someone who is guilty of some kind of crime. In the case of a criminal act, we are inflicting it upon someone who is innocent. This difference is what transforms what would normally be criminal acts to acts of punishment. Obviously it isn't simple to determine the guilt or innocence of a person. That is why we have an arduous and complicated processes to try to ferret out the truth. In the case of Negan, we the readers are in a privileged state where we can easily see his guilt.

A second reason, also given by Rick, is that they would be *worse* than Negan. Negan had opportunities to kill Rick and others, but didn't take them. Negan is clear, he kills to send messages, and killing Rick wouldn't send the message he wants to send. This is a narrow justification; it only applies to this particular scenario. What message would Rick be sending by executing Negan? Don't do what Negan did? Most people already wouldn't do what Negan did! Let's imagine that there was another character who did similar things to Negan. This person is executed, and Negan sees this. Negan doesn't strike me as the kind of person who would be deterred by a spectacle of this sort. So exactly who is this execution going to deter? Rick's choice not to execute might stem from a recognition that the death penalty may not be an effective deterrent at all.

The message that Rick wants to send is a different message, which brings us to the third reason: The rule of law. Rick wants to build not just a community, but a civilization; communities that are inter-dependent upon each other. However, Rick also wants to avoid making the mistakes that our civilization has made. The innuendo here is that the death penalty is among the mistakes of our civilization that Rick wants to avoid. Later in the comics, Maggie lectures Carl, "We don't kill anymore remember? Maybe they deserved it. . . . But that doesn't matter. We don't kill." If this is the message that Rick wants to send, then it's a powerful message indeed. The message that killing other people is *so* wrong that even when the criminal deserves it, we will continue to refuse to do it, might foster a culture in this society that encourages people to be less violent to one another.

Rick's underlying strategy here is to point out that the Saviors, his group, and all of mankind have a common enemy: the walkers. Rick wants to dis-incentivize killing other people, so that they can concentrate on dealing with the larger threat. Human lives are precious and few in this post-apocalyptic world. If execution were the deterrent for murder in this new civilization, then we would reduce everyone's ability to survive, since civilization, at this point, depends upon increasing numbers for greater communal co-operation and skill specialization. People can't learn to be blacksmiths if they also have to forage for food and defend their home and themselves from walkers. With more people to distribute "housekeeping" work, individuals can become specialized in particular kinds of work, and benefit the community as a whole.

Obviously, we have plenty of people in our world, but there is a possible analogy to this line of reasoning for us. If we execute individuals in our society, it demonstrates that human lives have less worth than if we don't. If people generally believe that lives are less valuable, then we may be less sensitive to the concerns of others, and more likely to harm them. This is called the "brutalization effect." Much like deterrence, the brutalization effect is difficult to prove conclusively. But there is some evidence to suggest that there is a connection. In most US states that do not have the death penalty, there are lower murder rates. FBI statistics indicate that states without the death penalty have had *consistently* lower murder rates per capita, on average, between 1990 and 2010. In nearly all European countries—Belarus is currently the only exception— there is no death penalty, and murder rates are lower. This is what Rick is rallying against; the possibility that the brutalization effect does occur, which could significantly alter the *character* of the fledgling civilization that he is trying to create.

Decaying Not Dying

The refusal to execute is not a refusal to punish. Rick tells Negan that he will watch Rick's community, and the other communities flourish without him, that it was Negan's leadership that was holding them back from prospering. Oddly though, Rick imprisons Negan in his basement, where he can't actually witness anything, other than what Rick and his few visitors tell him. Negan's punishment, life imprisonment, is the alternative that most people opposed to the death penalty offer as a reasonable alternative to execution. It gives a dis-incentive for people to follow the law that is plausibly strong enough to deter most people from committing crimes, and at the same time respects life enough to avoid the brutalization effect.

No punishment will work perfectly to deter all crime, but punishments that do deter the majority of people from crime accomplishes the goal well enough. If perfection is demanded, then we should throw out all of our punishments, since none of them work perfectly. This should be reason enough to think that the perfection standard is flawed, not just as a counterargument to punishment but for any argument in general. Requiring perfection, in virtually all circumstances, is an unreasonable standard.

But does Negan's punishment avoid the brutalization effect? It's not equivalent to life imprisonment in our world. Negan's prison is a small make-shift prison in Rick's basement. It's never been shown, nor is it likely, that Negan gets an opportunity to leave his cell to exercise or enjoy fresh air. He's given food and water, but for the most part, his imprisonment is long stretches of mostly isolation. He has no cellmates to commiserate with, only Rick as his jailor and the occasional visitor who reminds Negan that he would kill him if given the chance. So Rick respects Negan's life enough not to execute him, but doesn't respect his life enough to treat him with any kind of real decency. If real-world prisoners were treated in this manner, we would claim that their human-rights have been violated. Negan's punishment is far from morally ideal.

Life imprisonment, in reality, has at least a few controversial features. Some argue that rehabilitation is not a possibility with this punishment, since the prisoners will never be allowed back into society to show that they have been rehabilitated. This objection suggests that punishments should at least aim to provide individuals education or reform to correct their behavior, or character defects. Rehabilitation would then be a specific kind of deterrence that focuses in on preventing the criminal from re-offending.

Another objection might be that life imprisonment disrespects an individual's dignity. Generally speaking, we treat prisoners like children. We tell them when they can eat, what they can eat, when they go to sleep, and what they can watch on TV. Most adults don't like being treated like children, and let's face it, children don't like being treated like children. People like being able to govern their own lives and make decisions for themselves; people like to exercise their autonomy, which we severely limit in prison. People sentenced to life in prison have no future to look forward to where they are allowed to once again make autonomous decisions, which may make life in prison even more disheartening.

Some argue that this is precisely what we want prisoners to experience. We want them to experience a kind of suffering because they inflicted suffering onto others. But surely there must be some kind of moral limit to this suffering that we inflict on others, even if they are guilty of crimes. If the goal was to simply make people suffer, we could make prison much worse than what Negan is experiencing. We could torture people for the rest of their lives and endeavor to extend their lives for as long as possible. But one of the reasons that we find Negan horrifying is the sadistic joy that he takes in inflicting pain on others. If we can learn anything from Negan, it is that we ought not to take pleasure in the suffering of others, including those who might deserve very bad things. Taking pleasure in the suffering of others is precisely the character trait that leads Negan to make life all the more arduous for others and prevents Rick and others from building a functioning civilization.

Negan in Need

Is there an alternative way of punishing Negan that could better accomplish the goals that Rick has? I think it's obvious that Negan's punishment of being locked in Rick's basement is antithetical to Rick showing Negan the success of his society. If we also want to truly rebuild civilization without the mistakes of our civilization then Rick might be falling into the mistake of reconstructing prison life modeled after a far worse form of prison, one that we as a civilization have already moved away from, where prisoners are isolated and alive, but not much else. The simplest improvement would be for Rick and his society to build (or find) a decent prison where Negan can serve the rest of his time in humane conditions. But this would simply be reproducing the old world, and perhaps the flaws that come with it. I believe that there is an alternative method of punishing Negan that could improve Rick's civilization: Restorative Justice.

Restorative justice is a process in which criminals are made to confront victims of their crimes and work towards a resolution where the harm that was done has been resolved or compensated, in symbolic form if not actually. It is typically used to supplement other forms of punishment, like imprisonment, not to completely replace it. Under this model, the victims of the criminal take an active part in the punishment process. For example, if my property has been stolen, I would confront the criminal (in a safe, mediated fashion) with the harms that have been done to me. I was deprived of my property, my sense of security in my home might have severely diminished, perhaps I lost wages from dealing with the fallout from being victimized.

Through these mediated meetings the criminal would be taking steps that would alleviate or compensate the wrongs that have been done to me. Perhaps, in this case, the person who robbed me would have to work to pay restitution for the property stolen from me and my lost wages, as well as a security system for my home to help restore my sense of security. Restorative justice is not purely unidirectional. I might hear about the criminal's history and the circumstances which led him to rob me of my belongings. For example, perhaps he was starving and needed something to pawn in order to get money to eat. This might affect the final amount of restitution that is ultimately negotiated between the criminal and me.

Restorative justice aims for several results. Criminals are no longer experiencing a punishment that is only abstractly connected to his or her victims. It personalizes his or her criminal activity, and makes plain how the crime affects people, rather than abstractly injuring society. In a small society like Rick's, it could arguably reinforce the importance of community and highlight the relationship between individuals and community. Restorative justice is both punishment and rehabilitation in one.

The obvious objection would be that there are some crimes that cannot be compensated for. Negan killed people, both directly and indirectly. What could Negan possibly do to compensate the loss that the victims' loved ones experience? How can Negan compensate the children who will grow up without their mothers or fathers? How can he compensate the people who he permanently disfigures? Compensation in these cases are indeed impossible.

What would be possible is fostering a situation where the survivors of Negan's crimes are able to heal and move on. Apologies and forgiveness are powerful actions that can aid in these processes for the survivors, as well as be transformative for the wrongdoer. Additionally, the wrongdoer could engage reparative actions that can additionally foster healing. For example, if one of his victims loved chocolate pudding, then Negan could help improve the dairy so that more pudding could be made for the community. The unfortunate reality is that some actions cannot be repaired and some people will never heal. But the conditions that restorative justice attempts to foster are the ones that most likely will genuinely aid in victim healing. Restorative justice models have been utilized in cases of murder, rape, and even implemented in South Africa as a response to apartheid. (Whether or not it was actually a process of restorative justice is under a lot of debate, but the spirit of the attempt is at least commendable.)

To some, restorative justice sounds like a hippy, or naive, way of dealing with dangerous people. Let's just get Negan and Rick to say they're sorry and let bygones be bygones. Negan could simply lie and say, "I'm really sorry Rick. I see the wrongness of my ways, and won't do it again." If Negan were to be freed, he might simply be the first example, in this new civilization, of criminal relapse or recidivism. Restorative justice is a long process that could take years to see through and could fail to result in the desired outcomes. Even if reconciliation or forgiveness takes place between the criminal and victim, it still might be a good idea to keep the criminal in prison. Restorative justice doesn't pretend to be a generic punishment, like imprisonment, to fit all crimes. Criminals will still need to be evaluated on a case-by-case basis, much like parolees, to determine if their imprisonment should be shortened or not.

This is not to say that there aren't some reservations that we should have about this model of punishment. Restorative justice revolves around a potentially uncomfortable confrontation between wrongdoer and victim. When Negan and Rick faced off, Rick slashed Negan's throat! Arguably, what makes Negan's current punishment unjust, is that Rick essentially gets to torment Negan when he pleases, by simply visiting him in his basement. Okay, Rick isn't tormenting Negan in the comics, but in the few meetings that we've seen between Rick and Negan there is no air of reconciliation, forgiveness, or even an attempt at rehabilitation of Negan.

It might be that Rick and others, might never be able to confront Negan in a constructive manner. Additionally, the guidance and mediation social structures that would ideally be present to foster healing and growth don't exist for Rick and Negan. There are no social workers, therapists, or probation officers, who can help mediate and foster true reconciliation between Negan and Rick. There's also something very unfair to Negan when the judge, jury, and *especially* the *warden* of his prison is also his victim. However difficult it would be to find people completely impartial to Negan, they could find someone else who at least could be more objective than Rick.

On the other hand, I think that because of the crimes that Negan could be found guilty of, crimes against society, and possibly civilization, a restorative justice approach could be helpful in achieving the goals that Rick wants to achieve. Rick wants to foster a world where human lives matter, so much so that people ought not be killed. If people are of such value, then Negan needs to be treated better than one of the Governor's walker heads floating in a fish tank. Negan's current imprisonment suggests that the human lives really aren't that valuable. Rick's actions communicate that people should not be killed, but neither should prisoners be given a chance to live. Perhaps most tragically, before Rick slashes Negan's throat, it appears that Negan could have been on the road to rehabilitation, as he seriously considers Rick's vision for the future. Rick's subsequent actions, slashing his throat and imprisoning him in isolation, may cut off any hopes of Negan valuing the society that Rick is trying to build. Had Rick followed a restorative justice model in the beginning, he could communicate not just that people shouldn't be killed, but that people are so valuable that we shouldn't give up on anyone.

Rick has a noble vision for civilization, but the way he treats Negan fails to build towards that vision. It works against it. Rick might have rid society of a terrible and ineffective punishment, but he reinforces the idea that the only way to treat criminals is to treat them as less than human. I don't know if a restorative justice model of punishment could or should ever replace imprisonment in the myriad of crimes that people commit against one another, but I can only admire a civilization that treats the worst of its citizens with decency and offers a chance of forgiveness.

III

Lose a Lot
of Soldiers and
Still Win the
Game

7
Machiavelli Advises the Governor

GREG LITTMANN

> I promise you, you'll never have to worry about whether you're doing
> the right thing or the wrong thing, because we will do the only thing.
>
> —THE GOVERNOR, 4.7 "Dead Weight"

What are you going to do when the walker virus breaks out and civilization collapses? Nail your front door shut and hide in the cellar? Scrounge some weapons and ammunition and take to the road? Or will you just give up, cover yourself in ketchup, and throw yourself to the shambling horde of undead?

Or will you instead gaze out over the gore-stained ruins and see an opportunity to get ahead in the world?

The Governor is a man who has taken advantage of the collapse of civilization in order to concentrate power in his own hands. He loses his ambition for a while in Season Four, after the loss of Woodbury, but when he's in top form, he'll do anything that it takes to gain control, allowing nobody to stand in his way. Unlike many ambitious leaders in history, the power itself isn't what is most important to him. As his adventures in Season Four protecting the Chambler family show, he gathers power because it is the only way he thinks he can be a part of a safe community.

Perhaps he's right. Woodbury is the safest community around when Michonne and Andrea first encounter it in 3.3 "Walk with Me." A resident explains to Andrea, "The walls haven't been breached in well over a month and we haven't suffered a casualty inside since early winter." The Governor elaborates, "People here have homes, medical care, kids go to school, adults have jobs to do." Yet in his pursuit of the power that promises such safety, the Governor is so ruthless that he's positively *Machiavellian*. Niccolò Machiavelli was a political philosopher of Renaissance Italy. In his masterpiece, *The Prince,* he lays out what he thinks are the ways in which dictatorial power can be achieved and maintained (a "prince" being his term for an independent ruler). His conclusions about how rulers should act have horrified readers for five hundred years.

Some scholars find his recommendations so shocking that they think he must be kidding and that *The Prince* must be a work of satire. I don't buy it. There's nothing unusual about original thinkers having opinions that seem horrible to others. That's just what political philosophers do!

Kill or Die

In this life now, you kill or you die . . . or you die and you kill.

—THE GOVERNOR, 3.16 "Welcome to the Tombs"

Previous treatises on government had urged rulers to behave virtuously. Machiavelli regards this as unrealistic. Someone who tried to be genuinely virtuous all the time would be at an enormous disadvantage in competition with someone who is willing to play dirty. Instead, Machiavelli advises that in order to get ahead and to maintain power, rulers should be willing to throw law and conventional morality to the wind, doing whatever it takes to reach their goals. A ruler should be willing to lie, cheat, kill and do anything else that provides an advantage.

Machiavelli would be impressed with the way that the Governor places gaining an advantage over obeying moral rules. We first meet the Governor in 3.3 "Walk with Me" when his troops kidnap Andrea and Michonne and take them as prisoners to Woodbury. Conventional morality would judge this a violation of their freedom, but for the Governor, people in his power are assets to be used to his advantage.

In 4.8 "Too Far Gone", the governor uses Michonne and Hershel as hostages, threatening to kill them if Rick's group does not surrender. In 3.7 "When the Dead Come Knocking," the Governor interrogates Maggie by making her remove her top and threating to rape her; when that doesn't work, he puts a gun to Glenn's head and threatens to pull the trigger if she won't talk. Perhaps most impressively, in 3.11 "I Ain't a Judas," he makes combatants of everyone thirteen and up, turning Woodbury into what Andrea calls "an armed camp with child soldiers."

Machiavelli regards killing as a particularly important tool for a ruler. Killing your enemies, as opposed to dealing with them in other ways, has the great advantage that dead people are incapable of retaliation. He wrote: "Men must be either pampered or crushed, because they can get revenge for small injuries but not for grievous ones. So any injury a prince does to a man should be of such a kind that there is no fear of revenge" (pp. 10–11).

Like Machiavelli, the Governor sees killing as an important tool. For example, when he learns the location of a downed military helicopter in 3.3 "Walk with Me", he butchers the survivors and takes their supplies. "Let's see what Uncle Sam brought us, shall we?" he invites his men, once he's shot the final, fleeing, soldier. Similarly, in 3.13 "Arrow on the Doorpost," he decides to kill Rick's entire group at the prison. The Governor's willingness to kill those who stand in his way extends even to Andrea, for whom he has genuine feelings. When she learns that he is planning to exterminate Rick's group and turns against him in "Welcome to the Tombs," he locks her in a room with the dying Milton, who will soon turn into a walker. In 3.5 "Say the Word," Michonne finds the Governor's diary, complete with a list of names along with tally marks to help him keep track of who he has wiped out.

To Machiavelli's mind, the Governor is simply doing what is necessary to ensure his own safety. A ruler must be brutal sometimes to stay secure, especially a ruler like the Governor, who only recently came to power over a group of people used to another form of government. Machiavelli writes, "A new prince, of all rulers, finds it impossible to avoid a reputation for cruelty, because of the abundant dangers inherent in a newly won state" (p. 54). Machiavelli might compare the way that the Governor kills people to protect his power with the way he deals with a walker-infected citizen inside the walls of

Woodbury in 3.9 "The Suicide King." The bitten man begs for help while a crowd gathers around him. Only the Governor has the sense and willingness to do the unpleasant thing that has to be done, shooting the infected man in the head.

This act of murder violates our normal standards of morality as the man has done nothing to deserve death, but Machiavelli would say that the Governor is only being sensible by removing a threat that has to be removed. He would compare the Governor favorably to Rick, who puts his life and his community at risk at least once a season by being reluctant to kill. In 1.3 "Tell It to the Frogs," Rick's unable to leave Merle to die handcuffed to a roof and returns to a walker-infested Atlanta to release him, though Merle is hostile and violent, and a danger to everyone. In 2.8 "Triggerfinger," Rick decides that he's unable to execute his wounded prisoner Randall and must set him free, though Randall's group have already fired on Rick's group, and Randall might reveal their location. In 3.15 "This Sorrowful Life," Rick decides that he can't send Michonne to die at the Governor's hands, though doing so might save everyone else at the prison. Even in Season Five, when Rick's become Machiavellian enough to slaughter an entire community of cannibals at Terminus in 5.1 "No Sanctuary," he still can't kill his dangerous captive enemy, ex-cop Bob Lamson, without agonizing over it first in 5.7 "Crossed." The Ricktadorship simply doesn't have the heart to make the decisions that are in its best interest.

Machiavelli admiringly holds up multiple historical rulers who achieved their position through murder, often on a grand scale. The murder of friends and family is as legitimate as the murder of strangers, as in the case of Oliverotto of Fermo (1475–1502). Oliverotto took over the city of Fermo by throwing a feast in honor of the ruler—his uncle and patron Giovanni Fogliani—and then having his men slaughter Giovanni and the noblemen of Fermo who had shown up to honor him.

This is certainly reminiscent of the way that the Governor murders his way into the leadership of the group of survivors gathered by his one-time lieutenant, Martinez. Martinez offers to share power with him. But the Governor doesn't believe that an effective ruler would look to share power and concludes that Martinez can't keep the group safe. He murders Martinez by shoving him into a pit filled with walkers, and murders the next leader, Pete, by dropping by his caravan for a chat and knifing him in the back.

Machiavelli would not be surprised by the ease with which the Governor assumes authority of the group, since "men willingly change their ruler, expecting to fare better" (p. 8). He believes that people are much more concerned with their present well-being than with the legitimacy of the means by which their rulers took power, writing that "men are won over by the present far more than by the past; and when they decide that what is being done here and now is good, they content themselves with that" (p. 77). As the governor puts it to Mitch as they plan to explain Pete's death as a glorious sacrifice on a supply run, "people believe what they want to believe."

In fact, Machiavelli might criticize the Governor for not being bloody enough, on the grounds that harming people without killing them invites revenge. For instance, if the Governor had killed Merle once he had condemned him as a traitor—rather than allowing him to escape—Merle wouldn't have returned to assassinate him, leading an army of walkers in tow. Likewise, the Governor could have saved himself a lot of trouble by murdering Michonne, Andrea, and Milton as soon as he had started to fight with them, rather than giving them a chance to turn on him.

More Machiavellian is the way that the Governor decides in 3.16 "Welcome to the Tombs" and 4.8 "Too Far Gone" that none of Rick's group are to survive his assault. Rick himself, of course, has often failed miserably to eliminate those he harms. From leaving Merle chained to the roof, to wounding Randall then saving his life, to throwing the convict Andrew out of the prison and into a yard full of walkers in 3.4 "Killer Within," to failing to assassinate the Governor when invading Woodbury in 3.9 "The Suicide King," to expelling the murderer Carol from the group in 4.4 "Indifference," again and again Rick gives people reason to hate him, then leaves them alive to plot revenge. As Carl accuses in "Welcome to the Tombs", just before throwing his sheriff's badge on the ground, "You didn't kill Andrew and he came back and killed Mom. You were in a room with the Governor and you let him go." If not for the way Rick murdered everyone in Terminus, Machiavelli would think him beyond rehabilitation.

Conquer or Be Conquered

I got more people. More firepower!

—THE GOVERNOR, 4.8 "Too Far Gone"

The Governor believes that he needs to conquer rival groups. Rick's group would much rather live in peace; in "Too Far Gone", Rick even offers to share the prison with the Governor and his people, but the Governor can't allow a rival power. In 3.13 "Arrow on the Doorpost" he declares, "We're going to have to eliminate Rick sooner or later. No way can we live side by side."

Machiavelli would approve. He warns: "there is no avoiding war; it can only be postponed to the advantage of others" (p. 12). Rulers must constantly be planning to expand their territory in order to be safe from their neighbors. Machiavelli holds the ancient Romans up as his ideal, on the grounds that they were never satisfied with peace but rather always looking for fresh conquests. So important is warfare that it should be a ruler's main preoccupation. Machiavelli writes: "A prince . . . must have no other object or thought, nor acquire skill in anything, except war, its organization, and its discipline. The art of war . . . is so useful that besides enabling hereditary princes to maintain their rule it frequently enables ordinary citizens to become rulers" (p. 47).

Just as military expertise is a ruler's most important skill, so a well-equipped army is the foundation of a ruler's power. Machiavelli warned that a state without a good military is bound to be conquered, while a ruler's "defense lies in being well armed and having good allies; and if he is well armed he will always have good allies" (p. 59). Soldiers are not only useful in warfare but also for keeping order among the ruler's own citizens. Machiavelli writes: "The main foundations of every state . . . are good laws and good arms . . . you cannot have good laws without good arms, and where there are good arms, good laws inevitably follow" (p. 40). Machiavelli's point is that a ruler's ability to enforce their power is more important for maintaining order than the specific laws they put into place.

The Governor likewise appreciates that military superiority trumps other forms of power. He's always keen to scavenge weapons, like those of the National Guard soldiers he has his men exterminate in 3.3 "Walk with Me" (compare this to Rick *giving away* rifles to a needy group of strangers holed up in a nursing home in 1.4 "Vatos"). When becoming the leader of Martinez's group gives the Governor control of a working tank, it doesn't take him long to work out how devastating it could be in a fresh assault against Rick's group at the prison. Perhaps Machiavelli would even regard the way that the Governor uses his soldiers to keep order among his citizens—as when the soldiers prevent them at gunpoint from leaving Woodbury in 3.9 "The Suicide King"—as an example of good arms ensuring good laws. The guys with guns are certainly keeping order.

Smiles and Picnics

You're not prisoners here. You're guests. If you want to leave, you're free to do so.

—THE GOVERNOR, "Walk with Me"

While Machiavelli thinks it's important for rulers to play dirty, he also thinks it's essential that they aren't seen to be playing dirty by the public. An *image* of virtue is essential for anyone who wants to maintain the people's trust. The ruler must appear to be "compassionate, faithful to his word, kind, guileless, and devout" (p. 57). Fortunately, people are easily deceived: "Everyone sees what you appear to be, few experience what you really are" (p. 58). Citizens care far more about their own wellbeing than they do about ferreting out the truth about the misdeeds of their leaders: "The common people are always impressed by appearances and results" (p. 58).

For all his brutality, the Governor is usually careful to maintain an image as a compassionate leader. He even pretends to the people of Woodbury that his murderous raids against other survivors are simply supply gathering. For instance, when he returns with the supplies of the soldiers his men kill in "Walk with Me," he claims that the soldiers were killed in a walker attack and his own men were only scavenging what was left. When Andrea and Michonne are first brought to the Governor as prisoners, he treats them with hospitality, telling them that they are guests and even offering them supplies. He's so convincing that in time, Andrea develops feelings for him and decides to stay in Woodbury, even though Michonne urges her

not to trust him. In 3.11 "I Ain't a Judas," when Andrea confronts the Governor about his attack on the prison, he claims
that he went in peace but was attacked by Rick's group. In 3.8
"Made to Suffer," the Governor lies to his people about the raid
Rick's group made on Woodbury to rescue their friends. He tells
the residents of Woodbury that the raid was "an attack by ter-
rorists who want what we have. Want to destroy us . . . or
worse." He presents his attempted conquest of the prison in
3.16 "Welcome to the Tombs" as simple self-defense, declaring:
"They're not going to stop until they kill us all!"

The Governor even arranges entertainments for his people
to make himself seem a beneficent ruler. For instance, in 3.5
"Say the Word," he hosts a picnic for all the residents of
Woodbury. He runs generators to supply cold drinks and tells
them, "Today, we celebrate how far we've come . . . we raise a
glass to us!" Of course, the most distinctive entertainment of
Woodbury are the gladiatorial fights in a ring full of captive
walkers. As dangerous as the sport is, it brings excitement and
diversion to the citizens, and the Governor enthusiastically
works up the crowd before a match. He even gives them fights
to the death, as in 3.9 "The Suicide King," when he decides that
Merle is a traitor and condemns him to fight Daryl. The mob is
delighted, bloodthirstily screaming for Merle to murder his
brother. Their pleasure may seem revolting to us, as it does to
Andrea, but to Machiavelli's mind, the Governor is doing the
sensible thing by harnessing his people's bloodthirstiness as a
tool to secure his own power. He wrote, "whenever that class of
men on which you believe your continued rule depends is cor-
rupt, whether it be the populace, or soldiers, or nobles, you have
to satisfy it by adopting the same disposition" (p. 63).

Yet despite the importance of appearing benevolent,
Machiavelli thinks it is even more important for a ruler to be
feared. Ideally a ruler should be loved as well as feared, but if
only one of these can be achieved, being feared is more useful.
He explains: "love is secured by a bond of gratitude which men,
wretched creatures that they are, break when it is to their
advantage to do so; but fear is strengthened by a dread of punishment which is always effective" (p. 54).

Appropriately, while the Governor makes an effort to be
loved by the citizens of Woodbury, he also makes it clear that
failure to obey him will have dire consequences. As noted

above, in "The Suicide King," when panicking residents try to flee out the gates in the wake of a raid by Rick and Maggie, they are turned back at gunpoint by Martinez and other security guards. The citizens are made to appreciate that disobeying orders means being shot. Even the gladiatorial fight between Daryl and Merle serves as a public warning as well as a public recreation. The Governor is demonstrating what happens to those who cross him. Machiavelli would regard it as particularly useful to make an example of a fighter like Merle, on the grounds that a fighting force, more so than ordinary citizens, can only be controlled through fear. He writes: "when a prince is campaigning with his soldiers . . . he need not worry about having a reputation for cruelty; because, without such a reputation, no army was ever kept united and disciplined" (p. 55).

However, Machiavelli also appreciates that being *too* brutal can make a ruler less safe rather than safer. He warns: "The prince must none the less make himself feared in such a way that, if he is not loved, at least he escapes being hated" (p. 54). The people will rise up against a leader they hate, or at the very least, will abandon him when the opportunity presents itself. The Governor should have heeded Machiavelli's warning. After massacring his own army in 3.16 "Welcome to the Tombs" when they fail to conquer the prison, the Governor loses the support of the people of Woodbury, who desert the town rather than tolerate his continued rule.

Courage and Cunning

We'll go in under a white flag, like we did with the National Guard.

—THE GOVERNOR, 3.8 "Made to Suffer"

Machiavelli believes that a ruler must maintain a balance between audacious boldness and calculating cunning. Audacity is so vital to a ruler that "it is better to be impetuous than circumspect" (p. 81). People who are too slow to take risks don't get anywhere. If the Governor had played it safe in the wake of the walker plague, he would have concentrated on survival in a hostile world and not taken on the additional dangers involved in trying to gain power over a force of fighters and a community of citizens. Machiavelli holds such successful gamblers up for our admiration, describing many examples from history of ordinary citizens who managed to claw their way to the position of dictator. Yet rulers must be cunning as well as aggressive, or they will succumb to the plots of their enemies. Machiavelli writes that a ruler "must learn from the fox and the lion; because the lion is defenseless against traps and a fox is defenseless against wolves. Therefore one must be a fox in order to recognize traps, and a lion to frighten off wolves" (p. 56).

The Governor has, at times, successfully been both lion and fox. When we first meet him, he's got enough of the lion's aggression to be the leader of a post-apocalyptic military force that he murders other survivors for their supplies; yet he also has enough of the fox's cunning to fool his people about the nature of these raids and his rule. He's also cunning enough to use walkers as troops, as in 3.10 "Home," when he destroys the prison gates to allow the walkers to invade the grounds. More innovative yet, he collects walkers in Woodbury with the intention of using them as a standing army. In 3.13 "Arrow on the Doorpost," he plots to trick Rick into handing over Michonne in return for peace, and nearly succeeds, though he intends to exterminate Rick's group all along. In 4.8 "Too Far Gone," he almost convinces Rick's group to give up without a fight by taking Michonne and Hershel hostage and threatening to kill them.

At other times, though, the Governor fails to be a lion or a fox when his circumstances call for it. When he loses Woodbury in 3.16 "Welcome to the Tombs," he loses his motivation with it; no longer a lion, he becomes so apathetic that in 4.6 "Live Bait," he doesn't even bother to defend himself when attacked by a walker. He finds motivation again only by committing himself to protecting the Chambler family and only rediscovers ambition when the need to protect the Chamblers forces him to start fighting again. He certainly finds his lion when he kills multiple walkers with his bare hands to save Meghan, crushing their heads and tearing out their throats.

The Governor is also, at times, outfoxed. In 3.15 "This Sorrowful Life," for instance, Merle successfully leads walkers to ambush the Governor's army by driving slowly down the highway playing loud music. Both times the Governor has attacked the prison, he's had superior military force to Rick's group. Not only the numbers, but the vehicles, grenade launchers and tank have been on his side. But each time he's lost because his opponents have had a superior strategy. Perhaps he should have studied battle more carefully, as Machiavelli suggests. In both "Welcome to the Tombs" and "Too Far Gone," the Governor leads his troops directly into ambushes inside the prison fence, resulting in costly and bloody defeats.

A particular weakness of the Governor is a tendency to let the lion in him overwhelm the fox, which is to say that his aggression can eclipse his reason. For instance, in 3.8 "Made to Suffer," Michonne "kills" the Governor's undead daughter, Penny, with a katana thrust through the head. The Governor responds by attacking Michonne in a rage, giving her a chance to stab him in the hand and eye. In 3.14 "Prey," he personally chases the traitorous Andrea, allowing her to trap him in a room filled with walkers. Likewise, in "This Sorrowful Life," he attacks Merle for his treachery, rather than calling on his troops. The fact that he wins is beside the point—taking on the champion of the Woodbury arena is a foolish risk. Indeed, in the end, the Governor dies because he lets his courage over-whelm his cunning. In both his assaults on the prison, he joins in the fighting personally, an act of great bravery, but one that puts him in peril. Machiavelli warns rulers not to rely on luck, and predictably, the Governor's luck runs out in 4.8 "Too Far Gone." Though the Governor almost kills Rick, Michonne stabs him through the back before he can finish the job. Nothing remains but for Lilly to shoot the dying man in the head, ending his quest for power.

Adapt or Die

I'm through holding their hands. We're at war.

—THE GOVERNOR, "The Suicide King"

Machiavelli's belief that a ruler must be able to act as lion or fox as the situation demands is a specific instance of a more general rule, which is that rulers must be prepared to tailor their approach to their situation, adjusting it as the situation changes. He wrote: "the one who adapts his policy to the times prospers, and likewise . . . the one whose policy clashes with the demands of the times does not" (p. 80). There is no one road to power and so one cannot stick with a single strategy, however successful it has been. Rather, power goes to those who can best change in response to their environment.

In some ways, the Governor has excelled in changing to adapt to his environment. When the walker virus broke out and civilization collapsed, he instituted an entirely new social order of his own devising, with himself at the top. He recognized the opportunities offered by the apocalypse and went from living as a private citizen to being a general and dictator. As noted, he's adaptable enough that while people around him are stuck in the old morality under which you can't shoot an innocent man, he's able to execute the victim of a walker bite, and adaptable enough to treat walkers as a military asset.

On the other hand, failure to adapt is also the Governor's greatest weakness. In "Welcome to the Tombs," he goes from ruler of the most powerful group in his area to an outcast. When the Governor's army is fleeing from the prison after being defeated in battle by Rick's group, the Governor is unable to adjust to changing circumstances and instead becomes pigheaded. He orders his troops to return to the fight, and when they refuse, he guns them all down, apart from Martinez and Shumpert.

Machiavelli urges leaders to be cruel to their soldiers and has no problem with soldiers being executed to make an example of them to their comrades. But when the Governor kills almost his entire army, he's just throwing power away when he should be forming new plans to snatch victory. The Governor even destroys his material resources out of annoyance, returning to the abandoned Woodbury and burning it to the ground.

Is Machiavelli Right?

MERLE: I ain't gonna beg! I ain't begging you!

THE GOVERNOR: No [*shoots him*]

—"This Sorrowful Life"

That's what I think Machiavelli would say about the Governor, but is Machiavelli right? It would be nice to be able to deny that anyone ever got ahead through lies and violence, but it isn't true. Characters like the Governor ring true because, as Machiavelli notes, history is filled with dishonest and bloody leaders who lied and killed their way to the top, and then lied and killed some more to stay there. Sometimes, doing things that other people would refuse to do on moral grounds can offer a distinct advantage over them.

Machiavelli is also right that military power can trump any other kind, if it is skillfully directed. If the Governor had had numerical superiority *and* the cunning of Rick's group, he'd own both Woodbury and the Prison, and would be eyeing the surrounding towns. Balancing military audacity against shrewdness correctly as Machiavelli recommends is quite a trick, of course, and it's easy for a leader to move too quickly or too slowly. But it can be done. Leaders like Julius Caesar, Genghis Khan, George Washington, and Napoleon were audacious *and* cunning, making careful calculations but seizing opportunities.

On the other hand, Machiavelli fails to note that there are other vital strategic resources than weapons. For example, survivors of the walker virus will need proper supplies of food and medicine, neither easy to come by after the end of civilization. When Rick's group is hit by influenza in 4.2 "Infected," it threatens to wipe them out. Similarly, a group that runs out of gas will be easy prey for raiders with vehicles; and without fresh breeding stock, inbreeding will destroy a community in a few generations. Our own pre-apocalyptic society relies on even more complex networks of resources, both for our military forces and to maintain our infrastructure. Survivors of the walker plague aren't the only ones who have to worry about the gas running out!

Machiavelli is right that it's dangerous to harm people without killing them. But while he offers this as an encouragement to kill, it also implies that if we aren't going to kill someone, we should avoid harming them. So for most of us, the practical implication will be that we should be merciful to people and try not to hurt them. Perhaps Machiavelli's most important observation is that success comes from adapting to the circumstances. There isn't one right strategy for getting ahead in life. Rather, we must change with the times to fit our environment. That means that if we don't want to be pushed around by people like the Governor, we have to make sure that our political environment isn't one where behaving like the Governor is the most effective strategy. We need to keep a careful eye on our politicians to make sure that their actions match their rhetoric and image. It will be better for us if the Machiavellians amongst us have to adapt to an environment where the most successful approach doesn't involve tricking us, killing us, or feeding us to the dead.

The Governor gazed out the window over the prison grounds triumphantly. All around, his people were at work, repairing, rebuilding, improving. He smiled and said, "I owe it all to you, Nicky! You've been a wonderful advisor. You don't mind if I call you Nicky, do you?" Niccolò Machiavelli did mind, but he wasn't about to say that to the Governor. He kept his eyes down and answered, "No, Governor."

"This one here would have had my eye out if not for you," the Governor observed, tapped on the glass of one of the fish tanks stacked up against the wall. Michonne's head responded to the sound and motion, biting at nothing. Dark braids floated in the murky water like the waving tentacles of some strange octopus, obscuring her face.

"And this kid! If I'd let him live, he'd have been sure to take revenge on me somehow." Carl's head was trying to eat his sheriff's hat. He gnawed on the water-logged brim, but couldn't seem to tear a piece off to swallow. But Machiavelli was in no mood for another head tour. He interrupted, "Governor, the prison is a good start, but the territory of what was once the United States is wide open for military conquest. You must act immediately."

"I don't know, Nicky. Now that I finally feel safe, I'm not sure I want to conquer any more. It's enough just to be Governor." Machiavelli grimly shook his head and answered, "There is no safety in stopping at Governor. You must gather your armies at once and run for President."

8
The Warring Dead

RICK MORRIS

Killing has been a part of human existence since long before Cain picked up a rock: early modern humans and Neanderthals both seem to have preyed on and eaten each other. Humans killed, and then ate, each other. In *The Walking Dead*, however, humans are killed . . . and then they eat each other. Much of the world after the apocalypse seems straightforward: try to survive, don't be eaten, try not to be turned into a walker, and be ready to kill anything that tries to kill you. Killing walkers seems equally straightforward: the person that once inhabited the body is gone, and only a primitive eating and killing machine, devoid of conscience and perhaps even consciousness, remains. If one attacks, you try to escape or kill it.

This gets a little more complicated, however, when the threat comes from another living human: unlike walkers, humans are persons; unlike walkers, humans have moral worth. If another human attacks you, we generally assume that self-defense is justified. What if they are not attacking you, but they're competing for resources you need? What if they haven't attacked you, but only a member of your group? What if the leader of your group tells you that they're a threat and must be attacked? Can you trust him, or must you investigate for yourself? Perhaps the post-apocalyptic world is more complex than we thought—and just when we figured that a clean gun and lots of ammunition would solve all our problems!

As it happens, philosophers have been discussing these questions for centuries in the form of just war theory. Just war theory is far too long and complex to discuss here, so instead we'll just talk about a concept referred to as the *moral symmetry of combatants*, and what two famous philosophers— Michael Walzer (*Just and Unjust Wars*) and Jeff McMahan (*Killing in War*)—have had to say on the subject. We're talking about war and philosophy, and here we will look at the war between the prison group and the group in Woodbury.

The Moral Symmetry of Combatants

Just war theory has traditionally concerned itself with two primary issues, which we can call "justice *of* war" and "justice *in* war." "Justice of war" looks at when it's right or wrong to go to war; "justice in war" at what it's right or wrong to do when fighting a war.

Philosophers who have written about justice of war have usually held that for a war to be just, the war must be defensive in nature, other means of resolving the conflict must not be available or must be unlikely to be effective, and war must be a proportionate response to the threat posed by the aggressor. If these conditions are met, the war is just; if these conditions are not met, the war is unjust. (This is a simplification of many views, but this is the standard we'll be using in this chapter.)

You may notice that these questions implicitly demand something of political leaders in particular. The populace as a whole may have some say in whether or not a war is pursued, but in general the obligation only to prosecute just wars falls most strongly on the decision-makers. At Woodbury, for example, the Governor (and perhaps his most important lieutenants and advisors) bears the primary responsibility for ensuring justice of war: he has the most information and he is making the political decisions, so it's primarily his job to be sure not to launch a war or an attack without good reason.

"Justice in war" concerns the morally proper conduct of war: minimizing suffering, minimizing harm to noncombatants in particular, using proportionate means to prosecute the war, and so forth. Typical standards of behavior involve treating enemy prisoners humanely and with respect, providing medical care to enemy wounded, avoiding the use of weapons of mass destruction, avoiding the deliberate destruction of civilian infrastructure, avoiding the deliberate destruction of hospitals, and the like. Although politicians can set policies which govern the behavior of combatants in war, you will notice that these obligations fall more heavily on combatant personnel. Justice in war, then, would be focused primarily on the actions of the Woodbury combatants: the people going on raids, the people guarding the gate, and so forth. They might not be able to do much about the justice of the war they are sent to fight, but they can be sure to fight it justly.

Some philosophers have seen these two issues as basically independent: a just war can be prosecuted unjustly; an unjust war can be prosecuted justly. Some historians and philosophers (including Michael Walzer) have argued that the dropping of the atomic bombs on Japan at the end of World War II was unjustified, but most agree that the war itself was just. If they're right, then World War II is an example of a just war (for the Allies) which was fought, in part, unjustly. By contrast, we might imagine a war which involved the invasion of another country in order to capture desired resources or territory, without provocation or threat. In such a war, however, military forces might carefully have avoided civilian casualties, treated prisoners of war with respect and dignity, and sought to minimize harm in general. The war would clearly be unjust, but the fashion in which it was fought would be just.

The implication here, for some philosophers, is that combatants need not concern themselves with whether they are fighting in a just war; their only moral concern is the justice of their personal conduct in the war. According to this view, one of the Woodbury combatants—knowing nothing about the prison group she was attacking except that they were shooting at her —might have no obligation except to refrain from harming one of the group who was not a combatant.

There is an important point here: in fighting a war, combatants have the right to kill other combatants. Regardless of the justice (or injustice) of our own cause, killing (or otherwise harming) enemy combatants is justified. Thus, the Woodbury fighter would do nothing wrong in killing Rick or Michonne, even though the fighter was part of an unjustified attack. Our Woodburian would only be doing something morally blameworthy if he were to violate the moral rules governing the conduct of war (for instance, by killing disarmed and wounded Hershel, harming Judith or Beth, and so forth). Similarly, the prison group's fighters would have the right to kill attackers from Woodbury, so long as the prison group otherwise fought in a just fashion.

This view—that combatants on all sides of an armed conflict are equally entitled to kill combatants on the opposing side—is called the *moral symmetry of combatants* (or sometimes the *moral equality of combatants*). Many people will instinctively be sympathetic to this idea. After all, enemy combatants are trying to kill you! Why shouldn't you be entitled to defend yourself and your friends? International law has generally made this the standard of behavior for soldiers in war, as well: so long as you only harm enemy combatants who are a threat, you won't be prosecuted—no matter how unjust your side in the war might be. Pragmatically, philosophers (like Walzer) have argued that this permissiveness makes sense. If a soldier believes that he will be prosecuted for fighting in an unjust war no matter how he morally he fights, he loses much of the motivation for restraining his own savagery. After all, he'll only be prosecuted if his side loses! He might as well fight as aggressively as possible, no matter who gets hurt, to ensure victory.

As you may notice, however, that argument is not moral but rather practical: many people think that waiving legal consequences for killing enemy combatants will help to reduce the suffering caused by wars. This does not mean that killing enemy combatants is itself always morally justified; it only means that it would be foolish to prosecute soldiers for doing so. In our discussion, we're interested in the morality of war when it comes to a post-apocalyptic world in which there is no rule of law. Consequently, we need to look at *moral* arguments.

Michael Walzer argues for the general permissibility of killing enemy combatants in war. One of his arguments for the moral symmetry of combatants is that soldiers generally occupy a specific role in society, a role in which they are "dangerous men" (in Walzer's phrase) who are trained to be servants of the state's purposes. Part of what it *means* to be a combatant is to be someone who participates in fighting as part of the group. If that person is attacked for reasons outside of their military duties, then the ordinary set of moral rules governing interpersonal aggression will apply. But if they are attacked as a combatant, no wrong is done because they are occupying the role of warlike public servant.

Combatants are inherently liable to attack. Consequently, combatants on each side are justified in killing combatants on the other. Killing an enemy combatant is not only a simple act of war; it is also self-defense. If a citizen of Woodbury had attempted to rob and murder Daryl after encountering him on the street, she would have done wrong. She wouldn't have done anything wrong if she killed Daryl during the fighting at Woodbury or at the prison.

When Self-Defense Doesn't Cut It

Jeff McMahan is one of the most prominent critics of the idea of the moral symmetry of combatants. He musters a number of arguments against the view that all (or most) killing of enemy combatants in war is morally justifiable self-defense, one of which I will sketch out with a popular analogy: suppose a criminal is robbing a bank and, while shooting at the customers, starts to receive fire from a police officer who arrives on the scene. The robber returns fire, killing the cop. Most of us, I think, would agree that the robber has committed murder here: the police officer had a right to live and the robber violated that right.

If self-defense is an adequate justification for killing, though, why would this not be true here? Why would the robber have done anything wrong? He was just defending himself from the police officer, after all. Similarly, soldiers in war—including unjust combatants—are often defending themselves against attack by someone who wants to kill them. If the robber does something wrong by killing in his own self-defense, then it seems that a soldier for the unjust side in war also possibly does something wrong. He certainly needs a stronger reason for killing a just combatant than merely that it was self-defense.

Perhaps we can evade this objection by pointing out that the robber is committing a crime already: if the police officer had attacked the robber without provocation, the robber would have had a right to defend himself and the cop would have been liable to attack by the robber; here, though, the robber was already doing something wrong by taking money from people who had a right to it. The problem is that the unjust combatant is in a similar moral situation: his cause is unjust. Those who might kill him are defending their own rights or the rights of others, not unlike the police officer. It seems that just combatants are not liable to attack by unjust combatants. So this evasion probably won't work. Perhaps we can argue that the robber has an immediate way to de-escalate the situation: he can throw down his weapons and then be taken into custody. Killing the police officer is not *necessary* to keep himself alive; he can do so without harming someone not liable to attack. Again, here, the unjust combatant has a similar option and presumably can surrender or refuse to participate in the unjust war.

The moral symmetry of combatants might still be true, but it seems that the simpler justifications won't work. We find two sorts of moral justification in McMahan: objective justification and subjective justification. If an act is objectively justified, then it is simply what the actor ought to have done. It does not take into account the actor's knowledge, personality, beliefs, or any other individual factor; the only consideration is the morally proper thing to do in the given circumstance. In other words, when trying to determine whether someone is objectively justified, we ask ourselves a question like this: what ought the person to have done?

If a person is subjectively justified, which McMahan typically refers to as *being excused*, then the person made the best decision to act that they could have, though it may actually have been the wrong decision. Subjective justifications include the sorts of things we normally consider to be an excuse: duress, ignorance, mental disability, and so forth. Thus, someone might be subjectively justified because they simply did not know any better, while being objectively unjustified because they still ought to have done something different. To simplify terminology, I will use the term *justified* to refer to being objectively justified, and *excused* to refer to being subjectively justified.

McMahan recognizes a number of different excuses for wrongful action, but I'll focus on two: coercion and ignorance. Consider Maggie's interrogation by the Governor in 3.7 "When the Dead Come Knocking": although she is intensely loyal to the group and willing to suffer for them, she gives up the location of the prison when the Governor threatens Glenn. I think most of us would agree that giving up the information isn't *right*, per se, as it enables the Governor to attack. Most of us would probably also agree that Maggie shouldn't be judged too harshly: she was faced with Glenn's likely death. This is coercion. Now suppose the group at the prison found a stash of food and ammunition in what appeared to be an abandoned house and took it. As it turns out, this stash belonged to other survivors who had left the home to forage. Had this happened, it's clear that the prison group would have done something wrong—taking supplies from people who desperately need them. It's also clear, though, that they didn't do so out of greed or even desperation, but out of ignorance. People who do the wrong thing in ignorance are often excused.

An unjust combatant who faces a prison sentence if he refuses to fight is under some level of coercion. Thus, he has an excuse for killing just combatants. Now, he may not be *fully* excused (which is to say he may be somewhat deserving of blame for fighting), but he is at least partially excused. Regardless of whether or not he is excused, however, what he does is morally unjustifiable and, therefore, wrong. Similarly, an unjust combatant who has been led by his government to believe (wrongly) that the next country over from theirs is planning an invasion will have an excuse for fighting: he shouldn't fight, but so far as he knows he is just protecting his country and their cause is just.

You may have noticed that being excused is not simply a matter of being excused or unexcused: you might be fully excused, partially excused, or unexcused; further, you might be excused for multiple reasons. It seems reasonable to think that, morally, you can be partially excused for two reasons which would allow you to be fully excused. Consider a citizen who has a suspicion that a war is unjust but isn't sure either way, who knows that his government will send him to prison for a brief period if he refuses to fight. While a short prison sentence inflicted on an innocent person (the citizen who refuses to fight) is preferable, morally, to killing innocent people (the just combatants against whom he might fight), it is a partial excuse on the grounds of coercion. If we consider that in light of the fact that he simply doesn't know whether the war is just or unjust—but he knows that his political leadership, which ostensibly understands the situation better, claims that the war is just—then it seems hard to blame the citizen for deciding to avoid the legal burden on himself and trust his country's government. I would consider such a combatant mostly—perhaps even entirely—excused. The interaction of different excuses is something that we can't forget when we evaluate the moral blameworthiness of unjust combatants.

So What?

In *The Walking Dead* (specifically, Season Three of the TV series), there are two belligerent groups which interest us: Woodbury and the survivors at the prison. In the show, we see tensions gradually escalate between the two groups. At first, they are not aware of each other's existence. We learn in 3.3 "Walk with Me," that the Governor is taking his men on raids to kill members of other groups and confiscate their supplies. This is clearly intended to show us that Woodbury is not the benign, comfortable refuge which the Governor wants us to believe it is; instead, it is a comfortable place which insulates its citizens from all of the terrible things which are done on their behalf. The tension between the truth about Woodbury, and what its citizens believe about Woodbury, allows much of the drama throughout the season.

After Andrea and Michonne are captured by the Governor, Michonne and Andrea diverge as they take radically-opposed views of both Woodbury and the Governor. Michonne grows more suspicious, finding captive walkers and fresh bullet holes in the vehicles captured in "Walk with Me." Eventually, Michonne leaves Woodbury, and the Governor sends Merle (with three henchmen) after her. Michonne escapes and Merle starts making his way back to Woodbury (without his three less fortunate companions). Both stumble across Glenn and Maggie, and Michonne watches as Merle takes them prisoner. At this point, we can identify at least two reasons for attacks against Woodbury: Michonne quite reasonably believes that the Governor will not leave her in peace but will continue to hunt her; Rick's group (now tipped off by Michonne) seeks to have Glenn and Maggie freed. Both of these seem to be ongoing threats which justify violence against the Governor (and, by extension, combatants from Woodbury who assist him), as a sort of proactive self-defensive.

Merle, meanwhile, holds a grudge against Rick and the rest of the prison group for having abandoned him on the rooftop in

Atlanta. It's worth noting here, however, that this is not a continuing threat against Merle: whether or not he ought to have been left on the rooftop (and we're clearly not supposed to feel sorry for him), Rick's group has no ongoing grudge against him and Merle can safely ignore them without a threat to his own safety. Thus, while he might have a good claim against the group for abandoning him, the situation is resolved and Woodbury would not be justified in attacking the prison group as a reprisal for abandoning Merle. Unlike the group seeking to rescue Glenn and Maggie, then—and unlike Michonne defending herself—Merle has no reason to initiate violence against the group.

During a return to Woodbury with Rick's crew, Michonne discovers the Governor's collection of heads, and his walker-daughter, Penny. Michonne kills Penny. The Governor, already inclined to root out the group at the prison in order to gain control of their resources, becomes committed to retaliation for the "death" of his undead child. Meanwhile, the group from the prison set to work trying to bust out Maggie and Glenn. They succeed in doing so, killing several armed citizens of Woodbury in the process. As a consequence of this attack and a second attack to rescue Daryl, the Governor is easily able to persuade the citizens of Woodbury that they face aggressive attack by the group at the prison. Of course, we know this to be false.

Watching the show, we know that those at the prison would prefer to be left alone and to live in peace with Woodbury. Under Rick's leadership, they generally seek to de-escalate and resolve the conflict (though given the meeting which occurs in 3.13 "Arrow on the Doorpost," perhaps not very hard). The Governor, however, is not interested in a peaceful end short of the group turning over Michonne (and, unbeknownst to them, clearing them out of the prison entirely). Clearly, then, we can take the prison crew to be fighting defensively and we can view their cause as justified. Since their war is justified, their acts of killing in specific battles seem also to be justifiable acts of self-defense.

By contrast, the people of Woodbury seem pretty clearly to be fighting an unjust war: their leadership has refused a diplomatic solution and lied about the reasons for going to war. There is no obvious need for competition, except that the Governor hopes to claim all of the resources of the prison for himself—and, of course, he hopes for revenge against Michonne. What of the individual fighters led by the Governor? Some of them, like Shump and Martinez, have been extensively involved in the Governor's morally unjustified raids on other groups of survivors. If anyone other than the Governor is capable of knowing the injustice of their cause, these men know or ought to know. If the moral symmetry of combatants holds, then these men—despite their knowledge of the war's injustice—seem to be justified in killing members of the group at the prison. Both the Woodbury fighters and the prison fighters are combatants on opposing sides of a war, and thus they are morally permitted to kill each other as part of the war. In a case like this, it seems counterintuitive to think that these fighters do nothing wrong in attempting to kill Michonne, or Rick, or Glenn, or Maggie: they are all enemy combatants, true, but they also seem to be doing nothing which makes them liable to attack beyond the fact that they are armed and potentially dangerous.

Excuses, Excuses, Excuses

If McMahan is right, then if Maggie were killed in the fighting, something morally wrong would have happened, and it would have been done by one of the unjust combatants from Woodbury. But how harshly do we blame them? Do they have any excuses available? We know that the Governor is fully prepared to use coercion to get his way—consider his attempts to control Michonne and Andrea, or later to kill Milton in retribution for his betrayal. It is not clear at all that the inhabitants of Woodbury at large are aware of this preparedness.

The Governor has certainly shown a willingness to force "traitors" like Merle prove their loyalty, but beyond this particular example he mostly seems to lead by force of personality. The inhabitants of Woodbury may feel some coercion as they stand in line waiting to be inspected for participation in the raid, but it does not seem to be such strong coercion that they are excused for not even voicing objections.

If we want an excuse for Woodburians, we may have more luck if we consider an excuse from ignorance. As the viewers, we are epistemically privileged—by virtue of being viewers rather than characters, we know something the characters don't. As viewers, we know that the people in the prison mean no harm to Woodbury and we have known them long enough to anticipate that they would probably endorse mutual collaboration in efforts to survive. The people of Woodbury, however, know only a few key facts:

1. **the prison group has attacked them on two occasions, killing several people from the town;**

2. **members of the prison group may have caused a breach which allowed walkers in to attack other residents;**

3. **the Governor, who has kept them all alive, insists that the members of the prison group mean to do the people of Woodbury harm.**

Given these apparent facts, it's easy to see why our hapless Woodburians might be excused for trusting the Governor's word: everything they've seen lines up with it. The alternate choice for them is to believe not merely that the Governor is bad (which would not entitle the prison group to attack Woodbury, and thus would make attacking the prison group possibly justified), but that the prison group has a legitimate reason to attack Woodbury. Ignorant of the attack on Michonne, attack on the prison, and kidnapping of Glenn and Maggie, it's easy to see why the citizens of Woodbury would tend to assume the worst of Rick's group and would see them as a threat.

At first glance, we're probably tempted to say that while killing the members of the prison group would be wrong, it would be hard to blame the citizens of Woodbury. They have a pretty good excuse from ignorance. On the other hand, consider all the men who are brought on these raids to kill and rob members of other groups. Are we to believe that no word of their activities has leaked out to the greater population? That seems unlikely. Perhaps the people of Woodbury actually have a better sense for the injustice of the Governor's decisions than we might first assume. Perhaps they believe the Governor because he tells them what they want to hear, rather than because trusting him is the most rational choice. This is speculative, however, and we cannot argue this point either way from what we're told in the show.

I'm inclined to think here that while it would be wrong for ignorant members of the Woodbury militia to kill members of the prison group, they are fully excused through their legitimate ignorance. Meanwhile, the members of the prison group will be justified in defending themselves with deadly force: they are being attacked, they have not been able to resolve the situation peacefully, and they are not interested in a massively disproportionate response (like wiping out the inhabitants of Woodbury). Ultimately, the culpable people here are the Governor and his lead henchmen, who are fully aware that the fighting is aggressive rather than defensive.

What the fighters of Woodbury have here (on McMahan's account) are excuses, but no justifications: their cause is unjust and, therefore, the morally right thing to do is not to fight. We haven't established the moral symmetry of combatants, so being fully excused is the best for which the Woodburians can hope. If Walzer is correct, Woodbury's war is still unjust, but most of its citizens are justified in fighting. A subtle difference between the two, but an important one.

None of us are likely to face herds of walkers any time soon, nor are any of us likely to band together for long-term survival in any sort of apocalyptic situation. It is well within the realm of possibility, however, that some of us may be called upon to fight in a war, and I hope I have shown that there is more for the ordinary citizen (and potential combatant) to consider than merely survival: there may be moral obligations to refuse to fight in an unjust war, or to refuse to kill the enemy. If McMahan's arguments are correct, then we are in danger of committing murder when we fight in an unjust war, and this is a risk which citizens surely ought to consider.

9
Anarchy, State, and Apocalypse

MICHAEL DA SILVA AND MARTY MCKENDRY

> I knew they were bad but, they had a code. It was simple, it was stupid, but it was something . . . it was enough.
>
> —DARYL describes life with the Claimers to Rick, 4.16 "A"

In *The Walking Dead*, United States government functions have severely contracted or completely collapsed due to a pandemic of virulent, reanimated corpses that feed on the flesh of the living. On the upside, there are no more taxes. On the downside, there is not much of anything else, especially police. Life is hard, with Season Four indicating that even peach schnapps has become scarce. Walkers, starvation, and murderous survivors all pose threats, and as Andrea said on her death bed, "No one can make it alone now."

Amidst the lawlessness and violence, many survivors have formed co-operative groups to secure defense, subsistence, and companionship. Some communities have even fostered cohesive identities and moral codes. These may constitute basic government structures. The Claimers, the town of Woodbury, the prison settlement, and the Terminus cult may all plausibly claim government status. But are these post-Apocalyptic would-be governments legitimate? If so, are they equally legitimate?

Answering these questions requires analysis of the important philosophical concept of political legitimacy. This concept can be applied to four systems of political governance that developed in the post-apocalyptic American South: anarchy, dictatorship, democracy, and quasi-theocracy.

What Justifies the State?

A central question in political philosophy is how to justify state authority. Philosophers working in this area often seek to justify or undermine the legitimacy of governments that exist in the present world. "Given the fact of government authority," they ask, "is that authority justified, and if so, why?"

In the world of *The Walking Dead*, political authority is scarce. Authority often seems synonymous with power, particularly in the Governor's case (more on that later). Some philosophers argue that this power narrative is all we have; even today, 'might makes right.' When looking at competing types of post-apocalyptic governance, a government that can effectively wield power has at least one form of legitimacy over those who cannot. As Shane said, challenging Rick's authority in 2.10 "18 Miles Out." "You can't just be the good guy and expect to live." Referring to Lori and Carl, he later added, "I don't think you can keep them safe."

But do any of the leaders in *The Walking Dead* have a moral claim to lead, as well as the practical power to do so? A possible moral justification for political authority is the idea of a social contract, whereby members of a community consent to be governed by one or more rulers, or by a system of rules (as in a democracy). The community's actual consent is not even required for the social contract to be morally valid. On this view, if a community would and should hypothetically agree to the contract's terms, it is valid. For instance, people born in the US today didn't agree to be bound by the American constitution, but if we can reasonably assume that every American would and should have agreed to be so bound (because the constitution establishes a free, just, and democratic society), that would explain why individual Americans can't rightly declare their own independent countries, or ignore the existing law. Further, if the hypothetical social contract is morally valid, then the government can legitimately use force to seize your property if, for example, you hole up in a weird rural compound with ammo, canned goods, and attractive cousins and stop paying your property taxes. Carl seems to flirt with this lifestyle when gulleting an entire tub of chocolate pudding.

Many social contract theorists, like the philosophers John Locke, Thomas Hobbes, and Jean-Jacques Rousseau, discuss the idea of a 'state of nature', a state before government in which chaos reigned; when everyone was free to do as they pleased but couldn't be assured of their safety or well-being. For example, a caveman was free to walk around naked and defecate in plain view, but a rival caveman could beat him with a club and steal his mate and mammoth meat. While the explicit ways that social contracts terminate the state of nature may vary, the idea is that we all (fictionally) surrendered certain freedoms to the state in favor of a system that protects our welfare and property. That is, we collectively agreed to end what Hobbes famously called a "war of all against all." By surrendering these freedoms, we granted the state a monopoly on the use of violence to maintain order (with a few exceptions, such as self-defense).

As noted above, in *The Walking Dead*, the pandemic has apparently destroyed the functions of the US government. The rule of law has disappeared from the American South, unless we consider a police officer like Rick or Dawn, or a soldier like Abraham, to retain vestiges of state authority. Perhaps these individuals may legitimately govern the survivors under residual martial law in an indefinite emergency period. Hence, theoretical questions arise as to whether the government's authority should endure if it is cut off from its purported citizens. If the US government's authority does endure, then replacing the government with a new one would arguably be an illegitimate and revolutionary act. In such a case, the previous rules should continue to operate under improvised enforcement mechanisms. Carl and the other children should pledge allegiance to the flag while pausing to reload and sharpen their machetes.

This idea has some support in *The Walking Dead*. For example, Rick wore his Sheriff's Department uniform in early episodes of the show and commanded respect accordingly; the "government scientist" Eugene kept "classified" the scientific explanation of the zombie virus; and small groups of police and military personnel continue to operate, perhaps retaining their command structures and mission objectives. However, if the American government exists to protect its citizens, it has failed to achieve that end. Never was that more clear than when we saw the Center for Disease Control go up in flames at the end of Season One. The horde of undead cannibals roams unimpeded and the government cannot even confirm its continued existence to the surviving population. In light of these considerations, new governance structures may be appropriate for the purposes of defense, subsistence, and companionship.

The two above noted features of government legitimacy—power and morality—jointly provide a test for comparing different forms of post-apocalyptic governance. Ideally, survivors want a government that strives to protect their welfare and property from internal and external threats and has the power to do so. In the absence of such a government, it may be in survivors' interests to remain in the state of nature and get what they can in an undead-dog-eat-undead dog world. This option would be the first type of 'government' we encounter in *The Walking Dead*: anarchy!

Yes, Anarchy!

Anarchy is a state of lawlessness—like the state of nature discussed above. Basically, anarchists may do whatever they want, unless a fellow anarchist is able to prevent their chosen action through persuasion, violence, or the threat of violence. Of course, anarchists can also constrain their personal behavior according to a moral code—if they want to be nice, it's up to them! Contrary to popular perceptions, anarchists need not wear black, pierce their unclean appendages, and cultivate scrappy purple hairstyles: anarchists simply must not let anyone tread on them.

In *The Walking Dead*, anarchy reigned as Rick slept—if Shane's descriptions are to be believed. By the time the onscreen action began, some semblance of public order began to sprout in small communities like the trailer park camp outside of Atlanta. Yet the anarchic spirit took root in lone wolf survivors—like Michonne when we first encounter her—and small, rag-tag groups like Tyreese and Sasha's band before they gained acceptance into the prison settlement.

The largest, most committed group of anarchists in the series is undoubtedly the biker gang led by Joe (the group that is sometimes called "The Claimers"). This group illustrates the benefits and perils of anarchy in the post-apocalyptic landscape. On the upshot, the group need not accept or retain weak and dependent members, enhancing their mobility and capacity to scavenge sufficient resources to survive. However, with a larger group of anarchists, there is greater potential for internal conflict—as illustrated when one biker murders another simply to take a nap on the best bed. To avoid violence, the anarchists need rules. They may even require some public authority to enforce them, contrary to the anarchic spirit. Indeed, later in Season Four, we see that the biker gang has developed a rudimentary way of adjudicating property disputes—essentially, the first person to "claim" something becomes its acknowledged owner. In 4.15 "Us", Len was able to claim Daryl's (presumably delicious) rabbit, even though Daryl shot it. Yet the claiming system is unsophisticated and may have limits. Could a biker have claimed another human being, such as Beth? What if the bikers disagree on this point? Adjudicating the claim system ultimately fell to Joe, the group's leader; in this larger group setting, anarchy appears to collapse into a power structure that resembles dictatorship.

Applying our two criteria for legitimacy to anarchy, we can see that the power and morality of individuals and small groups is driven by the capabilities, character, and values of individuals or group members. With larger groups, anarchy can tend towards violent conflict (as it is often caricatured), making it an unsustainable mode of governance in the long-term if groups acquire new members. On the other hand, Michonne did quite well on her own from a survival perspective (though she was unhappy because of her social isolation, as we discover in Season Four).

The Governor and the Rick-tatorship

An alternative to true anarchy is collective acknowledgment of a public authority figure. One could argue that Joe filled this role in the Claimers. He was able to make decisions for the group, regardless of the input of others. If this accurately describes the Claimers case (which is unclear from what appeared onscreen), *The Walking Dead* also shows us how anarchy can evolve into our next form of government: the dictatorship. Contrary to anarchy's central tenets, public order is restored, but private lives are no longer under your own command. Members of the group are safer, but less free—like wolves turned to dogs. Regardless of what you think of Joe's authority, the dictatorship is arguably the most prevalent form of governance in *The Walking Dead*. The contrasting leadership styles of the Governor and Rick suggest that dictatorship can be malevolent or benevolent, but both men show characteristic signs of the dictator: they make unilateral decisions for the group, and they wield this power primarily through use of force and control of resources.

The Governor's status as a dictator is not difficult to establish. He ruled Woodbury with an iron fist and killed those who got in his way, including innocent non-members of the group—such as soldiers in a small military encampment. He conducted odd, risky experiments with walkers that seemed beyond the moral pale. He wore a sinister, pirate eye-patch. And ultimately, the Governor's story arc demonstrates the folly of following a charismatic leader without moral scruples or accountability. In the end, the Governor, like many dictators before him, turned on his own citizens when the going got tough, killing numerous loyal Woodburians after their failed attack on the prison settlement. The Governor's rise and fall as a dictator even recurred when he became the ruler of Season Four's trailer-based compound. Again, most members of the community wound up dead, directly or indirectly by the Governor's hand.

Yet Rick's rule in Season Three, which paralleled that of the Governor, was equally authoritative and suggests that dictatorship can take a more benevolent form. We've seen that Rick is a good man; yet he explicitly took authoritative control of his group of survivors in the name of security at the end of Season Two. In 2.13 "Beside the Dying Fire," he famously accepted a leadership role by proclaiming "This is not a democracy anymore!" Recognizing the need for strength and decisiveness to secure the group's safety, Rick took absolute control. Inefficient democratic decision-making just wasn't cutting it.

Rick's leadership may be benevolent. When Rick ruled with absolute authority at the prison, the group consented to his rule, seemingly fulfilling a social contract criterion. The distinction between this situation and that of Woodbury is that the Governor concealed the methods and consequences of his rule. We have also seen that a hallmark of Rick's leadership is a demand that any killings be justified through self-defense (though in the case of the Terminus cult, he also seems to allow executions to pre-empt threats—even to third parties—and to denounce actions beyond the moral pale). In addition, Rick permits group members like Michonne to leave despite their knowledge of the prison's defenses.

Yet even Rick's arguably benevolent dictatorship reveals a practical problem with dictatorships in general: the concentration of power in the hands of an individual makes the exercise of that power subject to individual fallibility. Even if the dictator attempts to act morally for the sake of the community, the lack of an oversight mechanism can mean that mistakes go uncorrected. Sound advice is not taken, and the stresses of leadership can lead to paranoia and impulsivity. Rick's unfair treatment of Tyreese and his band—keeping them under lock and key—is a good example of Rick's poor judgment that ran contrary to the group's wishes. Further, considering that the prison community was set to expand, the people who would have presumably faired the best in emergency situations were those with the strongest personal relationships to Rick (such as Carl, Hershel, and other original group members). For instance, would Carl and Tyreese have received equal rations during a food shortage? We think not. The Rick-tatorship may have been better than Woodbury, but it was not a just society.

Democracy Lite

Eventually, even Rick realized that his dictatorial rule could not survive. Faced with the Governor's absolute rule, Rick's belief in his own benevolent dictatorship crumbled and, in 3.15 "This Sorrowful Life," he told his group, "I won't be your Governor." The Council replaced him. While the establishment of this council took place off screen, and though its composition and procedures were unclear, the Council's purpose was to represent the people of the prison community and Rick was not a member.

Democracy means "rule of the people" in Greek. In ancient Athens, communities were sufficiently small that all citizens (an admittedly restricted class in ancient Greece) had a voice. Arguably, the prison community was sufficiently small that they could have adopted a similar structure, perhaps excluding minors. But they appear to have adopted a more modern representative view whereby a select group is said to represent the people and makes decisions on their behalf. In the modern world, these representatives are usually elected.

It's unclear whether the community elected members of the Council to serve a true representative function, but their group-based decision-making was still a proxy for the interests of the collective. We can probably assume that the majority did not intentionally use its power to oppress a minority by, for example, deciding that the original members of the group get the best food. Indeed, the risk of "the tyranny of the majority" is why modern democracies usually have constitutionally-guaranteed individual and minority rights enforced by an independent judiciary.

As an aside, had the Council not sought to represent the interests of the collective, rather than a democracy, it would have more closely resembled on oligarchy—a dictatorial structure whereby several individuals share power. The arrangement at the hospital in Season Five somewhat resembles an oligarchy, where Dawn makes most of the command and control decisions, but effectively shares her power with Dr. Edwards by virtue of his medical expertise. Indeed, we see Dr. Edwards kill a newly arrived injured doctor to maintain his position.

Regardless, the prison community's Council clearly had the consent of the governed. A social contract appeared to be in place whereby everyone in the community followed the rules for their own good. Yet breaches of Council authority did occur during their reign. Even if their authority was legitimate, the Council sometimes failed to wield real power. As occurs in many post-dictatorial states, a previous rule undermined the Council's governance. In 4.4 "Indifference," Rick reasserted his leadership by exiling Carol from the community following her unilateral decision to kill Karen and David after their infection. While Carol believed that she was acting in the group's best interest, she had no authority to take such drastic actions. She effectively made herself secret dictator for a day. The same, however, could likely be said for Rick's decision to banish Carol. While he justifies his decision by noting that no one in the group could trust her after learning of her actions, the democratic ideal would require him to share this information with the group (or their representatives) so they could make an informed decision together. How could the Council continue to trust Rick? Did he not betray the group for their own good, as Carol believed she did?

Despite these hiccups, the Council-led community briefly secured the safety of the population and employed a well-developed moral code. The Council developed a fair test for citizenship eligibility—the three questions:

1. **How many walkers have you killed?**

2. **How many people have you killed?**

3. **Why?**

The three questions are helpful for both ensuring the safety of the community (by barring psychopaths from membership) and the integrity of its moral values. While the fact that Rick invented the three questions weakens its democratic flavor, this fact helps add to the legitimacy of the program by giving it a foundational constitutional and moral force; both Rick and the Council held the moral truths revealed by the three questions to be self-evident, so to speak.

We have discussed the perils of dictatorship, but we can similarly imagine the perils of a council of the weak or the foolish: what would have happened if the Council's judgment was in error and in conflict with Rick's views? Would Rick have been right to retake power by force? These questions do not have easy answers. In the end, both Rick's dictatorship and the Council's rule succeeded insofar as they were effective and moral. But conceptually, Rick's view of morality—or the view of any individual—may be flawed, and the Council may likewise err in moral judgment or fail to achieve consensus. In such cases, we might wish they had direct access to an absolute moral code derived from an infallible divine source. Like, oh say, God.

Quasi-Theocratic Cannibal Cult (Also a Great Name for a Heavy Metal Band)

This brings us to theocracy, Greek for "rule by a god." The problem with theocracies is that it is impossible to determine the authenticity of a divinely, mystically or magically inspired moral code. There is no rational test to determine the truth of supernaturally-based factual or moral claims derived from the Bible, Greek mythology, Charles Manson, witches' cauldrons, or Pink Floyd acid trips.

Practically speaking, it's also impossible to apply a divine code of moral governance except through human interpreters, who are subject to the fallibility problems associated with dictators. There are several reasons why these considerations do not lead many people who live in theocracies to revolution or even protest. They may stay silent out of fear and even we are nervous to use certain examples in a zombie essay!. They may be systematically kept ignorant of alternatives or indoctrinated in their youth by the government that rules them. Alternatively, they could simply accept the familiar.

Then, there is also the consideration that theocracy has a certain appeal, because inherent to the idea of a theocracy is that *your theocracy is special*. By being a member of an exclusive society, you become better and more deserving than other people. You and only people like you have seen the light. As to everyone else—who cares?

In *The Walking Dead*, the quasi-theocratic Terminus cult illustrates these problems in spades. By the end of Season Four, we know that members of the cult cannibalize people seeking safe refuge, serving them up in a folksy southern BBQ picnic bench area, replete with a matronly, seemingly-less-racist Paula Deen figure: "Let's get you settled and we'll make you a plate . . ."

The first few episodes of Season Five confirm the extent of the community's depravity, as the hunters discuss the flavor of their prey, not content with mere subsistence. We learn that they have a quasi-religiously-derived "ethical" system that justifies their *Homo sapiens* feed-downs, which—if atmosphere is any indication—feature bibs and BBQ sauce. We know there is a quasi-religious basis to the community from the freaky, candle-and-such filled worship chamber that Rick and company flee through, and where Carol confronts the cannibalistic Paula Deen-esque figure.

Everywhere, the weirdo temple is decked out with slogans like "We First, Always." This implies that members of the cult see themselves as a special class (inedible), as distinguished from non-members of the cult who are not special (good eatin'!). While the cannibalism of the group grabs the headlines, what makes the group quasi-theocratic is that its moral code is rooted in secret "knowledge" and ritual. Their creed, the necessity of which they claim to uniquely grasp, is, "You're the butcher or you're the cattle." The quick destruction of the Terminus cult makes it difficult to fully assess their views to determine whether they truly believe that they were following the will of a deity, but their belief that their status as a chosen group gives them some authority for their actions seems clear.

It is possible that some members of the cult don't sincerely buy into this false morality and are simply satisfied with the group's power to provide subsistence and defense. Yet the Terminus cult's deranged approach to governance should raise some red flags about the potential problems of an extreme theocracy. Like any society, a theocracy can be judged as powerful or impotent, moral or immoral; but a theocracy uniquely claims that its moral system is immune to rational criticism. Some historical quasi-theocracies—such as the Aztec empire—featured human sacrifice. And even non-theocracies can seem crazy when their leaders claim to have a direct pipeline to divinity for specific policy decisions. After all, do you want your president consulting a ouija board?

Most philosophers aren't big fans of theocracies. Conceptually, we reluctantly admit, it is possible that a legitimate theocracy could exist (and each one claims that it is in fact legitimate). However, a hallmark of current and historical theocracies is an inability to demonstrate legitimacy, since the foundations of their belief systems are not rationally-based. But prove us wrong, theocracies! Prove us wrong!

Terminus

Anyone finding themselves in a post-apocalyptic hellscape should seek a community that both wields power and respects the moral good. If only one of these values is available at a given time, you will have to decide which is more important to you: survival or human dignity. Alas, such are the quandaries of life in an undead hellscape.

In *The Walking Dead*, we think the Council's imperfect democratic rule is preferable to the alternatives that we see. This echoes Winston Churchill's famous quote, "Democracy is the worst form of government, except for all the others." A related lesson from the series is that effective and moral governance must not be taken for granted—it involves a constant struggle for the public good against private interests and outside threats, especially cannibal cults who live at train stations.

If I Don't Save the World I Have No Value

SETH M. WALKER

"Eugene's a scientist, and he knows exactly what caused this mess" (4.11 "Claimed"). At least that's what Sergeant Abraham Ford and any others that they came across were led to believe in the televised series.

Abraham's "mission," we all know, has been to get the mysterious Dr. Eugene Porter to Washington, DC, as soon as possible so he can meet up with other scientists to help save the world. Before we found out Dr. Porter was really Mr. Porter (and the only *doctoring* he was good at was doctoring up one big hoax), we understood the importance of that mission and the value Eugene had in this crumbling world. But his revelation to his companions near the middle of Season Five (5.5 "Self Help") might have changed the nature of that value and his place among the others—especially Abraham.

The case of Eugene Porter is unique. Inherent value, most believe, applies to everyone, equally. But, it doesn't really work out too well as an underlying rationale, since adults would be just as valuable as children, and yet, in many instances, that doesn't appear to be how the characters always feel or act. Instrumental value has its own problems, too: children and newborn babies are obviously not as useful as resourceful adults to the survival and longevity of others. But, that little tidbit seems to get ignored in many situations throughout the series as well. Eugene Porter, however, is a great example of how these two problematic perspectives come together.

So, let's take a step back for a moment and pretend we haven't seen "Self Help" quite yet and have no idea Eugene was full of rotting walker muck. Let's also pretend we don't know he was deliberately stalling the DC road trip along the way, trying to delay his looming confession for as long as possible. Before we found out he was lying about being a scientist with The Human Genome Project and his ability to save the human race, Eugene's value was well beyond the possibility of *just* being inherent: he could have been truly *instrumental* in saving what's left of the world.

Okay, now go ahead and trigger that memory we just briefly suppressed. Eugene's a fraud. He knows it, and now all of the others know it. So, how does this affect any sort of inherent or instrumental value he might have at this point in the series?

The thing to keep in mind is that Eugene knew his life was dangling by that little fib of his anyway. Before his Season Five confession, and Abraham's knock-out blows, he confided in Tara Chambler that he sabotaged the fuel line of the bus they had taken from Father Gabriel Stokes to delay their arrival in DC, in case they got there and he was unable to work his magic:

EUGENE: The bus crashed 'cause of me.

TARA: No, it didn't.

EUGENE: Yes, it did. I put crushed glass in the fuel line. Light bulbs I found in the church. The vehicle should have failed before it ever got to the road. . . . I know empirically and definitively that I cannot survive on my own. I cannot.

TARA: So you killed the bus?

EUGENE: If I don't cure the disease, if I don't save the world, I have no value.

In other words, he's well aware of the fact that his value to the group seems to rest solely on his ability to help them save the world, and by extension, their own lives. Without that, he's nothing but a somewhat socially awkward gamer who enjoys watching a good, live-action bookstore romp, and one who's rather inept when it comes to defending the group (though let's not write him off completely quite yet . . . he's still a little bit more useful in that area than Judith, right?). And when he does reveal his lie to everyone later in the episode, that's pretty much what it comes down to. Or does it?

The conversation between him and Tara continued:

TARA: That's not how it works.

EUGENE: If I don't fix things, there's no way you people would keep me around, share resources, even protect me.

TARA: Of course we would. We're friends. We have each other's backs. That's it. That's how it works. . . . You're stuck with us. Just like we're stuck with you. No matter what.

Granted, she wasn't responding to *the* confession, but the point is there: it's not about your usefulness to the group that keeps them wanting you around, and it's not necessarily about the inherent value individuals may or may not have. There's something much more powerful and *connective* involved: community, friendship, love, and perhaps a shared existential angst that makes all of their trials and tribulations easier to get through together (sort of makes Tara's "GREATM" sound a little bit cooler now, huh?).

But, let's not forget that, well, this Eugene *is* one pretty smart Tennessee Top Hat-wearing-fellow, scientist or not. And we haven't seen cunning like his since Dr. Edwin Jenner almost tricked Rick's entire group into an explosive suicide in Season One, or since the Governor's various escapades throughout Seasons Three and Four. Maybe he isn't very fast, and maybe he doesn't really know how to properly use a weapon, as Tara notes (5.7 "Crossed"). And she's right: lacking those qualities does make you pretty useless in this sort of world. Then again, maybe Eugene will surprise us with some new, unforeseen resourcefulness on a par with his fire hose death-spray when he recovers from Abraham's little outburst. He did have *one* skill that kept him alive, Tara reminded his bitter companions: "We're supposed to be mad at him because he used it?"

Well, we can't deny there's some animosity brewing among his companions, and maybe they won't be as adamant about *his* protection relative to others anymore. But, in the words of

Sergeant Abraham Ford, the only way to make it in this world is to "find some strong, likeminded comrades and stay stuck together like wet on water" (4.11 "Claimed"). Simply put, people need people.

And indeed, the more, the better.

10

We're Not Free to Save Lee

COLE BOWMAN

For the many players who have taken up the mantle of Lee Everett in the *Walking Dead* videogame, it can feel like the decisions you make on his behalf don't really matter. No matter how carefully you plan and scheme, Lee dies at the end of Telltale Games's popular contribution to the *Walking Dead* corpus.

Though the game has been designed specifically to simulate the ramifications of making hard choices in everyday life, the question still rings clear as a shotgun blast: do any of these decisions matter?

While, yes, there are many options involved in the gameplay, they have little impact on the ultimate outcome of the game itself. Even right up to the end, the player controls many of the elements surrounding the outcome. For instance, you can choose whether or not Clementine kills Lee or simply leaves him to turn. Your choices also determine just how many people are waiting for her once Lee is gone and just how hard she has to fight to get out of Atlanta. Regardless of this, though, he will always die.

Spoilers Ahead

The first thing that any new player to the *Walking Dead* series videogame will notice is its rather revolutionary interactivity. During the gameplay, the story unfolds not in the linear, methodical fashion that gamers have come to see as standard form for most games on the market, but rather as a series of interactive scenes intricately interlaced to create a narrative.

Unlike many other videogames, this one is very "story heavy," focusing more on narrative than on any other element. This narrative relies predominantly on player choice in order to move forward. Whenever there is an impasse or a critical juncture, the player is made to decide between a number of *possible* actions, with each action leading to specific ramifications within the storyline. Each choice that a player makes helps to "tailor" the game experience to her individual choices. In this way, the *Walking Dead* game mimics life in a startlingly realistic way, except in a few subtle, but important ways.

When you make a decision in *The Walking Dead* it acts as a mechanism for progressing the storyline. More specifically, to progress in the game, you must make decisions. The option to abstain from active choice does not really exist (unlike in life). Even in the moments when there is an option to do nothing, choosing to do nothing is often detrimental in the game, forcing your character into precarious positions that benefit no one involved. This mechanism is maintained so that you cannot passively move through the plot. This means that there is not an option to be able to avoid a situation entirely as there almost always is in life.

Let's look at an example to help clarify this difference. During the first episode of the first season, Lee has made it to Hershel's farm outside of Atlanta. After a rather tense conversation with the aforementioned veterinarian, there is a commotion over by the fence where Hershel's son, Shawn, and Kenny's son, Duck, have been fortifying it against walkers. Lee *must* proceed to the fence at that point. Once he's arrived, he can decide whether to save Shawn, Duck, or neither from the oncoming zombies. In the game, choosing neither leads to the necessary consequence that both Hershel and Kenny will begrudge Lee for standing by rather than attempting to save their son. In life, the matrix of decisions is not nearly so simple. If it were real life, several other options would be available to Lee. He could go for help. He could throw himself in the way of the oncoming zombies in an attempt to save them both. Lee could also simply leave the scene, unhindered by what he saw. In life, you do not necessarily need to participate in the events at hand. Passive participation is not an option for the people in game. Lee must decide.

Perhaps the easiest way to think about the mechanism of choice overall is like that of a "choose-your-own-adventure" story. To get from Scene 1 to Scene 2, you must pick from a list of up to four options: *A*, *B*, *C* and *D*. All of these impact the actual details of Scene 2. Therefore, in moving from 1 to 2, if you choose option *A* as your choice mechanism, you end up with scene 2*A*, rather than 2*B*, 2*C*, or 2*D*. All of these vary slightly in their design and each will impact what happens later in the game. Where you end up in Scene 2 depends on which choice you made in Scene 1.

While this system is fairly straightforward, the clever game designers coded the game in such a way that the decisions you make can carry through various other stages of the game. For instance, if you are on Scene 1 and you choose option *C*, your decision might not have much of an impact on Scene 2. Instead, it could show itself at a much later scene, intricately tying into the string of all of the other choices you have to make. Perhaps it isn't until several scenes later that this exact decision makes an impact. So, when you reach the point in which a choice from much earlier on pertains, it "triggers" the permutations of your exact play-through. When you reach Scene 12, you come to it loaded with all the potential of your previous choices. So rather than having Scene 12 simply determined by your choices in Scene 11, *all* of your choices up until then matter. The scene you witness in 12 is determined by the interplay between the other one that have come before. 1*A*, 2*A*, 3*C*, 4*D*, 5*C*, 6*A*, 7*C*, 8*D*, 9*A*, 10*A*, 11*B* could be entirely different than 1*A*, 2*A*, 3*B*, 4*D*, 5*C*, 6*A*, 7*C*, 8*D*, 9*A*, 10*A*, 11*B*. The only difference between these two long strands of information is what you decided at Scene 3, yet it can (and most often will) have resounding impact upon your experience with the game.

This is evident in many of the choices you make in the *Walking Dead*. For example, whether or not you befriend Kenny changes the outcome of the rest of the game, if you help the high-schoolers it will change your relationship with Lilly, how you introduce your relationship with Clementine will alter the rest of the group's perception of you. Perhaps the most stark example of this mechanism comes with the scene in which your group (whoever they may be), comes across a car abandoned in the woods. It is fully stocked with survival supplies and you can choose whether or not to take these supplies.

This choice seems insignificant for a long time in the game. That is, until you reach the final episodes in Atlanta in which you meet the former owner of that car and he's holding Clementine hostage. Suddenly this decision is a *really* big deal.

But why is any of this philosophically interesting? What makes this important? Well, it all closely illustrates a long standing discussion in philosophy about a concept called "determinism." Determinism is an interpretation of reality in which your choices matter to a small enough degree that no matter what you do, the outcome is always the same. The impact of this paradigm is most starkly felt when considering the nature of free will. In our conversation, however, the "free will" that is of most concern is not necessarily Lee's. It's the player's. So, how does this reflect life as we know it? And what do videogames have to do with the nature of reality?

The Nature of Choice

First, we must understand the nature of choice before we can truly discuss the philosophical implications of the game. There are two extremes by which choice can be easily understood: absolute freedom of choice and complete lack of that freedom. Both models have been hotly debated by philosophers, but each have something to offer to help understand the problem of free will in *The Walking Dead*.

Let's start with the idea of complete lack of freedom of will. This is not an uncommon perception about reality amongst not just philosophers, but many theologians, physicists, and other great thinkers. In this scenario, there is nothing that your mind, what you do or how you intend for things to be, that makes a difference in the outcome of your life. This is the true basis of determinism, in which each and every action you take is determined by a causal action that preceded it. To take this principle to the extreme is to take the entirety of the universe on this basis, in which every event can be viewed as a necessary consequence of every previous event. It is true cause and effect.

Eighteenth-century thinker Pierre-Simon Laplace devised one of the most definitive thought experiments on this subject in his ruminations on a "demon." Laplace, a mathematician and physicist, spent a great deal of his scholarly time on trying to figure out the nature of reality, eventually coming to a strictly deterministic view through the following experiment.

Laplace imagines a hyper-intelligent "demon" who has the ability to calculate the trajectory of each and every particle in the universe. Because Laplace's thought experiment was grounded in Newtonian physics, which says that every action is preceded by a causal force, this is an entirely reasonable position. It only works, though, if the demon knows the activity of *every* particle in the time leading up to that moment. If the demon were to know the position of every particle that constitutes a walker and the velocity at which they are moving, it could calculate exactly how far it would shamble the next day. Extrapolated across the entirety of existence, the demon could calculate the exact movements of every walker. *And* every human, horse, and tiger in the apocalypse.

What this sort of conception would mean for the reality of a videogame is this: nothing you do as a player matters. No matter how badly you want to make Clementine understand how to stay safe in the apocalypse, you will not be able to keep her from getting hurt at least a couple of times. The particles that make up her every movement and glitch are already set into motion.

It goes way beyond even just that, though. More than just the actual in-game choices is concerned: *Your* very existence is already *entirely* predetermined. Whether or not you choose to tell the group about Lee's murder conviction has already been determined. You have no control over the matter. You either will or you won't and your opinion on it has nothing to with what happens. Your thumbs cannot possibly strike a button other than the one to which they were already heading. Even your apparent choices to purchase the game and play it in the first place weren't your choices to be made.

The counterpoint to this problem comes with the idea of radical freedom, a principle originally posed by twentieth century French existentialist philosopher, Jean-Paul Sartre. Very much unlike his predecessor Laplace, Sartre argued that people are radically free at all points in time in everything that we do. Regardless of the factors leading up to an action, Sartre's model proposes absolute autonomy of action. According to Sartre, people so badly want to avoid responsibility for these actions that we employ intricate strategies to deflect blame onto anything else. These strategies are what he called *mauvaise foi* or "bad faith."

One example of this "bad faith" occurs back with Lee's interactions on Hershel's farm after zombies have penetrated the flimsy fence. We've seen that the player has the choice to try to save Hershel's son Shawn, Kenny's son Duck, or neither. Regardless of the player's decision at that point, Shawn is eaten by the zombies that have toppled the fence, but there are people who demand answers of Lee in the aftermath. Either Hershel or Kenny are angry that Lee didn't attempt to save *their* son over the other man's. A little later in the episode, the player has to choose how to account for her decision. The most popular answer that players give at this point was: "I thought I could save both." In this situation, Sartre's bad faith is expressed by the player's unwillingness to take command of her decision, to own it.

Sartre would probably argue that the very idea of determinism might have been constructed as a means of avoiding the responsibility of our freedom. Laplace, in turn, would argue that Sartre was always bound to make that conjecture. The real philosophical problem with strict determinism versus absolute freedom is that we don't really know which is valid. Some authors, like William James, even argue that we *can't* know whether or not there is a determinist principle governing the universe. This does, however, bring up some interesting questions about the nature of reality.

Are You in a Videogame?

The strange and confounding truth of reality is that we very well might be in some kind of computer simulation. Not just Lee and Clementine. You and me. Recent philosophical thought has begun to explore this concept at length, which has been coined the "Simulation Hypothesis." This hypothesis states that there is a possibility that reality as we know it is, in fact, a computer simulation and our consciousness is made to interact within this simulated reality.

Nick Bostrom, noted philosopher and professor at Oxford University, postulates this in his simulation hypothesis treatise "Are You Living in a Computer Simulation?" Bostrom's answer is a resounding "Possibly." Bostrom argues that, if the rate at which computers have been progressing continues as it currently is, eventually (probably sooner rather than later) the advances in technology necessary to compute a consciousness will exist. He then proposes this in a simple logical syllogism, in which the option of a post-human civilization running a computer simulation in which we are all simply programmed consciousnesses is presented as an outcome. Bostrom then does the math in order to support his thesis, illustrating through an elegant designed equation that we are *more likely* in a simulation than we are in an authentic "reality" in his proposed future.

While no major philosopher at present believes that this is a *probable* permutation of reality, some have estimated that it has about a *twenty percent* possibility of being true. (Both Nick Bostrom and David Chalmers, a modern philosopher, who is no stranger to zombies, working from the Australian National University, calculate this same probability.) Given Bostrom's argument, the Simulation Hypothesis seems a little less ludicrous, if a bit jarring. But why is it jarring? What is it about the nature of a simulation that makes us so uncomfortable? Do you think of all those times you went back to replay a videogame just to see if a character dies again? Are you that character in someone else's simulation? If so, why does it matter? The short answer to all of these questions is this: we like the idea of having free will.

Lee is your avatar for the first season of the *Walking Dead* game, meaning that, through him, your will is exercised. He can do nothing without you. What is strange, though, about the paradigm of a videogame is the confines it puts upon your will. That is, your will can only make the choices apparent to your avatar while you're actively participating in the game. You cannot choose to capture a walker if it is not presented as an option for Lee, even if you think it would be the best possible choice to make.

When you sign on to the game, you enter freely into these restrictions of absolute free will. These restrictions are placed upon you for many reasons, not the least of which being the practical consideration of the actual game itself. There is only so much that can be programmed into a game. While having a game with infinite possibilities is an appealing thought, it is in no way a practical stance on game making. At least at present.

The most important lesson within Bostrom's treatise is not necessarily the soundness of the Simulation Hypothesis at all, but rather what it would mean for an individual if it were true. If you were the actual character in a computer simulation, your decisions would likely be played out much like the ones within the *Walking Dead* game's narrative. While there are no "right" answers for any of the problems that are presented, there definitely are better decisions that can be made. There are, however, the aforementioned defined parameters. Despite what it might seem at first, this is from where your freedom of will truly emerges.

This situation suggests something known as fatalism, which would help to resolve the problem of free will versus predetermined outcomes of a videogame. Fatalism exists somewhere between the two extremes mentioned before: radical freedom and absolute lack of freedom. Also known by some as "soft determinism," it suggests that determinism and free will are compatible ideas, in which a person loses no agency to act out her motivations while navigating causally set events. Many philosophers, such as Arthur Schopenhauer, David Hume, and Carl Hoefer, have tried to justify something like this scenario, in which there are determinist parameters (like you would find when in a game) but also room to move around within them. This paradigm suggests that there are a certain number of "set" occurrences and that the time between them can be used in various ways. Say, for instance, you must kill a man. The cards are dealt and this has to happen. While you are unable to extract yourself from this fate, you can choose the method of his death. This is the case with Clementine and Lee at the end of Season One.

A good way to think about this is like an itinerary, which lists a number of necessary elements that must happen in a certain sequence, but leaves time for other events that might arise. What this sort of paradigm stresses is that, even with necessary points of time factored in, your free will is still valid. What you do in between these benchmarks is what really defines your character. What really defines your version of Lee's character, therefore, is what you do during gameplay, not what happens during the cinematics.

Why Your Choices Matter

On the internet, there are several databases detailing the statistics of player choices for the *Walking Dead* seasons. They show, much like each episode does at the end of the gameplay, the percentage of players who made each choice possible at every major junction. The game statistics initially showed most decisions skewed distinctly toward one decision or the other, with most players choosing the morally "higher ground" in dire situations, according to Telltale's marketing director Richard Iggo in a 2012 interview.

What is especially interesting about the statistics at hand, however, is the way that they have changed over time. Around the same time as the interview, the statistics for the second episode "Starved for Help" were drastically different than they have become since. The major difference between the two might help to highlight something about the nature and importance of choice. As Iggo said, the majority of players at the time tended toward the perceived "right" option. This option tended to be the one that spared the most lives or were typically considered the most morally "correct." Iggo points out that this is in the face of many options in which the decisions were specifically occupying some kind of morally grey area. He reported to *GamesBeat* magazine:

> It's fascinating because even when we offer players a decision where the apparently darker option might make sense from a purely logical point of view, they'll often try to choose the 'higher' ground at personal cost even if that means being put in danger or having a relationship with another character suffer because of it.

While this trend continued to be true throughout the first season, with such morally grey decisions tending toward the "highest possible good," the nature of the statistics began to change the longer that each of the episodes was available to players.

"Starving for Help" (June 2012) had a number of tough decisions to be made, just like any of the other episodes in the series. The initial end of game reports of these decisions showed that eighty-five percent of people chose to chop off high school band director, David Parker's leg in order to free him from the bear trap even though walkers were bearing down on the group at that very instant. As of December 2014, that decision was at 61 percent. When confronted by the crazed woman in the woods, Jolene, 87 percent of initial players waited to shoot her. Newer statistics put that decision at 52 percent.

When faced with the decision to help Kenny kill the unresponsive Larry after a heart attack, 68 percent of players chose to attempt reviving him. Newer statistics put that decision at now at 49 percent.

This shift in statistics is not isolated to just this episode, with the numbers continually crawling closer to the center of the statistical curve. While it's entirely possible that the new players with different priorities are shifting the curve, this distinct progression toward an equal division between the decisions suggests otherwise. What's more likely is that the people who have played through the episode (or even the whole season) have gone back and intentionally "tested" out the other options. This "testing" is typical if any choice leads to undesirable ramifications. But why?

Game theory may have a few answers for this kind of behavior as far as *The Walking Dead* is concerned. Eric Rasmusen states in *Games and Information* that games must contain four essential elements in order to be fully defined: the *players* of the game, *actions* and *information* available to each of these players and the potential *payoffs* for each of these actions. During the initial play-through, three of these four essential elements are present. The player is defined and they are given immediate access to their potential actions and the information surrounding each of these actions. What is not defined, however, is the payoff for their decision.

Let's look at one of the aforementioned decisions as an example: whether or not to save high school teacher David Parker. Firstly, the person at the controller knows herself to be the *player* of the game, therefore satisfying the first game element according to Rasmusen. Secondly, the player knows that if she does not save David from the bear trap, he will be eaten by walkers, seemingly satisfying the element of *information*. Thirdly, the player knows that she can either save David or not save David, outlining the possible *actions* available to her.

During an initial play-through, however, the player does not have access to the final element of Rasmusen's set, the *payoff.* While it's reasonable for her to make assumptions about the possible benefits of adding more people to the group, the actual payoff isn't defined until after her decision has been made. This lack of knowledge of the payoff also impacts the critical information that the player has access to. In game theory, this situation is known as a game with "imperfect information."

What follows is an imperfect play-through of the season of *The Walking Dead* in which our player might regret her actions earlier in the game, and hope for a different outcome. When she reaches Scene 12, she now regrets not playing Scene 5 differently. This ultimately leads players to retry by starting over. In imperfect information games, the desire to replay is entirely normal behavior according to game theory. What is most interesting about the application of these sorts of theories to our player is that, given a choice in the matter, all well-formed games tend toward an equilibrium of sorts.

While the decision making-process is difficult in this particular game, players tend toward what they consider to be the "right" decision, but there are many factors working against them. For instance, when there are walkers barreling down on Lee the player may accidentally slip and hit a button she did not anticipate. Perhaps she hits *A* instead of *B* as she had intended and doesn't do what she wanted. This kind of action is also accounted for in game theory, in the "trembling hand perfect equilibrium" equation. According to this, even unintended actions eventually lead to an equilibrium, given enough time and enough choices made by players. That is, no matter what game is being played, every available action will be utilized a normatively equal amount of times so long as they are beneficial to the player. This is why the numbers for later playing have been skewed so much from their original outcomes when the episodes first appeared. Because players have gone back with new "perfect" information in order to equalize their own unintended consequences.

But why is this the case? Why do people try to "fix" the outcomes of the game like this? This answer is both exceptionally simple and maddeningly complex. We want to be right. Depending on your own moral standpoint, you are able to choose between several "grey" moral outcomes.

Now, to bring it all into perspective, consider again the paradigm of determinism. But instead of a religious figure or the laws of physics deciding the outcomes of what happens, it's a group of human game designers. One of these designers, Jake Rodkin, acknowledges this mechanism in a Telltale Games interview: "every single thing you say to every character is tracked and is available to the writers of subsequent episodes to use and to flavor your play-through and make you feel like you ruined everything." At its core, a videogame is a playable story. Stories have a certain progression, which includes a set beginning and an ending. While sometimes the ending depends on the story's play, it must end.

Despite this, though, we are compelled to play again and again, erasing "bad" decisions where we can in order to make the best possible play-through. Because all along, the game has been all about the player in the first place. Even though Lee, your avatar, dies you can still shape his story so that it most reflects your desired outcome. It is the choices themselves that matter because they are your choices. The way that these decisions turn out does not define the story, but rather the player. And it is up to the player to decide whether or not these choices were meaningful.

In the end, what comes to the surface of the story is just that: the story. We are telling ourselves a story of our moral selves when we play this videogame. We, the players, are exercising our will in a way that is much more directed than can be done in real life. Whether or not we have free will or we live in a reality ruled by determinism will likely never be parsed out for certain. But the knowledge of this fact can help to inform our choices, and it is as powerful a philosophical tool as there has ever been. If we know that there is a possibility that our choices matter, we will always choose the higher option. This is why, in the Telltale Games *Walking Dead* videogame, we will always regret not being able to save Lee.

IV

Look at the Flowers

11
I Ain't No Hollaback Girl!

MELISSA VOSEN CALLENS

"*Look at the flowers*" is a seemingly benign sentence, but for fans of AMC's *The Walking Dead*, it is a sentence that is all too haunting. Before killing Lizzie, a child with an obsession and dangerous affinity for walkers, Carol desperately instructs Lizzie to "look at the flowers," in the hope she'll find a brief moment of peace before her death.

Many audience members were shocked at this scene, and some suggested the writers had gone too far. Even in 2014, the death of a child in such a horrific manner is rarely seen on television, and if a death of that nature is part of the storyline, it is usually just implied rather than shown. In post-apocalyptic Georgia, it still seems like a horrendous, unthinkable turn in the plot. Lizzie's crimes that prompted her execution, however, went beyond her precarious infatuation with the undead; her infatuation led her to kill her younger sister, Mika. After she killed Mika, she watched and methodically waited for Mika to reanimate. I find the outcry from fans odd, however, because in many ways this outcome was foreshadowed much earlier in the season (4.2 "Infected").

In "Infected," we gain a better understanding of each of the girls and how they view and cope with the apocalypse. In the episode, Lizzie and Mika's father dies and turns into a walker. Once he turns, Lizzie volunteers to end his life, but after trying to, she breaks down and is unable to do it. Carol tells Lizzie she must be strong in order to survive the apocalypse; Mika, however, suggests Carol is wrong in her assessment. Mika argues that her sister is not weak—just "funny in the head." At the time, viewers assume that Lizzie simply cannot kill her father, even in walker form. It seems plausible that a young girl would not want to stab her own father despite the danger he now poses as a walker. Patricide is quite uncommon. We later learn, however, it is because she has a fascination for walkers. Throughout her time on the show, she names them. She plays with them. She feeds live rats to them through the fence at the prison. Some may even argue she befriends them—all of which are very dangerous behaviors, behaviors that eventually lead to her execution.

Carol ending Lizzie's life was obviously a difficult scene not only for the audience to watch, but also for the actors and production crew to shoot. It was not a scene shot lightly. Melissa McBride, the actor who plays Carol, struggled to deconstruct the scene when asked to do so on the wrap-up show *The Talking Dead*. But, still, after nearly four seasons of carnage and the loss of main character after main character, was it all that much of a surprise? Does the audience not remember young Carl shooting his reanimated, just-gave-birth-to-his-baby-sister, mother?

In *The Walking Dead*, characters are continually confronted with a barrage of moral dilemmas, like the two described above. The dilemmas are played out in a tense sixty-minute sequence of events, and the characters' decisions are influenced by the apocalyptic landscape. To help us understand the character's moral decisions, it helps to think in terms of Lawrence Kohlberg's theory of moral development. Kohlberg claims that individual humans, starting as little children, go through definite stages of moral thinking.

Kohlberg dedicated most of his career to studying the moral reasoning and development of both adults and children by presenting study participants with several moral dilemmas, asking them to explain what they would do in the given situation. One of the more common dilemmas Kohlberg used, the Heinz dilemma, asks participants if it's morally okay to steal a drug that would save their partner's life.

Kohlberg's Stages of Moral Development

Level 1 (Pre-Conventional)

1. Obedience and punishment orientation (*How can I avoid punishment?*)

2. Self-interest orientation (*What's in it for me?*) (*Paying for a benefit*)

Level 2 (Conventional)

3. Interpersonal accord and conformity (*Social norms*) (*The good boy/girl attitude*)

4. Authority and social-order maintaining orientation (*Law and order morality*)

Level 3 (Post-Conventional)

5. Social contract orientation

6. Universal ethical principles (*Principled conscience*)

Kohlberg's six stages and three levels of moral development. Little children start out at Stage 1. Stages cannot be skipped, and regression back to an earlier stage never (or almost never) occurs.

The dilemma facing Carol would have interested Kohlberg as well. On the surface, Carol's decision to kill Lizzie seems unforgivably immoral. It certainly would be in today's world—without the ever-present danger of walkers. Carol's reasoning, however, was very complex; she hoped to save not only the little baby that she was caring for, as she could not be sure of Lizzie's intentions toward her, but also to save the possibility of sustained human life. On two separate occasions, Lizzie had nearly killed Judith. At one point in the series, Lizzie put her hand over a crying Judith's nose and mouth to avoid being heard by walkers (4.10 "Inmates"). In 4.14 "The Grove," she sat near the reanimated Mika, with a defenseless Judith nearby. If Carol and Tyreese had failed to show up at the moment, Judith could have easily been Mika's dinner because of Lizzie's inaction. This careless behavior demonstrates that Lizzie was a threat to any human she met, especially defenseless ones like Judith.

This is the moral dilemma posed: is killing one person okay if doing so can save many? When Carol discusses the situation with Tyreese, she states matter-of-factly, "She can't be around other people" ("The Grove"). While Tyreese suggests Lizzie could perhaps change, that they could make her change, Carol argues that it's too late. It's just who Lizzie is, and there are no resources available to help her. There's no other solution which will ensure their safety and the safety of others.

What would have happened to Lizzie before the walker outbreak? While she would not have been executed, because of her age, she would probably have faced prison time, in a juvenile or an adult facility or a combination of both. At best, she might have been committed to a mental institution. In post-apocalyptic Georgia, none of these are options. Carol knows this and makes her decision accordingly.

In Kohlberg's highest level, the postconventional, people define their values by ethical principles they have chosen to follow. People in this stage, unlike the conventional stage, believe that laws can be rewritten and changed for the good of others; in addition, decisions made by people in this stage are often driven by self-chosen principles or their conscience. If posed the Heinz dilemma, people in this stage would argue it is okay to steal a drug that could save their partner's life—as human life is valued over property. Carol would likely steal the drug.

Unlike other characters, Carol recognizes that the laws of the pre-apocalypse no longer apply in this new world. For Carol, protecting the group is more important than protecting the lives of the individuals, a perspective not supported in the pre-apocalypse. When she kills Lizzie, or Karen and David earlier in the series, she uses this justification; she was merely protecting the collective health of the group. She also recognizes that the makeshift laws her group established post-apocalypse are not an appropriate response given the severity and gravity of the situation with Lizzie.

In *The Walking Dead,* we see tremendous growth in Carol; in the first few episodes of the series, we see a battered wife, fighting for a chance to live another day. She fears the living, particularly her husband Ed, as well as the living dead. Both threaten her survival. We then see her as a grieving mother after the death and reanimation of her daughter Sophia. She, however, manages to channel this grief, accepts Sophia's fate, and becomes a surrogate mother to other children—children orphaned by walkers. When examining Carol's moral development, it is particularly interesting to explore in comparison to other primary characters, characters who are often thought of as masculine and as leaders: Rick, Hershel, and Daryl.

You Oughta Know

As we watch the moral decisions made by the Walking Dead characters, episode by episode and season after season, we can see that something more than Kohlberg's theory is required. Ultimately, we see that the characters' moral development, in most cases, depends on whether or not their basic physiological and safety needs are met. As viewers, we understand that these needs—for water, food, and shelter—are always in danger of not being met. So the characters' moral thinking is heavily influenced by their immediate situation of danger.

Here we have to turn to the theory of Abraham Maslow. Maslow describes the needs all human beings have by using a pyramid; the needs at the base of the pyramid must be secured in order to move to the next tier, the highest level being self-actualization. At the base of the pyramid are the most urgent physiological needs such as food and water, above that the need for safety or security, above that, love and belonging, above that, the need to feel good about yourself, and at the top, self-actualization.

After humans' physiological needs are met, they focus on safety needs such as on security of the body, mental health, and resources. This is where we could describe Rick in Season Four, as he's reeling from the loss of his wife Lori. Despite the physical security the prison provides, he is unable to cope with her death. The next tier, once security needs are met, is love and belonging. At this stage humans can focus on friendship and intimacy. In Season Four, characters such as Glen and Maggie are likely in this stage. In the show, we see their bond form, moving beyond sex (physiological stage) to intimacy (love and belonging stage), particularly when they are separated from one another. Their search for each other is not for sex, but for being lost without one another. The next stage is esteem. Esteem needs focus on respect and confidence: respect for others, respect and confidence in oneself. It is here that I put Daryl in Season Four and even Season Five.

The final stage is self-actualization. Self-actualization refers to the desire of self-fulfillment, when a person seeks personal growth and experiences. Self-actualizing people are able to resolve the contradictions inherent in dichotomies, like Carol in the moment described above. The key to self-actualization in the apocalypse is simply an acceptance of the situation, the understanding that these needs might be threatened at any given moment. This is why Carol is very different; she is higher on Maslow's hierarchy and because of this, able to reach a higher moral stage compared to the others.

Maslow's Hierarchy of Human Needs

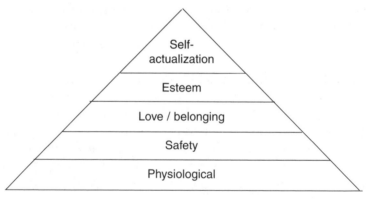

Maslow's hierarchy of needs is shown as a pyramid with the more fundamental needs closer to the base. An individual will not be highly motivated to satisfy 'higher' needs until more basic needs are satisfied.

I Will Survive

Many of the characters' choices, particularly in Season One, could be described as examples of Kohlberg's first level of moral development, a stage typically occupied by small children and characterized by a "looking out for number one" attitude. Physical consequences often determine the goodness or badness of any given situation in this level of moral development. Carol is clearly past this stage by Season Four; she makes tough decisions based on the needs of the group. Other characters, however, struggle greatly with this; ultimately, this struggle impacts their moral development.

Because the basic physiological and safety needs of *Walking Dead* characters are in danger of being denied at any moment, it is easy to understand how some of the characters can only focus on the immediate physical consequences of their actions. There are, however, several other instances throughout the series in which characters depart from Kohlberg's first few stages of moral development—some instances which, unlike the situation with Carol and Lizzie, could more easily be defined in pre-apocalyptic mindset as an example of moral decision-making. In 4.5 "Internment," Hershel risks his own life to care for those who are afflicted with a deadly flu virus. Throughout the series, Hershel has shown similar compassion, but his decision to put his own life in danger in this instance can partially be explained by where and when the illness struck and its relation to Hershel's physiological needs.

The prison had been secured for what the audience can presume was quite some time (at least thirty days), and the immediate threat to Hershel's physiological needs was not an issue. Hershel is likely in Kohlberg's second stage: the conventional stage. In the conventional level, people are concerned most with pleasing others and maintaining social order—something that Hershel is often concerned about. This is not to suggest that his desire to please and to maintain order is a bad thing; he shows great compassion, but ultimately puts himself and others in great danger, all in the name of providing the sick with a dignified death.

In many instances such as the one above, as the characters' basic survival needs are secured, their responses to moral dilemmas do change. Previously, in Season Two, Hershel took in survivors at his farm; he, again, was a caregiver of sorts. He did not, however, hesitate to ask the group to leave when he felt his own way of life and his physiological needs might be threatened. As soon as he realized Rick and his group viewed the walkers differently, that they wanted to kill them, he wanted Rick and the group gone. He only remained with the group, however, when the farm was overtaken, and his own basic needs were in danger. He needed others in order to survive.

After the prison was secure, law and order amongst the group was established, and the group attempted to define moral values both collectively and individually, drawing mostly on Rick and his view of the law prior to the apocalypse. Most group members were propelled into Kohlberg's conventional stage along with Hershel. Viewers often heard Hershel proclaim, "We all have jobs to do." And they did—and do. For example, Hershel's job, as one of the only members of the group with a medical background, was to care for the sick. Former leader Rick, in a hazy mental state, decided to become the group's farmer, with Hershel's guidance. Finally, Daryl served as a makeshift leader as Rick seemed uninterested in the previously held position. Maintaining defined roles seems to be the driving force behind much of the prison season, and their strong desire to replicate, in some small fashion, their previous lives.

If we combine Kohlberg's levels of moral development with Maslow's hierarchy of needs, we can see that those who are more self-actualized are more capable of higher moral development. Qualities of those who are self-actualized, and of those with higher moral development, include: perceiving reality efficiently and tolerating uncertainty; accepting themselves and others for what they are; being problem-centered (not self-centered); being concerned for the welfare of humanity; and having strong ethical standards. In many ways, the list reads like a description of Carol. Carol, unlike many of the other characters in *The Walking Dead*, is able to accept this new reality and make choices that may be unpopular. In some cases, her decisions would be illegal in a pre-apocalyptic world, but they are all too necessary in this new one. Carol is the one character in *The Walking Dead* who achieves self-actualization and consistently reaches the postconventional stage of Kohlberg's moral development.

Bad Reputation

For Kohlberg, moral reasoning was more important than actual behavior, an issue taken up by many critics. It wasn't what they did, but the reasons they appealed to for what they would do. After "passing" a level, Kohlberg believed the person would not regress to a lower stage. This, of course, is not true in *The Walking Dead*. Since at any given movement something could go terribly wrong, it is impossible not to have the threat of regression looming. We see several characters bounce between levels within a season, if not an episode, based on what needs are met or not met.

Carol Gilligan in her book *In a Different Voice*, has criticized Kohlberg's theory, arguing that men, or those with masculine traits, are more concerned with issues surrounding justice, whereas women, or those with feminine traits, are more concerned with issues surrounding care and responsibility. Throughout *The Walking Dead,* we see Carol move on this justice-care continuum. At one point in Season Four, Carol decides to kill David and Karen, the first two members who fall ill with the deadly flu virus Hershel is trying to eradicate. While the two were quarantined, Carol believed it was necessary to kill them, to prevent an outbreak. Her decision to do so ultimately meets with mixed responses. Rick banishes her from the group, and Hershel is shocked by her behavior and approves of Rick's punishment. Like her father Hershel, Maggie is also okay with this punishment, or at the very least, indifferent. Other group members, however, are more sympathetic and even seemingly angry, like Carol's confidant Daryl. Carol's loss of care, or at least some of it, is what actually makes her post-conventional in the apocalypse. In Season Two, she cares too much for Sophia, her daughter, who has gone missing. She becomes consumed with finding her and reels with grief. The Carol we see in Season Four and Season Five, however, is very unlike the Carol of Season Two. By the mid-season finale of Season Five, she rests in the middle area of the justice-care continuum.

Her loss of care in Season Four and Season Five, as well as her disregard for pre-apocalyptic justice, explains Carol's actions as well as Rick and Hershel's reactions. While Rick argues that banishing Carol was for her own good as he worried how others would react to her behavior, he also was adamant to Hershel that he did not want Carol around his children, which was likely the deciding factor in his choice. In the conventional stage, Rick is still holding a pre-apocalyptic notion of justice. He expected to see the Carol of Season One or Season Two and was shocked we he found out she had killed Karen and David.

Just a Girl

Carol is matter-of-fact when asked about the killings; she says to Rick, "You don't need to like what I did, Rick. I don't. You just have to accept it" (4.4 "Indifference"). This acceptance she asks for, the acceptance of the situation and their situation, is impossible for Rick because he hasn't achieved self-actualization yet. Accepting would be a marker of high moral development.

Achieving self-actualization means making difficult decisions. For example, while Carol has demonstrated her love for children time and time again, she also is unwilling to tuck a sick child in—not wanting to expose herself to the virus. If the child does survive the flu, she knows the child's best chance of survival is with a healthy adult. Carol is willing to make unpopular decisions and risk her standing in the group; she is problem-centered, not self-centered, another characteristic of self-actualized people. The group, unfortunately, interprets her actions as self-centered.

Gilligan argues that women are more concerned about caring and responsibility than their male counterparts; she also contends that women seek nonviolent resolutions. For Carol, killing David and Karen and burning their corpses is a far cry from a peaceful resolution to the danger the group faces. On the other hand, the way in which Carol handles the imprisonment of her group at Terminus is an example of this. While she could have gone in and murdered the Termites, the people who held her friends captive, she decided to create a distraction, destroying a propane tank, which allowed her friends to escape. This is certainly not a nonviolent resolution, but it is a decision that saved the lives of her friends and showed great compassion for the Termites, as many of them lived. She doesn't abruptly execute anyone. On the other hand, we see Rick, a character who is more on the masculine side of the continuum, summarily execute Gareth for his cannibalism.

We can further see Carol's compassion and care in the opening episode of Season Four, she commends Daryl for helping strangers, for welcoming them to the prison to share their limited resources and their home. She chimes, "Give the stranger sanctuary, keep people fed, you're gonna have to learn to live with the love (4.1 "30 Days Without an Accident"). She is, however, acutely aware of their situation and how it could change at any time. Their new reality always informs her decision making process and puts her where she needs to be on the justice-care continuum, achieving post-conventional status.

R.E.S.P.E.C.T.

Carol also believes in training the children in how to use weapons. This is another point in which she disagreed with Rick; while Rick did not want the children around weapons, Carol believed it was necessary for their survival. Rick, in the conventional stage, believes that children using weapons is wrong, as defined by pre-apocalyptic law and thought. On the other hand, Carol, in the postconventional state, recognizes that there is a need for children to learn weaponry. In order to train the children without Rick knowing, she invited the children to story time. Instead of reading the children stories, she taught them how to handle different knives and kill walkers. It is ultimately this training that saves Tyreese as Lizzie saves Tyreese from one of the Governor's soldiers.

Rick did not always feel this way. While he never was enthusiastic about teaching Carl, his young son, to use a gun, he did because he knew it was imperative for his survival—both from a fending-off-walkers standpoint and a gun safety standpoint. After the loss of his wife Lori, however, Rick breaks down and turns to a life of farming. He even gives up his own gun and leaves the rest of the group to deal with the walkers that accumulate daily outside the prison gates. Despite the security the prison offers, Carol reminds him that there's still a world full of walkers just beyond the prison gates, and it's only realistic to accept that at some point there will be a breach or some other threat to their safety. She proclaims, "You can be a farmer, Rick. You can't *just* be a farmer" (4.4 "Indifference"). Rick, however, is not in the right frame of mind to accept the reality that Carol so accurately describes.

Whereas Carol is at the top of Maslow's hierarchy—she is self-actualized and able to perceive reality efficiently—Rick is preoccupied with the second tier of Maslow's triangle: safety. But, rarely does anyone stay in one tier, particularly in a post-apocalyptic world. Throughout most of the series, we do see Rick as a capable leader. Due to the death of his wife, however, he is suffering from post-traumatic stress and is seemingly stuck in Maslow's safety stage. Even when we see him as a capable leader, his idealism and preoccupation with pre-apocalyptic justice seem to prevent him from moving beyond the conventional moral development stage.

One of the other male leads, Daryl, is less idealistic and is someone, like Carol, who does what needs to get done regardless of how horrendous the situation or act might be. Some may argue that Daryl is self-actualized and thus post-conventional, but I would say that he is in the esteem stage of Maslow's triangle and in the conventional state of moral development. Because of his complex relationship with his flawed brother, Merle, and the abuse he experienced as a child, his self-confidence is not quite as honed as Carol's—although it is certainly close. After the prison falls, and he loses his only companion, Beth, he joins a rag-tag group of criminals not because he likes them as people, but because he recognizes it is what he needs to do in order to survive. He does not protest Carol's banishment from the group because he is stuck in the esteem phase—following the unspoken rules established by the group. Daryl may be the closest to Carol's level, however, because his pre-apocalyptic world was not as rosy as Rick's or Hershel's. He has better ability to adapt and accept reality.

Finally, others may argue that Hershel is self-actualized, but he has had difficulties accepting the situation—and holds dearly to his previous way of life. When we first meet Hershel, he is keeping walkers in his barn, ultimately hoping to cure them. At the prison, while admirable, he attempts to remove the sick, walker-turned dead, and kill them away from others who are ill. This, however, is dangerous because at any moment, the walker could overtake him, a frail, one-legged man. Although we don't see Hershel in his pre-apocalyptic life, we hear about it. It is likely that Hershel may have been self-actualized in this world, but not in this new one.

For the men of *The Walking Dead*, it is hard to let go of their previous lives and their previous notions of justice, which is ultimately what causes them to struggle with achieving self-actualization and a high level of moral development. On the other hand, Carol thrives in this world. She understands that her responsibility is to the group, and sometimes that responsibility comes with difficult decisions, decisions that she never would have concluded to her a pre-apocalyptic world. While fans widely cry for Daryl's immortality, I say this: If Carol dies, we riot.

12
They Just Want Me to Be Like Them

HEATHER L. CASTRO AND DAVE BEISECKER

In Season Four of *The Walking Dead*, a year and a half has passed since the undead outbreak. While the production of the series in real time might confuse viewers as to this relatively short progression of the story, one aspect of time's passage is immediately noticeable: the kids are growing up, and are now confronting a crossing every bit as irreversible as transforming into a walker: that into adulthood. Even the characters recognize these inexorable changes, as indicated by Patrick's comments about storytime in 4.1 "30 Days Without an Accident": "I go sometimes," he admits to Carl, "I'm immature. You wouldn't like it—it's for kids."

As we all know, however, storytime with Carol definitely *isn't* just for kids. The show's prior emphasis on adults preserving the innocence and helplessness of children—epitomized by the popularity of the "Where's Carl?" meme—has by this time given way in the changed landscape of the post-apocalypse, so that growing up means growing up *fast*. Season Four presents us with poignant examples that raise philosophical, life-shaping questions for those about to make the inevitable transition to adulthood, as well as those who've already crossed over.

What is a growing, maturing child to do and to value in the world of *The Walking Dead*? Just as important, what are the obligations of parents and guardians to their potentially traumatized charges, especially when those obligations conflict with broader obligations to promote group security?

She's Just Messed Up

Spoiler alert—Lizzie dies (but you probably knew that already!). However, never was there a *Walking Dead* character with such a death wish—or controversial ending. Lizzie's affinity for the walkers of her world appears to arise from a psychological condition termed 'prolonged grief disorder,' or PGD. (Though not yet accepted as a defined disorder, the *International Statistical Classification of Diseases, 11th Revision* has proposed PGD as a new diagnosis.)

The "prolonged" aspect of PGD is the primary aspect that marks its difference from regular grief; the symptoms must continue beyond the six-month mark which, within the timeline of the show, confirms Lizzie's condition. She also displays PGD's other symptoms:

> persistent yearning for the deceased and associated emotional pain, difficulty in accepting the death, a sense of meaninglessness, bitterness about the death, and difficulty in engaging in new activities. (Bryant et al., "Treating Prolonged Grief Disorder.")

The presence of walkers in *The Walking Dead* world opens up wildly novel ways in which someone may manifest such a "yearning for the deceased." And it is through their active presence that Lizzie finds personified outlets for transforming her grief into an acknowledgement and embrace of the lives 'lived' by the undead.

The preteen—her age is never actively revealed, though the actress was ten at the time of filming—is a former resident of Woodbury. We first encounter Lizzie in 4.1 "30 Days Without an Accident" as the group of kids hang out by the fence making up names for the zombies. Together with Mika and Luke, Lizzie calls to the walker wearing a nametag by name: "Nick! Nick! Over here! . . . Hi, Nick!" Carl and Lizzie's resulting exchange reveals her difficulties with loss:

CARL: You're naming them now?

MIKA: Well, one of them has a nametag. So we thought all of them should.

CARL: The hell are you talking about? They had names when they were alive. They're dead now.

LIZZIE: No they're not. They're just different.

CARL: They don't talk. They don't think. They *eat* people. They kill people.

LIZZIE: People kill people. They still have names.

CARL: Have you seen what happens? Have you seen someone die like that?

LIZZIE: Yeah, I have.

CARL: They're not people, and they're not pets. Don't name them.

This acknowledgement of previous loss, within the context of identifying walkers by name, alerts us that Lizzie exhibits a post-apocalyptic PGD symptom of denying death, though here that denial is nuanced into separating walker death, or undeath, from people death, or final death. Her difficulty in accepting walkers as both exhibiting *and* serving as vehicles for final death manifests itself in several ways, the first being in her feeding them rats.

While the offering of food to the dead is a human tradition dating to ancient cultures, it is a custom that is nonexistent in present-day North American life. By enacting it, Lizzie is not exhibiting an ancient affinity for honoring the dead; she is, rather, feeding those whom she perceives to be not-dead. This activity continues past the abandonment of the prison; "I'll bring you more tomorrow," she croons to another walker stuck in railway tracks, with all the compassion of someone feeding a starving puppy.

The source of this initial confusion of states of life is revealed after the walker attack in Cell Block D in 4.2 "Infected." Lizzie attempts to complete the "final" death strike against her father, who was bitten in the attack. With Carol standing nearby, she holds the knife, ready to drive it into her father's head, but breaks down into tears. Carol takes the knife and, comforted by Mika, the sisters turn around to face a bunch of flowers. Lizzie begins shrieking, and Mika says: "Look at the flowers, Lizzie . . . one, two, three . . ." Following their father's death, the girls sit beside the prison fence, where Carol confronts Lizzie and accuses her of being weak.

Lizzie, rather than defending herself, spots the (finally) dead walker "Nick" and howls: "He's dead. He was special and now he's dead."

Lizzie's grief has prompted a psychological transference of her father's death onto Nick; the emotions that should be directed to her dead father are now placed upon the dead walker. Within this moment, Lizzie's social identification permanently changes; she has no qualms over gunning down the Governor's invaders, but she begs for and weeps over the undead lives of walkers. We see this again and again, combined with the "Look at the flowers" admonishment by Mika, in the atmosphere of the refuge house in 4.14 "The Grove."

Things Don't Just Work Out

The now infamous line regarding flowers is uttered with a frequency that implies that it is used regularly to distract the traumatized Lizzie from incidents of death. PGD patients typically exhibit avoidance strategies to suppress their emotions and minimize distress. Avoidance, as a maladaptive coping skill, is known to lead to further mental health issues and, specifically, aggravates both PGD and PTSD symptoms.

However, Lizzie's flowers are an avoiding focal point that is not chosen by the preteen herself; rather she is directed to it by her sister and maladaptive parenting figure, Carol. By suppressing Lizzie's emotional state through avoidance, her companions are contributing to her unresolved grief symptoms, thus not providing for an open environment for Lizzie to actively engage with her emotions.

This suppression becomes important when considering Carol's role in Lizzie's traumatic state. Having promised at their father's deathbed to "look after them like they're yours," Carol's approach to rearing preteen girls has undergone a radical change in the post-apocalypse. In addition to calling Lizzie "weak," Carol also calls her "confused" and berates Mika for being too sweet: "You have to change now—everyone does. Things don't just work out."

This emphasis on change, from Carol's point of view, is meant to toughen the girls for a safer life in the post-apocalypse, a life where the run-and-hide strategy Carol taught Sophia is no longer effective and an active, violent defense is.

However, this 'change' in Carol's parenting style is not so much a true change as an adaptation from her pre-apocalypse reality; her survivalist skills could have evolved from the battered person syndrome's "run-and-hide" avoidance techniques she taught Sophia to a more aggressive, hyper-vigilant survivalism, but it remains basic survivalism—rational with no emotions, no feelings, and no active processing of the truly changed reality of the post-apocalypse. She does what she feels she must. Lizzie's response to this approach, however, is influenced by her PGDed identification with walkers.

During the confrontation with Carol over a game of tag with a walker, Lizzie outwardly expresses her association of the final death of her playmate with Carol herself. "You killed her! It's the same thing! What if I killed you? What if I killed you?" (4.14 "The Grove") asks the preteen before repeating again and again, "You don't understand." And of course Carol doesn't understand; not only is this statement a stereotypical expression of teenage emotion, but Carol has repeatedly actively suppressed Lizzie's emotions so as not to *have to* understand. For Carol, walkers are solely active threats, as they have been and ever will be; but for Lizzie, they are an alternate consciousness, a viable option for not-death/life before a person's final death and the onset of survivor grief.

Unable to communicate her grief issues to the group, Lizzie embraces walker undeath, rather than the enforced flowers distraction, as her chosen PGD avoidance tactic of the constant presence of final death—with predictably tragic results. Lizzie's ugly, scary passage into growing up (to paraphrase Carol's dialogue) emerges as a change not from childhood to adulthood but of living under constant threat to accepting the living death of walkers as a viable option. "They just want me to change," Lizzie says by the railroad tracks after feeding a trapped walker. "To make me be like them. Maybe I should change. I can make you all understand."

After flirting with the walker's jaws in front of a horrified Mika, Lizzie decides to "transform" her sister. The act, at least in her eyes, is not murder, but rather registers her appreciation of post-apocalyptic walker existence over traditional human life. In her attempt to change Mika, Lizzie jumps past the potential grief at the loss of a family member and moves her sister into a state of existence that, as the show has demonstrated so far, is relatively eternal so long as Mika can withstand a head injury.

Thus, Lizzie's grief at death is overcome through realizing not only the value inherent in life as a walker but the relative safety of life as a walker in the post-apocalypse. In doing so, she gives new meaning to the notion of being a survivor in the *Walking Dead* world. Of course, Carol closes off that option with a proverbial and decisive bang. Look at the flowers, Lizzie . . .

What if I Killed You?

By the end of "The Grove," it is clear that things have gone terribly wrong—even by the grim post-apocalyptic standards of *The Walking Dead*. The manner in which Lizzie processes her grief by challenging what it means to be truly human poses a clear and present danger to all (survivors) around her. Mika is not merely non-alive but genuinely dead, first by Lizzie's hand and then by Carol's.

There appears little realistic hope for Lizzie's eventual rehabilitation. Her traumatic identification with the zombies is so transgressive that she becomes perceived as a monster far more threatening and psychologically dangerous than the walkers themselves. "She can't be around other people," judges Carol, especially with Judith also in her care, and so Lizzie needs to be put down, much as one might put down a vicious dog.

But whatever you might think of her, Lizzie is neither vicious nor a dog! She isn't evil like the Governor and, though damaged, you can still reason with her. Unlike the genuinely innocent deer that Carol sees shortly after taking Lizzie's life, Lizzie had an idea of right and wrong which could still be cultivated. Indeed, Lizzie should be praised for developing any sense of moral concern at all. Having little to no recollection of how things used to be before the rising, she refuses to surrender to moral nihilism by crafting post-apocalyptic values. Those values happen to include what appears to be an emerging or incipient moral concern for the non-dead. It should come as no surprise, then, that older folk who acquired their values before there were ever any walkers might find such concern wholly perverse. But that doesn't make Lizzie's attitudes any less legitimate, or even dangerous.

It's Carol who might seem to have abandoned her moral sensibility in the face of the apocalypse. She simply does what she feels is required for survival. Carol doesn't want to kill Lizzie. We can see that by the tears in her eyes and hear it by the tremor in her voice. Nevertheless, she thinks she must for the good of the whole. At the same time she is not blameless for what has gone so terribly wrong.

We've suggested that Carol's overbearing guardianship contributed to Lizzie's inability to address her grief in a more healthy manner. Unlike Sophia, Lizzie wasn't a little child anymore. Her ideas about the walkers shouldn't have been quashed quite so quickly, no matter how deviant they might have seemed. Instead of abruptly dismissing the idea that Lizzie knew what the walkers wanted as "confused," perhaps Carol should have worked out with Lizzie how she came to have such a bizarre idea in the first place. Then Lizzie might have had a chance to attain a healthier understanding of the grief and loss with which she was already contending and displacing upon the walkers. Lizzie—and Mika, for that matter—would have stood a much greater chance of survival and redemption, if only Carol had tried harder to understand her and take seriously the values that Lizzie was trying to express, no matter how strange and deviant those values might have seemed to Carol. Although she tried to live up to the vow of protection she made to the girls' father, it strikes us that she did both of the girls wrong.

Carol's struggles in the wake of Lizzie's death prompt her to confess to Tyreese that it was she, not Lizzie or the Strangers, who killed Karen and David back at the prison. Once again, she did as she felt she had to for the overall safety of the group. As is so characteristic, Tyreese is forgiving. We can perhaps look to him in order to see a better alternative to Carol's brand of guardianship.

Recall that immediately following the prison attack, Tyreese was stranded alone with Judith and the girls before reuniting with Carol in 4.10 "Inmates." Tyreese's interactions with the girls are much more supportive and positive than Carol's. In striking contrast to Carol's admonishment of Mika's weakness, Tyreese builds her up: "That's okay. We all get scared." Later in the forest he reassures her, "Look at me. You can handle this. You're tough." Moreover, he exhibits an appreciation, which Carol apparently lacks, for how the girls need to find their own separate paths for navigating a zombie world. "Don't be sorry," he says to them, "You each do things your own way. But you both get it done."

Such comments suggest that he, not Carol, possesses the wisdom and patience for talking things through that is required of fostering an adolescent's moral development. We saw some more of this at the beginning of Season Five with Noah. Alas, that relationship—like his with Lizzie and Mika—was tragically short-lived. *C'est la vie.* Such is the world of *The Walking Dead.*

It's an intriguing exercise to wonder how Lizzie's fate might have been different if Tyreese had remained her primary guardian. Perhaps things wouldn't have turned out so badly. In light of this, one might even think that his willingness to let Carol take such complete charge of the girls after their reunion is itself somewhat problematic.

Maybe I Should Change

Finally, the conclusion that Lizzie is a mere child in Carol's eyes is also reinforced in the *manner* of her death. Evidently, the fateful shot that ended her life as she stared down at the flowers was aimed at her head. For shortly thereafter, we see Carol digging a grave and Tyreese bearing Lizzie's enshrouded corpse. Hers, then, was a final death. But we have more than ample reason to believe that this would not have been the way she would have wanted to go. Part of the heart-wrenching tragedy of the Lizzie story is that Carol never afforded her the courtesy of crossing over into the walker "life" for which she longed. Carol closed off any opportunity to frolic with her kind or to "play tag" and be fed rats by any like-minded children that might happen along. More to the point, Carol refuses Lizzie a final chance to "make her understand."

Generally, we aim to respect the wishes of our dear departed companions. As Jim approached death way back in 1.4 "Vatos," he expressed a desire to reanimate so that he might join up with his family, who had preceded him down the walker path. The group accommodates this dying wish, and he is left beside a tree to die and presumably rise again. While the series closes with Jim by the tree, the comic nicely cuts back to the tree to show that Jim is no longer there.

So Lizzie's presumptive desire to be allowed to cross over to "experience life" on the other side isn't altogether unprecedented. That Jim's wish was respected while Lizzie's was not only reinforces the sense that Carol regarded Lizzie as little more than a child for whom decisions had to be made, rather than a developing young adult with beliefs and desires of her own.

Before the sad events in "The Grove," Carol tells Lizzie that at some point the fear will all go away, "And then one day you'll change." A shame that it wasn't the type of change that Lizzie would have preferred.

13
Carol's Transformation

Robert A. Delfino and Lea R. Lesinski

Her husband abused her, zombies destroyed her civilization, and they killed her only child, Sophia. Suffering of this kind would have shattered most people, but not Carol. She bent, but did not break. She survived and kept fighting.

Choices matter. In the movie *Gladiator*, the Roman general Maximus, played by Russell Crowe, tells his soldiers before battle that "What we do in life echoes in eternity." While poetic and moving, it also suggests an important philosophical point made centuries ago by the ancient Greek philosopher Aristotle—that the actions we perform help forge our personality and our moral character. Aristotle's famous work on ethics, his *Nicomachean Ethics*, is about moral character. Aristotle says that your moral character is formed through habitual action—actions that you perform over and over. For example, telling the truth once in a while does not make you an honest person, but telling it consistently over many years does.

While our free choices are important to forging our moral character, there is, of course, more to the story. We don't make choices in a vacuum. Each of us lives during a specific time and within a specific kind of community. Each of us has different talents and limitations, and often we have to act in the face of serious obstacles and hardships. Our environment and life experiences can influence our behavior, as many psychologists have argued. So, to obtain a good understanding of Carol's transformation as a person, we need to study both her psychological history and how she chose to respond to the significant events in her life.

I Didn't Think I Could Be Strong

In 1.3 "Tell It to the Frogs," we learn that Carol has an abusive husband, Ed. That's putting it mildly; Ed is an asshole. In the scene by the lake he is verbally abusive to Carol and to the other women present, and then he physically strikes Carol in the face. Unfortunately, we learn in Season Four this is not the only time he has hit his wife. After Carol fixes Sam's dislocated shoulder in 4.4 "Indifference," Rick asks her if she learned how to do that from Herschel. Carol explains that she learned how to fix her own dislocated shoulder on the internet because it was "easier than telling an ER [Emergency Room] nurse I'd fallen down the staircase a third time . . . Just fixed what needed fixin'."

It's hard to imagine the amount of verbal and physical abuse Carol endured during the years of her marriage to Ed, but it must have been quite bad. One indication of this is how Carol treats Ed's body in 1.5 "Wildfire" after he has been killed by walkers the night before. Ed has to be stabbed in the head so that he will not reanimate. One good strike would do it, but Carol violently strikes him five times with a pick-axe, while releasing powerful emotions that she had kept repressed inside.

Later, in 3.9 "The Suicide King," we learn that Ed made Carol feel like she deserved the abuse. Speaking initially of Merle's manipulation of Daryl, she says:

> Men like Merle get into your head; they make you feel like you deserve the abuse . . . I'm hardly the woman I was a year ago, but if Ed walked through that door right now breathing and told me to go with him I'd like to think I'd tell him to go to hell.

From this we get a sense of how difficult things have been for Carol. Even though a year has passed since Ed's death she still isn't sure whether she could tell her former abuser to go to hell. And in Season Four's "Indifference," we learn that Carol still carries some shame with her. Calling herself "Stupid" twice, while recounting to Rick her earlier life with Ed, she says "I actually convinced myself I was happy with him . . . Stupid. Stupid. I didn't think I could be strong. I didn't know I could."

Psychologically speaking, Carol suffered greatly prior to the apocalypse. Some of this suffering stayed with her and, unfortunately, during the apocalypse she experiences even more suffering. In 4.14 "The Grove," Carol comments on life in the apocalypse, telling Lizzie "It's ugly and it's scary and it does change you." And Carol should know. She says this after having secretly killed two ill members of the group, Karen and David, which we learn about in the back-to-back episodes 4.2 "Infected," 4.3 "Isolation," and 4.4 "Indifference." When asked point blank by Rick, in "Isolation," if she killed Karen and David, she answers matter-of-factly "Yes," without remorse, and then walks away. In the next episode, aptly named "Indifference," Rick confronts Carol about what she's done. Disturbed by what she has become, he no longer trusts her and banishes her from the group.

The killing of Karen and David is an important event that signals a significant transformation in Carol's personality and moral character. Before analyzing this event from an ethical perspective, let's briefly trace the development of Carol's personality from her early days with the group up until this fateful moment.

No Longer Scared of Her Own Shadow

In the first season, Carol is clearly one of the weakest, if not the weakest, of the main characters in the group. In "Tell It to the Frogs," when Jacqui asks out loud how come the women are doing all of the traditional housework, such as washing clothes, Carol responds with an air of resignation—"It's just the way it is." Later, when Carol's abusive husband tells her to come with him, Andrea sticks up for Carol and confronts Ed, saying "I don't think she needs to go anywhere with you, Ed." But a submissive Carol obeys Ed's command and meekly responds to Andrea, saying "Please, it doesn't matter." The death of her abusive husband in "Wildfire" is a traumatic event for Carol, but it sets the stage for her to grow in Season Two.

Unfortunately, Carol's personal growth in Season Two is at times both slow and painful. For example, although she is given an opportunity to learn how to a shoot a gun in 2.6 "Secrets," she doesn't take advantage of it. Then things get worse for Carol. After weeks of desperately searching for her daughter, Carol recoils in horror when Sophia emerges as the walking dead from Herschel's barn in 2.7 "Pretty Much Dead

Already." A distraught and crying Carol collapses to the ground and is held back by Daryl, as Rick steps forward and shoots Sophia in the head. In the next episode, 2.8 "Nebraska," we see Carol alone in the field, crying and tearing apart the Cherokee roses (symbols of hope) that Daryl discussed four episodes earlier in 2.4 "Cherokee Rose."

Psychologically speaking, this is one of Carol's lowest points. Few things are more devastating than losing a child. As time passes, it becomes clear that the enormous trauma and stress that Carol has experienced has taken its toll. For when it comes time to decide whether to kill Randall, who is being kept as a prisoner in 2.11 "Judge, Jury, Executioner," she can't handle it. She asks to be left out of the decision, saying "Stop it. Just stop it! I'm sick of everybody arguing and fighting. I didn't ask for this. You can't ask us to decide something like this. Please decide—either of you, both of you . . . but leave me out."

In Season Three, we start to see more significant changes in Carol. As the group begins to take control of the prison, in 3.1 "Seed," Rick notes that Carol has become a pretty good shot. She climbs the watch tower and uses a rifle to shoot walkers in the prison yard. Later, after mentioning that her back was hurting from the rifle kickback, Daryl gives her a massage. At this point Carol is in good enough spirits to joke about a romantic encounter with Daryl, and both laugh. Indeed, in this season Carol grows closer to Daryl and other members of the group, such as Lori. She asks Glenn in the next episode, 3.2 "Sick," to help her kill a female walker so she can practice performing a C-section on it in preparation to help deliver Lori's baby.

As Season Three progresses, there's no doubt that Carol is becoming a stronger person. But there are also signs that she has become more cold and calculating. Our first glimmer of this is in 3.11 "I Ain't a Judas." Whereas in the previous season Carol wanted no part in the decision over Randall's fate, she now actively counsels Andrea to kill the Governor in his sleep. After informing Andrea that Rick killed Shane, Andrea replies that "Rick's become cold," which sets up Carol's dark proposal to her—"The Governor, you need to do something. . . . You need to sleep with him. Give him the greatest night of his life. You get him to drop his guard. Then when he's sleeping, you can end this." It's obvious at this point that Carol has changed considerably. Even a brute like Merle takes notice, telling her, in

3.15 "This Sorrowful Life," "You ain't like you was back in the camp—a little mouse running around, scared of her own shadow . . . you don't seem scared of nothing anymore."

In Season Four, Carol's personality and moral character undergo more changes, as she takes several significant actions. In 4.1 "30 Days Without an Accident" Carol can be seen reading to the children in the library. But things are not as they seem. Shortly after Lizzie's and Mika's father, Ryan, leaves the library, Carol begins to teach the children how to fight walkers with knives. Her secret plan is discovered by Carl, and she asks him not to tell Rick. In the next episode, "Infected," Carl asks Carol if she plans to tell the parents of the children what she is doing. Carol reveals that she has decided not to tell the parents because they might not understand and she does not want to take that risk.

At this point we can see that Carol is not only capable of acting on her own, but also that she feels justified in making decisions that will affect others without consulting anyone. In the case of the library, she's trying to teach the children how to defend themselves from walkers, which is certainly a good skill to have. Nevertheless, for those of us who believe in parental rights, her actions are troubling because we feel that Carol should have informed the parents and obtained their consent. But this is merely a taste of things to come. In the next two episodes, "Isolated" and "Indifference," we learn that Carol, without consulting the others, has killed Karen and David. She has become the judge, jury, and executioner that she resisted becoming in Season Two.

Is it possible that, despite appearances, Carol made the ethically correct choice in this situation? Or was Rick right to criticize her and banish her from the group?

Just Fixed What Needed Fixin'

To evaluate Carol's actions from an ethical point of view we need to have all of the relevant information, including her motive, the circumstances, the specific actions she performed, and the consequences of those actions. Concerning the circumstances, in "Infected" we learn that Karen and David were coughing and had the flu-like illness that killed Patrick. Herschel and the others agree that they should be quarantined in the Tombs—locked in cells so that in case they die and reanimate as walkers they will not be able to harm the others. However, at the end of "Infected" Tyreese discovers that Karen and David have been killed.

As to her specific actions, from all the blood on the floor it looks like Carol stabbed them in their cells and then dragged them to the courtyard where they were burned. Confirmation that she burned the bodies comes in a flashback scene in 5.6 "Consumed." Although Carol never divulges the exact method of execution, we do learn during her confession in Season Four's "The Grove" that she tried to kill them as quickly and painlessly as possible. She explains her motive for the killings in "Indifference," arguing to Rick that "They would have drowned in their own blood. They were suffering. I made it quick. We needed the bodies gone. We needed to stop it [the illness] from spreading. They were the only ones who were sick. They were a threat. I was trying to save lives. I had to try. Somebody had to."

Carol, whether she realizes it or not, is making a utilitarian argument. Utilitarianism is an ethical theory that stresses the *consequences* of an action in determining whether it's good or bad. John Stuart Mill, in his famous book *Utilitarianism*, summarizes the theory this way:

> [Utilitarianism] holds that actions are right in proportion as they tend to promote happiness, wrong as they tend to produce the reverse of happiness. By happiness is intended pleasure and the absence of pain; by unhappiness, pain and the privation of pleasure. ("Utilitarianism," p. 330)

In other words, an action is morally good if it maximizes happiness for the greatest number of people.

At first glance it might seem that, according to utilitarianism, Carol's choice was the ethically correct one. This is because she was trying to maximize happiness for the greatest number of people by eliminating threats to their existence. For if the flu-like illness spread it could have killed others in the group, jeopardizing the survival of all of them. As the case of Patrick shows, if the illness spread to even just one other member of the group that member could die and awaken as a walker in the middle of the night and start killing people and creating more walkers.

While we're sure Carol meant well and was sincere when she told Rick she was trying to save lives, we think there are serious ethical problems with Carol's choice—even on utilitarian grounds. To begin with, in its classic formulation, your good (or bad) intentions are irrelevant in utilitarianism. All that matters is the results of the particular action you performed—did your action maximize happiness for the greatest number of people? And it's clear that Carol's actions did not do this for at least two reasons. First, Carol's killing of Karen and David did not prevent the spread of the illness. Second, several members of the group who found out about Carol's actions were very unhappy about them, including Rick, Maggie, Herschel, and, of course, Tyreese, though he eventually forgives her.

So far we have been judging Carol's action based on what is called act-utilitarianism—did her particular action maximize happiness for the greatest number of people? However, there is another version of utilitarianism called rule utilitarianism. According to rule utilitarianism, what is most important is that we follow rules that are designed to maximize happiness, under most circumstances, for the greatest number of people. According to rule utilitarianism, as long as we are following the rules we act in an ethically correct manner even if the consequences of a particular action end up not maximizing happiness.

However, Carol's action falls short, ethically speaking, even under the standards of rule utilitarianism. If killing Karen and David were the only way to protect the group, then Carol's action would have been ethically correct. Within the context of rule utilitarianism, we can envision a rule that says "Only kill an innocent person to save the lives of others when there is no other option." But this rule would not apply to Carol's situation for several reasons. First, we know it's possible that Karen and David could have survived the illness because Glenn and Sasha did. Second, Karen and David were quarantined in jail cells and so even if they died and became walkers they could not have harmed anyone. Given these circumstances, we think Carol should have waited and given them a chance instead of killing them "in cold blood" as Hershel described it in "Isolation."

We understand that Carol has experienced a lot of trauma and stress in her life both before and during the apocalypse; and we understand that these experiences have predisposed her to think and act more negatively and aggressively. But, ethically speaking, Carol still had a choice. She didn't have to give in to these negative temptations; she could have resisted them and tried to do what is right. Our actions make us who we are, and as Dale warned in "Judge, Jury, Executioner" what is at stake is our very humanity and civilization. Ultimately, by murdering two innocent members of the group, Carol weakened the group and caused a lot of pain and suffering within it. We don't blame Rick for banishing her, because how can you trust someone who is willing to murder innocent people in secret?

Confession, Absolution, and . . . Redemption?

After her banishment Carol returns in 4.10 "Inmates." She rescues Lizzie, Mika, and baby Judith from walkers while Tyreese was away investigating some screaming he had heard. Tyreese returns and is happy to see Carol, as he still does not know that she killed Karen and David. Together, they decide to follow the train tracks to Terminus, and in a later episode, "The Grove," they come upon a pecan grove with a nice house on the property. What follows are some of the most disturbing scenes in the entire TV series, and in them Carol takes another significant action. Before analyzing her choice from an ethical and psychological point of view, let's set the scene and give some necessary background.

In "Infected," as he is dying, Ryan asks Carol to look out for his daughters, saying "Lizzie and Mika . . . Can you look out for them? Like they're yours?" To which Carol replies, "Yeah. Yeah, I can. I will." Though they can never replace Sophia, these girls become her adopted daughters. Skipping ahead to "The Grove," there is a scene in which we see Carol, Tyreese, and the girls sitting in the living room of the house at night while light from the fireplace flickers. Carol is cracking pecans and talking with Lizzie, while Mika is playing with a doll she found. For a moment things seem almost normal and pre-apocalyptic. Tyreese alludes to this, saying "I'm not used to this . . . We're in a living room in a house." A little later Mika says to Tyreese "We should live here," prompting Carol and Tyreese to seriously consider it.

As the episode unfolds, both Carol and Tyreese have a serious discussion about living in the house. Tyreese tells Carol

"Maybe we don't need to go to Terminus. I've been thinking. Mika's right. We can stay here. We can live here. I know Lizzie and Mika. I know Judith. I know you. I trust you and I don't know if I can get that anywhere else." A day later, while out hunting for deer, Carol responds positively to Tyreese's idea, saying "The girls like it here. We could build it up, plant more food. We could find a car for an escape route just in case. If you don't want to go to Terminus we could stay."

For the first time in a long time it looks like Carol might be able to start over and live something of a normal life in the apocalypse. But it was not to be. Shortly after their conversation about the house, Tyreese mentions how he misses Karen and how he dreams about her every night. Feeling more remorseful about killing Karen and David, Carol almost confesses, but holds back. After a hug, they decide to walk back to the house. And then horror greets them. Carol and Tyreese see Lizzie standing over the dead body of Mika, her hands covered in blood and holding a knife. It soon becomes evident that Lizzie has killed her own sister. Adding to the horror, Lizzie tells them "Don't worry she'll come back. I didn't hurt her brain," followed by an awkward smile.

As Carol reaches to take the knife away from her, Lizzie points a gun at Carol, saying "No, no, no! We have to wait. I need to show you. You'll see. You'll finally get it." It's hard to imagine what is going through Carol's mind at this point. Shocked and horrified, she probably realizes for the first time just how severely mentally disturbed Lizzie is. But it's not like there were no signs of this earlier. In "Infected," Carol tries to console Lizzie after the death of her father. Emotionally upset and standing outside by the prison's barbed-wire fence, Lizzie says to Carol "He's dead. He was special and now he's dead. Why'd they kill him? Why'd they kill Nick?" Carol, who initially thought Lizzie was talking about her father, looks puzzled. She didn't realize that Lizzie had been giving names to walkers. After Lizzie runs away, Mika says "She's messed up."

At that time, Carol did not realize just how messed up Lizzie was, but over time she does come to some awareness of it. Early on in "The Grove," she tells Tyreese, "She's confused about them, the walkers. She doesn't see what they are. She thinks they're just different." And in the same episode, Carol tries multiple times to teach Lizzie that walkers are not people and that they are very dangerous. One example occurs about midway through the episode when Carol notices that Lizzie is "playing" outside with a walker. Carol rushes out and kills the walker, trying to explain to Lizzie that she could have died and that the walker wanted to kill her. But Lizzie, clearly delusional, screams "You don't understand . . . She didn't want to hurt anybody! She was my friend and you killed her!"

A second example occurs shortly after Lizzie feeds a mouse to the walker who is stuck on the train tracks. Mika, who arrives seconds after the feeding, tries to convince Lizzie that walkers are bad. But Lizzie disagrees, saying "I can hear them. . . . They just want me to change. They can make me be like them. Maybe I should change." During their conversation more walkers come and the girls run back to the house. There Carol, Tyreese, and the girls shoot the walkers. Carol, who sees this as a positive step for Lizzie, later asks her "Do you understand what they are now?" In response, Lizzie turns toward Carol, looks her into her eyes and says "I know what I have to do now."

As she stares into Lizzie's eyes, after the death of Mika, perhaps Carol finally understands what Lizzie meant by those words. Perhaps Carol also realizes that she indirectly taught Lizzie how to do what she did to Mika when she trained her to knife fight in the library. Whatever is going through Carol's mind, it's clear she wants to get the gun away from Lizzie and to protect Judith, who, as Lizzie reveals, was her next target. After defusing the situation, Tyreese and Carol later agree that Lizzie "can't be around other people." Carol takes Lizzie outside to pick flowers for Mika and then, crying, she shoots Lizzie in the back of the head.

Psychologically, this is devastating. Carol has already lost her own daughter Sophia. And now she has lost both of her adopted daughters—one she had to stab in the head to prevent her from reanimating, the other she had to kill herself. Her brief dream of living happily in the house by the pecan grove is over, and it is clear that Carol is haunted by what she has done. Did Carol do the right thing by killing Lizzie? Or did she make another bad choice, as with the killing of Karen and David? Ethically speaking, it is time to analyze her actions.

In this case, for several reasons, we think Carol made the right choice in killing Lizzie. First, if Carol and Tyreese keep Lizzie with them, she might kill them and thus she poses a serious threat. Second, Carol has already tried several times to teach Lizzie about the true nature of walkers and each time it has failed. Lizzie is delusional and disconnected from reality, and the chance of her changing seems slim to none. Third, there is no psychiatric hospital or institution that could treat her and separate her from others. Fourth, if they abandon her in the woods she will most certainly die, either through starvation or from walkers. Fifth, if she is abandoned and picked up by other humans she might harm them.

Certainly, by the standards of utilitarianism, killing Lizzie is the ethically correct thing to do. But many philosophers have argued that there are problems with utilitarianism and that it is not the best ethical theory; after all, we've just used utilitarianism to morally condone the execution of a child. What, then, would other ethical theories say about Carol's action? We don't have the space to treat multiple ethical theories here. However, probably the strictest form of ethics when it comes to treating other persons can be found in natural law theory, which began in the West in ancient Greece and was further developed philosophically in the Middle Ages by Christian thinkers, such as St. Thomas Aquinas. Since Carol identifies as a Christian, wearing a cross in the early seasons and telling Carl in "Judge, Jury, Executioner" that Sophia is in heaven, let's look at this theory.

In the natural law ethics of Aquinas, each human person has dignity because he or she possesses intelligence and freedom and therefore is in the image of God. To live in harmony with your nature, and with other persons who share that nature, is good. Conversely, it is unethical for a person to harm their own nature, or the nature of other persons. However, there are some exceptions that apply in this case. Aquinas argues that it is

> lawful to kill an evildoer in so far as it is directed to the welfare of the whole community, so that it belongs to him alone who has charge of the community's welfare. Thus it belongs to a physician to cut off a decayed limb, when he has been entrusted with the care of the health of the whole body. Now the care of the common good is entrusted to persons of rank having public authority: wherefore they alone, and not private individuals, can lawfully put evildoers to death. (*Summa Theologica*, II–II, q. 64, a.3, reply)

Aquinas says that only the proper authorities should execute evildoers. However, in the apocalypse all such authorities have been destroyed—only individuals and small groups remain. Therefore it falls to Carol and Tyreese to act on behalf of the common good, as Aquinas suggests in one of his replies to objections: "It is lawful for any private individual to do anything for the common good, provided it harm nobody: but if it be harmful to some other, it cannot be done, except by virtue of the judgment of the person to whom it pertains to decide what is to be taken from the parts for the welfare of the whole."

Of course, under normal circumstances, we are sure Aquinas would advocate placing Lizzie in a hospital where she could receive treatment. But that's not possible in this case. Given the apocalypse, how dangerous she is to other humans, and how all attempts to teach her to change have failed, we think killing her for the welfare of the human community is the right thing to do according to natural law theory.

Shortly after killing Lizzie, Carol confesses to Tyreese about killing Karen and David. This is another significant action for Carol. Unlike earlier with Rick, she now shows full remorse for her actions. She even slides her gun towards Tyreese, telling him "Do what you have to do." Through the horror and the pain, Carol has grown much. She has accepted full responsibility for her actions and is willing to pay for them with her life. Head held low, she waits to die—but Tyreese forgives her. Later, after she has risked her life to rescue the others from Terminus, in 5.1 "No Sanctuary," Rick forgives her too.

A Phoenix Reborn from the Fire

Carol's personality has undergone serious changes throughout the series. Metaphorically, she has died and been reborn several times. Perhaps the greatest representation of this is in Season Five's "Consumed." In need of a place to sleep for the night, Carol leads Daryl to an abandoned women's shelter that she stayed at once with Sophia during her marriage to Ed. While there, they discover a mother and daughter who have become walkers. Carol moves to kill them, but Daryl tells her "You don't have to."

The next morning Carol awakens to see that Daryl has taken care of it, and is burning the bodies. As Carol stares into the fire, she is staring into her past. She is no longer the meek and abused woman who once stayed at that shelter. The burning corpses are symbolic of Carol's old self dying and a new self being reborn from the ashes. Later, she tells Daryl:

> Me and Sophia stayed at that shelter for a day and a half before I went running back to Ed. I went home, I got beat up, life went on, and I just kept praying for something to happen. But I didn't do anything. Not a damn thing. Who I was with him . . . she got burned away. And I was happy about that. I mean, not happy, but . . . And at the prison I got to be who I always thought I should be, thought I should've been. And then she got burned away. Everything now just . . . consumes you.

Like a phoenix, Carol has been reborn from the ashes several times. Though much stronger now, she still struggles, of course. In this episode, we learn that she is struggling with her Christian faith. She tells Daryl, "I don't know if I believe in God anymore or heaven, but if I'm going to hell, I'm making damn sure I'm holding it off as long as I can."

Will Carol re-find her faith in God? Will she continue upon the path of moral decency? Or will she degenerate like Shane did? We don't know what will happen, but we hope for her success, and we are sure her development will be fascinating as it unfolds in future episodes. Good luck, Carol.[1]

---

[1] We would like to thank the following people for their suggestions on this chapter: Wayne Yuen, Marialena Delfino, Jennifer Musico, Phil Drucker, and Angelo Contino.

WALKER BITE

Innocence in Shambles

WAYNE YUEN

Young children are innocent. Lizzie, Mika, Sophia, and most especially Little Ass-Kicker come in to the world with a clean moral slate. They haven't done anything wrong, and even if they do things that we might find morally questionable or wrong, they generally wouldn't be able to understand that what they did was wrong.

Children lack the rational capacity to judge, in a moral way, their own actions. So when young children rip a toy from the hands of a playmate, even though he's done something wrong, we attempt to explain the correct behavior, we don't think that they are morally bad. He simply didn't know better. On the other hand, if Rick were to simply take Daryl's crossbow out of his hands so he could play with it, he's done something wrong. I'm sure that Daryl's admonishment would be more than words, and he would be justified in judging Rick's actions to be wrong, and perhaps hold Rick's character in less esteem.

But innocence also says something else about children in our society. It also means that there are certain kinds of demands or obligations that we shouldn't put on children. For example, we don't typically think that children should be earning a wage so that they can pay for their share of the rent. Parents and adults should insulate them from difficult choices. Parents will often maintain their marriage solely for the sake of their children, even if they no longer love one another.

When Lizzie kills Mika in 4.14 "The Grove" it is shocking, in part because she is an innocent child and she clearly does not know the moral gravity of her actions. But at the same time, we know that, given the opportunity, she would act in a similar fashion towards other people. She's living in a world where dead people come back to life and live again. She doesn't recognize that it's not the same person who returns to life, but rather an empty shell of a human being. When Carol tells Lizzie to "Look at the flowers" the audience is torn in two directions. We want to excuse Lizzie because of her innocence, yet we also understand that Carol is justified in cultivating Lizzie's botanical interests.

But this is the end of the story. Perhaps we should start closer to the beginning. In 2.6 "Secrets" Shane and Rick are leading a gun training class for the group of survivors. Shane sees Carl and offers to teach him how to shoot. For me at least, this is a jarring scene. Children shouldn't be handling guns! But in this world, it makes sense for Carl to know how to shoot. His life is in danger and he needs to be able to at least protect himself from a walker. This is the same reasoning that Carol uses in Season 5, the children need to learn to protect themselves. So she secretly shows them how to use knives to defend themselves against walkers.

Why the secrecy? To other survivors, this could be ending the innocence of their children, exposing them to things that they should be insulated from. Children shouldn't be responsible for their own defense; that's what adults are for. But we all know that the adults can't always be around and walkers can be anywhere. We, in the real world, wouldn't have to teach our children to use knives to defend themselves, but it's a luxury that Carol, in particular, knows all too well that they do not have. If Sophia was a little less innocent, then perhaps Carol wouldn't have the twinge of sadness in her eye since Season Two.

It might be strange to think of the innocence of children as a luxury, as I just did. Surely it isn't just a luxury in our world. There are definitely benefits to children being shielded from adult situations and responsibilities. We shouldn't want to hurry the mental development of children for our own convenience. But *The Walking Dead* is a useful analogy to a particular kind of life in our world: impoverished and developing countries.

As in *The Walking Dead*, children in impoverished and developing countries don't necessarily have the securities of food, shelter, or safety, and perhaps worse, they don't have the ability to simply walk into an abandoned home and gorge themselves on 112 ounces of chocolate pudding either.

What children do have is their labor. They can trade their labor for a meager income, so that they can support themselves, because their family can't. Child labor is routinely denounced in developed countries as unconscionable. Children are subjected to harsh working environments, literally risk their limbs and their lives around heavy machinery and toxic chemicals to bring home a small income to supplement food for themselves and their families. Worrying about walker attacks might be an improvement for some. This is certainly not ideal. But if innocence is a luxury, then it isn't a necessity. What is a necessity might be the dollar that they bring home in order to buy food, or patch a water jug.

In the comic series, Lydia is a sixteen-year-old girl who is captured camouflaged amongst a group of walkers and interrogated by one of the ever-expanding cast of the group of survivors that we follow. Why was she, a young girl, sent out to blend in with walkers, camouflaged? She answers, "There are no children anymore. Childhood was always a myth brought about by the illusion of safety. It was a luxury we could never really afford" (Issue 135 "Face to Face"). In the real world, safety isn't entirely an illusion, so it is a luxury that we can afford. Unfortunately, it isn't that way everywhere.

When the next news story comes up about how we exploit children working in sweatshops, instead of being outraged that corporate America would exploit children, perhaps we should pause and ask ourselves: How can we make innocence an affordable luxury for these children?

14
Carol Didn't Care

Wayne Yuen

"Just look at the flowers." Bang! Carol shoots Lizzie in the head and makes the world a safer place. But did Carol do the right thing? It's pretty easy to defend what Carol has done. After all, Lizzie killed her sister, almost killed Judith a number of times, and doesn't seem to understand the dangers that the walkers pose to people in general. I agree with all of these facts, and yet I can't but think that something bad has happened here.

I don't think that Carol was necessarily wrong in executing Lizzie. I think that given the options available to her and the post-apocalyptic setting that she finds herself in, Lizzie needs to be executed. There isn't a reasonable hope for rehabilitation and keeping Lizzie with the group would be unmanageable. Someone would need to watch Lizzie at all times so that she wouldn't kill other people, maybe even as the others slept. But just because something isn't wrong, doesn't mean that it is good either. I think that Carol had alternatives available to her that might have been morally better choices than execution. But to understand why the alternatives choices that I'm going to propose are even *plausible,* on a moral level, we need to understand the reasons behind a shift in thought of one of the more popular moral theories out there: Utilitarianism.

You Can Lead a Horse to Water . . .

Generally speaking, utilitarians have a singular goal, to maximize net utility, utility being traditionally defined as happiness or pleasure. This is how Jeremy Bentham, the father of utilitarianism, formulated the theory. He noticed that there were all sorts of happiness that were not being taken into consideration, like the happiness of animals, and suggested that in order to be moral people, we would need to take into consideration the pain and suffering that animals are experiencing, since pain and suffering detract from a net pleasure in the world. Let's call this "classic" utilitarianism.

Classic utilitarianism works pretty well most of the time. Should I kill the Governor? Sure, since killing him would probably make more people happier, especially after he reveals himself to be the monstrous person he is, and since more people are happy, that usually maximizes net utility (although not always).

But there are cases in which classic utilitarianism doesn't seem to give us the right answer. For example in 5.10 "Them," when Aaron leaves water on the road for Rick and his group, nobody dares to drink it, fearing that it might be poisoned. But in the end, we find out that Aaron's intentions are noble, and that it would not have been bad for them to drink it. Eugene volunteers to be the guinea pig and drink the water, but the group doesn't let him. Why? If Eugene drinks the water and it turns out to be poisoned, only one of them would die, Eugene. This would make the group unhappy. But if he drank the water, and it wasn't poisoned, they could all drink, and the group would be very happy, considering the state that they're in. If they don't let Eugene drink, they never get to know if the water is safe or not. Is Eugene's life really so important to the happiness of the group, especially at this point in their travels, that it isn't worth the risk?

I'll Pass on Happiness, but Thanks Though!

This is basically a math problem and that is the way that Jeremy Bentham imagines classic utilitarianism to be. We have two options available to us, use Eugene as a guinea pig, or don't, and there are three possible outcomes:

1. **He dies.**

2. **He doesn't die and we drink.**

3. **He doesn't die and we don't drink.**

Let's imagine that the math works out to be something like this: If Eugene dies, everyone is unhappy that they lost a member of their group, even Abraham! So the group experiences suffering worth minus 20 points.

But if the second outcome comes about, then the group is *really* happy. They get something like 100 points of happiness total. But if they prevent Eugene from drinking at all, they don't lose the happiness that they could have lost if he died, but they don't gain the happiness that they could have gotten if he lived.

But Eugene is a little upset that he didn't get to *try*. So there is still a net loss of utility, of minus 5 points. The problem here is that we don't know what the odds are of Eugene living or dying, to help us make this "bet."

But there is something strange about this scenario, that transcends the math. Nobody is thinking about happiness in this situation (well, except Eugene). They all would rather give up the potential happiness, for something that they want more, safety. They know they're alive now, why risk a member of their group for a potential benefit? Despite Eugene's desire, the group's overwhelming *preference* is for nobody to die. Happiness has taken a back seat to satisfying the group's preference.

The philosopher R.M. Hare argues that utilitarians should be substituting *preference satisfaction* over maximization of happiness, because maximizing happiness can sometimes lead to some bizarre conclusions. For example, let's say that Father Gabriel is really hot in his religious garb. *The Walking Dead* being set in the South this would be expected during the summers. He would be cooler if he took off his collar and probably more if he took off his shirt. But Gabriel prefers to keep his shirt and collar on, maybe as a kind of penitence, or maybe because he would prefer to have a visible sign, for the world to see, that he has dedicated his life to his faith. But it couldn't be denied that it would make him more comfortable and thus happier, if he took off his collar and shirt. Should that matter?

There are lots of things that make us happy or unhappy that we wouldn't prefer to subject ourselves to. It doesn't typically make a person happy to go to the dentist, but we prefer to go. It would be very pleasurable to be injected with heroin, but most of us prefer that we weren't. Our preferences are *more* important to us than our happiness and the type of utilitarianism known as *preference utilitarianism* reflects this.

There Are No Morally Bad Dogs

When Carol executes Lizzie, she doesn't have a direct preference to kill her. She would prefer not to kill a young child. You can see it in her face and hear it in her voice when she tells Lizzie to "Look at the flowers."

She executes Lizzie primarily because Lizzie is dangerous. Much like how people might put down a dog that is dangerous, people aren't blaming the dog or thinking that the dog is morally bad; but at the same time, to ensure safety, the dog might need to be euthanized. If we're preference utilitarians, this sounds reasonable since we prefer to be safe, despite the unhappiness that might result from euthanizing a dog (and of course, Lizzie isn't *actually* a dog, which would affect our preferences too).

But we're forgetting that there are other preferences that need to be taken into consideration, namely Lizzie's. Lizzie wouldn't want to be executed! Although the dog in the hypothetical scenario might not want to be euthanized, it would be a hard case to make that the dog understands what euthanasia is and why he wouldn't want it.

However the preferences of Carol, Tyreese, and Judith for safety could plausibly trump Lizzie's preference not to be executed. On top of this, Carol and Tyreese have additional preferences, like preferring that Judith isn't killed by Lizzie. They prefer that Lizzie doesn't hamper their ability to survive. To maximize the preference satisfaction, Lizzie needs to be eliminated from the group. We can rarely satisfy all of our preferences and in this case, the preference that loses out is the preference not to kill Lizzie.

However, Lizzie's preferences don't all have to be unsatisfied, simply because she needs to be eliminated from the group. We could imagine that one morning when Lizzie wakes up, she won't be in her bed, but tied to a tree. Unfortunately, if the scenario plays out like how Carol describes it to Sam in 5.13 "Forget", Lizzie still will be dead. Carol would have still killed Lizzie, only indirectly. But Lizzie has a preference that none of the other characters have seem to exhibit: she doesn't prefer to avoid the walkers. She likes to play with them. She doesn't think that they're bad things, which is why she kills her sister. She wants to show Carol and Tyreese that they are wrong about the walkers.

If Lizzie thinks that it's not bad for Mika, her sister, to be a walker, then it's likely that she doesn't think that being a walker is bad at all. If given the choice between a death where Lizzie would reanimate versus a death where Lizzie wouldn't reanimate, I think it would be reasonable to believe that Lizzie would prefer a reanimated death, where she could be a walker! She could live a life that she seems to value, if walkers could value things, however strange it may be to most. We might doubt that Lizzie would still *be* Lizzie as a walker, but this doesn't change her preference for this to happen. You can have a preference for something that will change you into something other than who you are now—it's still one of your preferences now.

Carol could have maximized preference satisfaction by executing Lizzie, but in a way that allowed her to reanimate. We don't actually see how Carol executes Lizzie, but assumedly she shoots her in the head. We see Carol and Tyreese finish burying Lizzie, forever interred. But Carol could have shot her in the heart, which would kill her quickly, and give her a chance to reanimate and be a walker that she has so much empathy for.

Now there might be a few objections to this line of action. We might argue that Lizzie is simply wrong about the nature of walker. They're mindless killers! But I think it's reasonable to view walkers as a kind of animal, that are neither good nor bad. A dog might hurt or kill people, but that doesn't make that dog an evil dog, as I pointed out earlier. Dogs lack the rational capacity to be behave according to moral rules that they give themselves. (Or if they do have this ability, we don't have a way to be sure that they do.)

Walkers are similar to dogs in this way. If they can conduct themselves according to moral rules, and they chose not to, they would be morally bad things. But everything we know about walkers is that they're mostly mindless, or are only about as rational as an ant. Carol and the others, seem to think that walkers are intrinsically or inherently bad. Sasha goes out hunting the walkers, in part because she's angry at them for killing Tyreese. But should we hunt down all the tigers in the world because one of them kills a human being, even one that we loved? Lizzie might have a point, if her point is that we're too harshly judging walkers to be *inherently* bad, but if her point is that they're simply misunderstood and inherently good things, that might be giving them too much credit.

Building a Better Walker

Another objection might be that allowing Lizzie to reanimate would make another zombie that could harm survivors. Adding to the army of dead isn't preferable, so we ought to ensure that she doesn't reanimate—by shooting her in the brain, not the heart. The easy response would be that a singular walker rarely poses a threat and the addition of one more walker to the population of walkers is unlikely to have any substantive effect on any individual's risk of being killed. Additionally, we could take steps to reduce the harm that Lizzie could inflict as a walker. We could pull her fingernails and teeth out, to make her less of a threat to anyone she comes across. We could tie wind chimes to her to alert the living of her presence. Perhaps we could build a cage or tie her to a tree to limit her movement. Any number of things could be done to render Lizzie a "safer" walker.

Another way to respond to this would be to say that it's inconsistent with the group's actions to deny Lizzie a walker life. Early in the series we see the group leave Jim behind to die. Although we don't see Jim turn into a walker, presumably he does. He doesn't have a gun, as he turns it down when it is offered to him. He prefers to die like this, and the group respects his preference. If the group was willing to respect Jim's preferences in this case, why not respect Lizzie's beliefs and allow her to reanimate?

This respect for the preferences of a living person, after they die is seen in our society too. While alive we leave behind wills that explain what our preferences would be for the estate that we leave behind, as well as what we might want done with our bodies after we die. On one level, it's strange to even *care* about what would be done with our possessions and bodies after we're dead, since we no longer exist, and what is done would not affect us. But most people think that it's important to satisfy these preferences, because honoring and respecting a person's preferences after they die is an extension of honoring and respecting the individual. It is our *last* opportunity to exemplify our love or respect, and satisfy their preferences, even if it is purely symbolic. This is a moral ideal, not a moral obligation; it would be great if we could do this, but we might not be required to do it. Again, Carol might not be doing wrong by not letting Lizzie reanimate, but she might be falling short of the ideal. Letting Lizzie reanimate as a walker would be like scattering a person's ashes in the place where they would want it to be scattered, it gives us one last chance to satisfy their preferences that is symbolic of our care for the individual.

Kids . . . What Do They Know?

The most problematic objection might be this: Lizzie might have preferences to be a walker, but we should ignore her preferences because she's merely a child. Children might have all sorts of preferences that we wouldn't think are *good* preferences. If Lizzie were living in our world, no doubt she might want to eat lots of candy, watch lots of TV, or spend all day using the computer or tablet. Typically, adults ignore the preferences of children because they lack full rationality. As they develop their rational abilities, we tend to give more weight to their preferences. If Lizzie wants to have a play date with Carl, we might find it acceptable and allow her preference to be satisfied because as her guardians, we might judge this preference to be reasonable, and without dangerous consequences. If Lizzie wants to have a play date with Carl after she kills him and turns him into a walker, we would try to prevent that preference from being satisfied. So why should Carol consider Lizzie's preferences in this case?

I think there are a number of reasons to that at least would make it plausible that we should give Lizzie's preferences some serious consideration. The first reason is Lizzie's attempts to reason. Although it isn't explicitly stated, Lizzie is about ten to twelve years old. At this point in her cognitive development Lizzie isn't completely irrational. Simply insisting that Lizzie is wrong would treat her as if her cognitive abilities are absent. She can reason, and she should be given the opportunity to exercise and develop her cognitive abilities, even if they seem to be supporting incorrect conclusions. Reasoning with Lizzie only happens on a superficial level, mostly in 4.14 "The Grove." Carol insists that the walkers were trying to kill her, not playing with her. Lizzie is the reasonable one when she admits to Tyreese that, "Sometimes you need to kill them. But sometimes you don't." Lizzie's perspective and values are consistently ignored and simply contradicted, so she struggles to find a reasonable way to justify her position to the adults. She finally resorts to a deadly experiment with her sister. Her attempts to be reasonable and the misguided attempt to prove her point lead to her execution. But her attempts at using reason at least requires us to give her significantly more respect. If Lizzie survived and started bringing boys over in Alexandria that Carol disapproved of, at some point we would need to respect her choices and values because of her rationality. Had her values been treated seriously she might not have resorted to such a misguided attempt to prove herself.

Re-evaluating Values

The second reason that would support that Lizzie should be allowed to reanimate are the very values that she holds. Lizzie has grown up in a world where the commonality of death is everywhere. It is a mundane fact that dead people get back up. This causes her to look and treat the world in a radically different way than others. The couple of years that Carl has over Lizzie (Carl is about thirteen or fourteen in Season Five) makes a significant difference in their perception of the world. Carl can likely recall a time when walkers were not the norm; Lizzie's memory of the pre-apocalypse is probably less distinct. Much of this comes out in a conversation between Carl and Lizzie in 4.1 "30 Days Without an Accident."

CARL: They had names when they were alive. They're dead now.

LIZZIE: No they're not. They're just different.

CARL: They don't talk. They don't think. They eat people. They kill people.

LIZZIE: People kill people. They still have names.

CARL: Have you seen what happens? Have you seen someone die like that?

LIZZIE: Yeah, I have.

Lizzie's age has made her more susceptible to a value shift that tends to happen between generations of people. In our world, older generations find it more difficult to understand homosexuality, since it was never accepted as normal. Increasingly younger generations find nothing strange about homosexuality because so many homosexuals are not living closeted lives anymore. It is normal to see them everywhere. If Lizzie sees walkers everywhere, she's more likely to consider this normal, and find no reason to be prejudiced against them. She hasn't been given reasons to be prejudiced against them, and her experiences tell her there is no need for prejudice. They're fun to feed and they like to play chase!

These value shifts aren't to be ignored by older generations, but rather used as an opportunity for older generations to really reflect upon their own values and change them if warranted. The values that Lizzie holds don't appear from nowhere either. We see instances of the "old guard" holding similar values. Morgan couldn't shoot his wife, The Governor couldn't let go of Penny. The real question isn't why Lizzie doesn't demonize the walkers, but why does everyone else prejudicially demonizes walkers? In 4.2 "Infected" when she discovers a walker that she had named "Nick" was killed Lizzie howls, "He's dead! He was special and now he's dead." Carol and the others find this to be strange.

Being the walking dead is certainly not a normal state of being, and calling it special is indeed not normal. But not being normal doesn't make a value wrong, bad, or incorrect. When Aaron and Eric are reunited in 5.11 "The Distance" it can be argued that their homosexual relationship is not normal, but none of the group complained that it was wrong *because* it wasn't normal. They simply accepted that Aaron and Eric loved one another, and that the object of their love is not a member of the opposite sex. Lizzie places a special value on being a walker. Is this value weird? Sure. Is it wrong? Perhaps. But the strangeness isn't what makes it wrong. If Lizzie thinks that being a walker is a "special" state of being, then what good justification do we have to say that she's wrong and deny her that state?

Wait, Why Can't I Pee There?

Finally, the last reason why we should respect this preference of a child is that this is a rather trivial preference. Many of the preferences that people and children have are, on the whole, not terribly impactful or important to a person's life or would radically affect other people's happiness. We don't think that our individual preference on what we wear or how we style our hair is going to significantly alter our lives. Is it really wrong to let children play in the dirt? Maybe if they get it inside the house, but hose them down afterwards and we haven't created lasting harm, and we've satisfied a preference. When people talk about ethics we're typically concerning ourselves with weighty issues, but not always. Should I use the handicapped stall in the restroom, even though it *might* inconvenience a handicapped individual? This is not a weighty issue, but it is a moral issue. Not all preferences are the same, and in the case of using the handicapped bathroom stall, for a little more room perhaps, my preference gets satisfied. But if a handicapped individual enters and needs to use the stall I'm occupying, his preference to use the stall is more important than my desire to flail my arms and legs around while I use the toilet. So it would be better for me to use the non-handicapped stall. I really can't explain why so many people prefer to use the handicapped stall. (Often people say they just like more room. More room for what?! This is my best guess for the need.)

Now, Lizzie's preference might not sound trivial, she wants to be a walker! But since it would be dangerous to let her live as a human being because we can't trust that she won't kill while people are sleeping to prove her point that walkers are harmless, the decision is really between death with no chance or reanimation, or death with reanimation. The weighty moral issue, to execute or not, has already been decided by Carol, the trivial issue is do we satisfy this strange preference by executing her in a way that would allow this preference to be satisfied? If we're good utilitarians, we should *always* maximize utility (in this case preference satisfaction) and squeezing one more preference being satisfied in this situation, if possible, is what we ought to do.

Carol didn't seem to give any consideration to Lizzie's walker preference. She simply didn't care, because this value was so foreign and strange to her that she couldn't give it a fair analysis. Lizzie's unusual values lead her to kill Mika, which causes Carol to execute her. But if Carol had known about preference utilitarianism, she might have been forced to look at Lizzie's preferences from a more open perspective, which might have prevented Mika's death. Preferences are preferences even if you don't understand why people hold them and our duty as preference utilitarians is to consider people's preferences and maximize the number of preferences that are satisfied.

V

Every Direction
Is a Question

15
My Zombie, My Self

RICHARD GREENE

"What the hell are those things?!?" If memory serves (a very big "if" indeed!), this is exactly what I was thinking as I sat in a midnight showing of George Romero's classic zombie movie, *Night of the Living Dead*, at the Briggsmore Theatre in Modesto, California, when I was twelve or thirteen years old (I don't think I slept very well that night!).

Since then I've seen literally hundreds of movies and television shows about zombies (not to mention, I've enjoyed countless novels, comic books, graphic novels, video games, zombie walks, performance art pieces, and philosophical essays on zombies). In the forty or so years since my first exposure to zombies, I've learned quite a bit about what zombies do (most notably, they lumber, slobber, eat brains, eat flesh, groan, and smell bad), I've learned quite a bit about how they come to be (the are the result of atomic bomb testing, they are infected by viruses, they are victims of Haitian voodoo rituals, they are living persons under the control of evil scientists, or they have encountered mysterious alien zombification substances), and I've learned quite a bit about how to stop them (typically a swift blow to the head will do the trick, but severing the head or burning them also works nicely), but knowing these things doesn't answer my original question—*What the hell are these things?*

How to Be a Zombie

As the above examples suggest, there are many different types of zombie, so there are probably lots of different answers to my question. For instance, Haitian voodoo zombies, such as the zombies in *I Walked with a Zombie,* are pretty clearly just people. Specifically, they are dead people whose souls have left their bodies, but their metaphysical status is no different from any other dead persons. Unlike most dead people, voodoo zombies move around and occasionally attack living people or animals, but they are not really doing it themselves; rather, they are being controlled by am evil necromancer who controls their bodies. Think of it like a puppet master who uses magic instead of strings to manipulate the movements of its puppets. So there is no great mystery about what voodoo zombies are.

While reports of zombie activity are usually restricted to fiction, there have been plenty of actual news reports of zombie activity in the Caribbean, Africa, and South America. Moreover, there is much documentation of Haitian voodoo rituals (and a host of closely related religious counterparts in non-Haitian culture). The speculation here is that these "zombies" are people who've been given a kind of poison that puts them in a near-death state, so that they are not quite dead, but lumber around in a trance. These are not really zombies, at all (at least not in the fun sense); they are just living persons lumbering around in a kind of stupor (not at all unlike college town fraternity boys on a Friday or Saturday night after imbibing a few too many).

Other voodoo zombies, like those seen in Victor Halperin's masterpiece *White Zombie*, are living persons under the spell of an evil genius, who controls his victims' minds, and by extension, their bodies using a combination of black magic and mentalist techniques. Again, there is no great mystery as to what these things are.

The same can be said of the Rage-infected zombies of Danny Boyle's *28 Days Later*. Rage is a virus developed by scientists. These "zombies" are regular living people who have become infected, so that they behave like the zombies of *Night of the Living Dead* (only they move much faster!)—they attack people and eat flesh, and their attack leads to the victim of the attack being infected, but unlike the zombies of *Night of the Living Dead* they are not undead. In fact, if not killed in the usual "kill a zombie" fashion, these "zombies" will eventually starve to death, which is a clear mark of being a real living organism.

While zombies like those described above—zombies who are either living persons who are infected with something such as Rage or are controlled by evil scientists, or zombies who are dead persons whose bodies are controlled by necromancers— are easy to explain metaphysically (they're just living or dead people), other zombies like those found in *Night of the Living Dead* and *The Walking Dead* are not so easy to explain. From here on out we can refer to zombies such as these as "*Walking Dead*-type zombies." *Walking Dead*-type zombies are said to be undead. That is they are not living, nor are they dead. So what is it to be undead? This is part of what my original question amounts to.

Those Are People Who Died, Died!

The first thing to note about the undead is that they are not alive. This seems obvious, but, as we've seen, it's not true of all zombies. Also, it's common to conceive of the undead as being both dead and alive (which, of course, requires that the undead be alive—to be both you have go to be each one). This, obviously, is a contradiction and cannot happen.

Stories about the undead are fictional and are not constrained by what can actually happen, but still part of what makes for good fiction (especially when it's horror) is a requirement that the main premise of the story (for example, that the dead have risen and are starting to eat living humans!) has to be, at minimum, a logically possibility. It has to make some kind of sense that it might happen. So if people conceive of the undead as something that can never happen under any circumstance, the story won't be as good.

Philosophers would make this point by saying that the story can be *metaphysically* impossible, but should be *logically* possible. This explains why *Attack of the 50-Ft. Woman* was a much better movie (and much scarier to those naive audiences of the 1950s) than *Attack of the 50-Ft. Round-Square*. The folks who write horror know this, and have been careful to define (or, at least, to characterize) the undead as dead, but not at rest, as opposed to both dead and alive.

So the undead have at some point died. Not everything that has died, however, is undead. Most things that have died are now simply dead things (or if they've decomposed sufficiently, they are no longer things at all. At some point, almost all things cease to exist altogether). So only a small percentage of things that die become undead. It's even smaller because, as far as we've seen so far, only humans become undead. Horses, pigs, and squirrels never seem to reanimate. Nor do the vegetables from the prison garden.

So we can think of the undead as things that have died, but are distinct from other dead things (or previously dead things in the case of those things that have died, decomposed to a sufficient degree, and no longer exist) in that they are not "at rest." The undead are ambulatory (they move around and change location), and they do things (for example, they attack, they make noise, in some cases the make plans, they initiate causal interactions with things in their surroundings).

Not everything that has died is dead. While having died at some point is a necessary condition for a thing being undead, being ambulatory, and performing actions, is a sufficient condition for a thing's not being dead. So the undead have both lived at some point and have died at some point, but in their undead state are neither alive nor dead.

Moreover, not everything that is undead is a zombie; there are many ways of being undead. So let's see if we can't narrow things down a bit. In addition to zombies, vampires, ghosts, draugrs, reanimated corpses (think Frankenstein's monster, here), wraiths, some skeletons, some mummys, banshees, and revenants (just to name a few) are also undead. So it would appear that along the way we will need to get clearer on the ways in which zombies are different from other undead creatures. But, as zombies like to say (or would no doubt say if they could), slow and steady eats the brains. So, first things first.

How Can You Tell if You're Undead?

So what exactly is death? Philosophers have changed their views on this one over the years. Up through the middle-ages a person was considered dead if they satisfied what was called "the putrification standard." This one is pretty self-explanatory: a person is dead at the point in which they become putrified. Certainly purtification occurs at some point well after death occurs. So why was this standard employed? Because, it's not always clear when someone is actually dead, especially before the advent of modern technologies, such as heart rate monitors and stethoscopes.

Someone who's unconscious or in a coma may appear dead to folks who don't have access to modern medical technologies, even though they are not dead. So the putrification standard served folks in the middle-ages quite well. If someone has begun to putrify, you can be pretty darned sure that they have died! This also points to an interesting distinction between someone's being dead and other people knowing that person is dead. Putrified people may have been dead for a long time before other people know it!

Eventually the putrification standard was replaced by the heart-lung standard. According to this standard, if someone's heart has stopped beating and their lungs have stopped breathing, they're considered to be dead. The heart-lung standard has now been replaced by the whole-brain standard. There were a number of reasons for this change.

First, given recent technological advancements, the whole-brain standard provides a more accurate way of determining when death has occurred.

Second, it better jibes with the modern notion that lack of systemic functioning is when death truly occurs.

Finally, and most importantly, there are a number of counter-examples to the heart-lung standard. A person who has clearly not died (for example, someone who is alert, conscious, and conversant), but has heart and lungs that have ceased to function would be considered dead by the heart-lung standard (here you are to suppose that a machine helps perform the functions of the heart and lungs). Similarly, there could be a person who is clearly dead (in fact, the person could have begun to putrify!), but (again, with the aid of machines) have a heart and lungs that have not irretrievably stopped. This is someone who, according to the heart-lung standard is alive, but clearly is dead.

The whole-brain standard is one of two standards for determining death currently being used. The other is the higher-brain standard. According to the whole-brain standard you're dead when there's no longer any activity in yourr brain. According to the higher-brain standard you're considered dead when you're cerebral cortex is no longer functioning. The higher-brain standard essentially involves a re-defining of the very concept of death. It's mostly used to determine when people can be removed from life-support, even though they are not completely dead. So for our purposes, the whole-brain standard seems to be the appropriate one.

Walking Dead–type zombies meet each of these standards. Perhaps, especially the putrification standard! In fact zombies smell so bad that even zombies can smell them. In 1.2 "Guts" Rick and the gang need to get through a crowd of zombies undetected. They do this by rubbing dead zombies parts (parts from zombies that they have recently killed) on their skin and clothing. The zombie smell masked their living person odor, and they could move slowly and safely through the zombie hoard. Zombies also satisfy the other standards. They have no heartbeat, their lungs don't function, and they have no brain functions (higher-brain or otherwise). So it's pretty clear that zombies meet every criterion for the ascription of death. But, as we have seen, they are clearly not dead in the typical way—*Walking Dead*–type zombies can move about, eat flesh, drool, grunt, rattle fences, climb on things, open doors, smash windows, and engage in what appears to be all sorts of intentional behavior.

So Why Exactly Aren't Zombies Alive?

I said earlier that the undead are not alive because they have died. This is a bit of an oversimplification, and also, while generally true of the undead, it is not always thought to be true. In most cases, the reason that the undead are not alive is because they don't meet the criteria for being alive. While able to move and so forth, *Walking Dead*–type zombies don't have living tissue, they don't have heart or lung activity, they don't have electro-chemical activity in their brains. Life, as a state, occurs so that we might actually do the things that living creatures are able to do. What this amounts to depends on the type of creature you are. Aristotle tells us that plants live to take nutrition and grow, animals live to do those things, and move about, humans, do those things and also use reason. These are the functions of living things (at least if Aristotle is to be believed). The undead don't require living tissue to perform these functions. Supernatural forces (or viruses or alien infections) will do the trick.

Moreover, it can be argued that some undead creatures are, in fact, alive. Frankenstein's monster, for example, can be conceived as a reanimated corpse. He is literally brought back to life. Others argue that for this reason Frankenstein's monster should not be counted among the undead. At minimum, undeath is a concept whose boundaries are not exactly precise. For our purposes, it will be useful to treat Frankenstein's monster and *similarly* reanimated corpses as though they are alive and therefore not undead.

At Least I'm Not a Banshee

So to this point we've established that (at least for the most part) the undead are currently neither dead nor living, but at one time were alive and at some later time were dead, and there are a variety of ways of being undead. Our interest, of course, is in *Walking Dead*–type zombies, or walkers. How do they differ from other undead creatures? Studying Socrates (by reading Plato, of course) teaches us that one good way to define things is to figure out which category something belongs in and then distinguish that thing from everything else in the category. (More technically, identify the genus, and then make it explicit how the species being defined differs from other species in the genus). Let's do this for zombies.

So like all undead creatures (we've already decided to exclude reanimated corpses, such as Frankenstein's monster from the category of the undead), zombies of the sort under consideration are undead (with all that that entails). They are also corporeal, meaning that they have physical bodies. Plenty of undead creatures are incorporeal (that is, they are made of spirit or non-physical substances). Ghosts, wraiths, and banshees are among those that are incorporeal in nature. So walkers are undead creatures that are corporeal. Notice that this doesn't, however, serve to exclude all undead creatures that are distinct from *Walking Dead*–type zombies from the species walker, so we'll have to look at other features they have, as well.

Walking Dead–type zombies are generally thought to be mindless. Of course, depending on the zombies you're talking about, some zombies are smarter than others. The *Walking Dead*–type zombies of *The Return of the Living Dead*, for instance, are quite intelligent. One clever zombie shouts over a police radio "send more cops," as the zombies were having a cop feeding-frenzy. Another pleads with his still living girlfriend, "if you love me, you'll let me eat your brains." The zombies of *The Return of the Living Dead* and similar works are outliers. In fact, it's best to think of such shows as satirical. They are not the norm. *Walking Dead* zombies, by contrast, are as described above—lumbering, slobbering, and mindless. They may grunt or make noises, they do not have higher-order brain function. Adding this criterion serves to distinguish zombies from other undead creatures such as vampires, some skeletons (such as the Lost Skeleton of Cadavra (in the unforgettable *The Lost Skeleton of Cadavra*), who exhibit a kind of super-intelligence) and some mummies (other mummies are more akin to the zombies of *I Walked with a Zombie* in that they are not actually undead. They are just dead creatures who are being controlled by someone).

So noting that *Walking Dead*–type zombies differ from other undead creatures in that they are corporeal and mindless gets us most of the way toward defining *Walking Dead*–type zombies, but it doesn't distinguish them from all undead creatures. For example, non-intelligent skeletons meet both of the above conditions, as do draugrs. Draugrs have both superhuman strength and magical powers (for example, they can enter into dreams). Skeletons have good hand to eye co-ordination and can move quickly (and in some cases have magical properties). Unlike draugrs, walkers do not have magical properties, and their strength is akin to what they had at the time they died— some zombies are strong, some are not, but none have superhuman strength. Unlike skeletons, walkers are not co-ordinated and do not move quickly. They lumber about. Finally, walkers are rotting away—they are continuing to decompose—whereas skeletons do not (they've lost all flesh, vessels, and organs, but they are not rotting, and they don't smell bad).

So now we have all we need to define walkers. They are creatures who

1. **Are undead**

2. **are corporeal**

3. **are mindless**

4. lack super strength and other magical properties

and

5. are continuing to decompose.

Anything that meets these conditions will be a walker. These are all necessary conditions, and together they are sufficient.

Might I Become a Zombie Someday?

As I raised my question—*What the hell are those things?*—at the Briggsmore Theatre's midnight showing of *Night of the Living Dead* in 1973 or 1974, I was terrified. Oddly, nowadays, zombies don't seem scary at all, and I sometimes wonder why they did at the time. I think it might have something to do with the prospect of that happening to me. "What if I become a zombie?" It's a terrifying thought. This raises the question: might I become a zombie someday?

It certainly appears that it could happen to anyone (or at least anyone who is not already a zombie). You are walking along, a zombie attacks you, you get bit, become infected, and lo, you are a zombie. Certainly shows such as *The Walking Dead* pay more than lip-service to this possibility. You hear characters saying things such as "kill me as soon as I begin to turn; I don't want that to happen to me." You also see people recognize zombie versions of folks they knew previously. (Recall the look on Carol's face when she sees the zombie version of her daughter come out of the barn in 2.7 "Pretty Much Dead Already.")

But you also see shows such as *The Walking Dead* suggest that you don't survive zombie infection, and that it's not the same person that is the zombie, as it was before becoming infected. Consider Carl's stony reaction that "she'll turn" when he was forced to go all old yeller on Lori in 3.4 "Killer Within." Carl, presumably, does not have to consider whether he actually killed his mother, because the zombie version of Lori is not the same person as her. It's more like some shell of her. This is an interesting case, because we don't really know if Lori is "dead" here since we didn't see Carl shoot her. Did her brain stop functioning because of blood loss? Was she actually dead or just unconscious? Did she reanimate? Or did Carl just prevent her from reanimating?

So what's the right thing to say here? Do we survive zombie attacks and actually become zombies or is it the case that once we're dead, we cease to be, and it's something else that's moving around in what was once our bodies doing unspeakable things to innocent people. Philosophically, this is an unresolved issue. Some theorists suppose that no one survives any change at all. On this view, just cutting your fingernails (or reading this chapter) is enough to change you into a different person altogether.

Other theorists hold that we can survive most changes but not the major ones. So, for example, getting your hand chopped off is not enough to change who you are, but dying is a significant enough change, that necessarily what remains is something else entirely. On this view, I would not be the zombie version of myself, nor could I ever be a ghost, banshee, skeleton, or a Frankenstein's monster. Certainly the Epicureans of ancient Greece would have held this line.

Other theorists hold that one is always the thing one is, until there is nothing left at all. According to this theory, after I die, I'm whatever remains. If I get reanimated, I might be a zombie, if not I might be worm food, but I'm still me, right up to the point where there's nothing left of me. This option, certainly makes for the most interesting narrative: I'm conceived, I live, I die, I lumber and slobber, I eat brains, I get beheaded (or burned or some such), I go back to being dead, I feed the worms, then I go out of existence.

Which of these views is correct? While each has its merits and its drawbacks, none compels me to choose it. Instead, I'm choosing on the basis of self-interest. The reason I watch horror movies and television programs, is to get just a little of that adrenaline I felt that night in the early Seventies. It doesn't happen very often at the movies, but I want to feel frightened. If what's required for that is to "believe" in some sense that I could become a zombie, then that's what I'm gonna do! In fact, I think I'll choose to believe that a full-fledged zombie apocalypse is just around the corner, just because it's more fun to do so! My thirteen-year-old self would expect nothing less from me.

16
The Truth about the Walkers

BRANDON KEMPNER

The Walking Dead is lying to you.

It promises answers and never delivers.

We can blame Robert Kirkman; we can blame the television producers. In the end, it doesn't matter. The series keeps hinting that it'll reveal the origin of the walkers and it never does. The television show is particularly cruel, as it has dangled these teasers far more prominently than the comic.

Think about Dr. Edward Jenner and the Center for Disease Control in Season One, or Dr. Eugene Porter and his mad quest to reach Washington, DC, in Seasons Four and Five. As loyal viewers, we get tricked into believing that the "Truth" of the walkers will be revealed, and when everything falls apart—as it always does in *The Walking Dead*—we wind up with nothing.

This shroud of mystery is a major violation of the zombie formula. Usually, your typical zombie story provides a clear (if stupid) explanation of where the zombies come from. Patient Zero infected the world! These chemicals turn people into zombies! A probe from Venus caused it! Those are the explanations offered in *World War Z, The Return of the Living Dead,* and *Night of the Living Dead.* By withholding any such pseudo-scientific explanation of the walkers, *The Walking Dead* refuses to give us any sense of cause, and with that, any possibility of a cure.

The conspiracy is bigger than that. By not revealing this key piece of information, *The Walking Dead* is keeping us in a continual state of philosophical suspense. As the comic proudly informs us in every collected volume, this is a "continuing story of survival horror." It's not a story about endings, happy or otherwise. It's certainly not a story about finding meaning. If we run this through the philosophical meat grinder, we'll come up with some tasty walker hamburgers, or, more precisely, an investigation of whether meaning is one or many things. This is a central philosophical debate of our times, as to whether the world around us contains one Truth (*transcendent and knowable!*) or a variety of truths (*multiple and unknowable!*).

As you can imagine, this philosophical fight can get vicious, so how better to explore it than through a TV series filled with vicious walkers? What we can claim is that *The Walking Dead*—the TV show, although the comic operates in a nearly identical way—takes us right into the middle of this philosophical swamp, forcing us to ask the question, Will we ever know where the walkers come from? Or, to frame that more philosophically, Will we ever know the Truth?

The Walking Dead plays with our desire to know, our desire for simple, clear, and rational explanations. By preying on this desire for a single cause, *The Walking Dead* sets its viewers up for disappointment and confusion—two emotions that go well with zombie horror. In the end, the series forces multiplicity upon us, rather than the comforting certainty of a single all-powerful Truth.

Where Do Survivors Go?

The Walking Dead, so far at least, has emphatically withheld any notion of cause. As such, we can approach the television show as a textbook example of deferred meaning. Instead of a linear journey to Truth (or safety, which is pretty much the same thing), we have a non-linear wandering that leads us to radial, branching paths of possibilities. One thing about *The Walking Dead* is that it can take you to some abstract places very quickly, so let's slow down and look at an actual example of this multiplicity problem.

In Season One, our hero Rick reunites with his family and best friend Shane. Shane, of course, has secretly slept with Rick's wife, but let's put that aside for the moment. These characters have joined up with some other survivors, and are currently camped outside the city of Atlanta. In short order, they're besieged by walkers. Bite, bite, bite. People die, and in the aftermath of all that death, they have to decide what they should do next.

They have several options: stay put and hope they can last out the winter, return to Atlanta, seek military aid, or head for the Center for Disease Control (more on that later). Here, the characters are confronted with a multiplicity of options. In a traditional philosophical reckoning, one of those choices would be right and the others wrong. One would presumably lead to safety, security, the government, a hot meal and a warm bed, and, eventually, a world untroubled by the walker curse. The other options would lead to death, ruin, and getting eaten alive. It's a classic "Either/Or" dilemma with one option being right and the others being horribly, horribly wrong.

In a post-modern philosophical reckoning, all these options are simply options. All the decisions, all the various paths, are equally right and equally wrong. None of them can lead to a singular "Truth" or "Safety" because a singular "Truth" or "Safety" no longer exists. Despite this, we still *want* the characters of *The Walking Dead* to find "Truth" and "Safety", even if we know those things are impossible. As such, we're confronted with the horror of multiplicity, numerous possible actions that we have no way of choosing between. Categories of "right" and "wrong" are done away with, as we undergo a shift from a centralized to a de-centralized world view. While multiplicity can be a disorienting, it can also be exhilarating, and once we understand the liberation of multiplicity, we can better learn to survive in the universe of the walkers.

Multiplicity and Philosophy

Let's get some philosophers on the table to walk us through this multiplicity problem. The French philosophical team of Gilles Deleuze and Félix Guattari has written extensively about the idea of multiplicity. In their most famous book, *A Thousand Plateaus: Capitalism and Schizophrenia*—that title just screams multiplicity, doesn't it?—they dismantle conventional notions of knowledge and Truth by arguing that there are thousands of stable resting places (plateaus) from which to survey the world. They go so far as to argue that schizophrenia—viewing the world in multiple ways at once—may be more natural, desirable, and human, than always having one philosophy, one mindset, or one sanity.

This philosophical project is as dense as it is broad: *A Thousand Plateaus* could just as well be called *A Thousand Ideas*, as it jumps all over the place in terms of its argument and analysis. That, of course, is exactly the point: that no one idea is central enough to explain/mold/organize all of human life. There's no one mountain peak to climb; there are just a thousand different perspectives on truth—no capital "T," just a small "t." Truth versus truths.

To apply Deleuze and Guattari, you simply pick one of the many plateaus and hike on up. For the purpose of this essay, let's consider the second chapter of *A Thousand Plateaus,* "One or Several Wolves?" Here, Deleuze and Guattari continue their long-standing war against Sigmund Freud, viciously lashing out at the Viennese psychologist for attempting to reduce the complexity of human experience down to one basic cause. In Freud's case, that's his Oedipal cycle, the idea that all human psychology flows from childhood experiences, namely the desire to kill your father and sleep with your mother.

Deleuze and Guattari take apart Freud's philosophical insistence on a "knowable cause" for all human behavior. In one of Freud's most famous cases, he treated a neurotic who had a childhood nightmare about wolves. The patient, whom Freud generously nicknamed the "Wolfman," kept having a dream about four or five white wolves in a tree, threatening him terribly. The Wolfman would then wake up in a state of absolute fear. Freud, in his long essay on this case, pulls an impressive rabbit-out-of-the-hat: the wolves are really his father, threatening to castrate the little boy.

Deleuze and Guattari vehemently object. They accuse Freud of fixing the results from the start. Since Freud wants to see one cause (castration), he finds one cause:

> For him, there always will be the reduction to the ONE: the little scars, the little holes, become subdivisions of the great scar or supreme hole named castration; the wolves become substitutes for a single Father who turns up everywhere. (*A Thousand Plateaus*, p. 31)

That phrase "the reduction to the ONE" is the central idea we can apply to *The Walking Dead*. There is a philosophical desire to reduce the walkers to "the ONE," to an intelligible, biological cause, and that's exactly what the show constantly denies us.

According to Delueze and Guattari, this is what traditional philosophers always want, to find a unity that no longer exists. Our lives—philosophical and social—are organized around these unities (the Subject, the Government, God, Science), all of which take the complexity of the world and reduce it to the ONE. By doing so, we avoid the confusion of reality. Instead of this cop-out, Deleuze and Guattari want us to embrace multiplicity: "What should have been done is the opposite, all of this should be understood in intensity: the Wolf is the pack, in other words, the multiplicity instantaneously apprehended." That sounds slick and all, but what can we do with this idea?

From Wolves to Walkers

Let's apply this Deleuzian idea to the walkers. Do we see the walkers as the "ONE," as an understandable disease, controllable and solvable, or as a "Many," a multiplicity, a pack, irreducible and uncontrollable? As a series, *The Walking Dead* poises us on this razor's edge, at times hinting that we'll discover a "cause" and thus a "cure"; at other times, the show implies that this walker curse is the world, and that nothing can possibly change.

What is at stake is the philosophical understanding of the series. Is this a narrative about redemption, where Rick eventually saves his son? Or is it a narrative of tragedy where everyone dies? Or does it need to be understood as something more? As a story of multiplicity? Deleuze and Guattari claim that multiplicity helps us to escape a false reliance on Unity or the ONE, which, according to them, is always made up. The ONE is a trap, an artificial way of thinking that distorts reality—and which might lead you open to be killed by walkers.

Don't fall into the trap of thinking this is relativism. Relativism throws its hands up and says, "Everything is probably equally true, so pick whatever you want." Multiplicity says, "There is no such thing as a singular Truth; it takes multiple causes to produce multiple effects." Relativism would have us believe that the walker point of view is just as valid as the human. I mean, why shouldn't the walkers eat? Who's to say that they're acting wrong?

Multiplicity is a different kettle of fish entirely. That's the point: the kettle is full of fish. One fish, two fish, three fish, four fish, red fish, blue fish a whole mess of fish swimming around in confusion. We can't look into that kettle and say "this fish is the fish." If we do that, we're saying more about our own desire for order than we are about reality. Multiplicity theory forces us to acknowledge the complexity of existence. We can't reduce reality down to the "One," relative or otherwise.

With this in mind, we can argue that *The Walking Dead* embraces multiplicity. The show feints towards Unity with the CDC and Dr. Eugene Porter, and then pulls the rug from under us. However, *The Walking Dead* is more than a "Charlie Brown misses the football" series, because the way it tackles this issue of knowability is philosophically profound. Whenever the characters try to find the "cause" of the walkers, to reduce the walkers from the multiple to the singular, they almost die. Think about Hershel's barn full of walkers, just waiting to burst out and kill someone. By not accepting them as walkers, but as something that can be "cured," Hershel invites danger into his very home. Hershel wants to turn those walkers back into humans (from the unknowable to the knowable), and that's what you can never do.

When our heroes accept the many walkers as simply being walkers, in all their multiplicity, they are better able to survive. Michonne's relationship to the walkers embodies this the most clearly: we see scene after scene of her walking in a crowd of walkers (sometimes with her pet walkers, sometimes not), and she's able to do that because she sees them as *walkers*, not as something to be understood. This is exactly what makes Michonne the most competent of our survivors: she accepts the walkers as themselves, as a pack, and this gives her power in the universe of *The Walking Dead*.

Baiting the Trap

Although the success of *The Walking Dead* seems like a given now, the show was far from a surefire hit. The idea of a hyper-violent zombie apocalypse on basic cable was something of a stretch. AMC took several precautions. They only ordered six episodes for the first season, and they also tinkered with the plotline of Kirkman's graphic narrative. They added in some eye-candy for the ladies (Daryl), and toned done some of the bleakness of the world.

One of the biggest changes, though, comes at the end of the first season, when they add a narrative arc not included in the comics: a trip to the Center for Disease Control (CDC). This is an important addition, because it allows the television show to tease the idea of an explanation—and thus a cure—early on. Since the CDC is both a government and scientific agency, it symbolizes the ability of humans to take control of their world. The CDC promises us a walker apocalypse that is knowable, intelligible, and, ultimately, stoppable.

This sense of control is exactly what is lacking in *The Walking Dead*. We can see how badly the characters want security. Consider this exchange in 1.5 "Wildfire":

RICK: I heard the CDC was working on a cure.

SHANE: I heard that too. Heard a lot of things. Before the world went to hell.

RICK: What if the CDC is still up and running?

SHANE: Man, that is a stretch right there.

RICK: Why? If there's any government left, any structure at all, they'd protect the CDC at all costs, wouldn't they? I think it's our best shot. Shelter, protection—

Here, we see the philosophical debate embodied by Deleuze and Guattari. In the CDC, Rick is hoping to find structure, order, safety, civilization, protection. All those things are predicated on the idea of the walkers being "knowable," of their being one definable cause. Like Freud, if Rick can find a cause, he can find a solution.

That's exactly where Deleuze and Guattari take issue, as it turns the complexity of human life into a simple logic game, one with clearly defined rules. What if there aren't rules? What if we never understand the cause of the walkers? While this might infuriate certain viewers, who want cleanly delineated plotlines in their television shows, it also opens up a new realm of understanding the world. When we cease to look for one cause/one effect, we can move beyond the limitations of traditional Western philosophy.

Therein lies the horror and genius of Deleuze and Guattari.

Back in the television world, Rick convinces everyone to head out to the CDC. Near the end of the "Wildfire" episode, we are introduced to a mysterious CDC scientist. We see him, fully swathed in an environmental suit, performing experiments on walker tissue. He accidentally sets off a decontamination process, which results in the burning of all his samples. The episode ends with the scientist drinking and ranting that "the tragedy of their loss cannot be overstated." The camera pulls back, exposing an empty CDC. To the empty room, our scientist says, "I think tomorrow I'm gonna blow my brains out. I haven't decided. But tonight, I'm getting drunk." The series plays this scene perfectly, allowing viewers multiple interpretations. Was the scientist making progress towards finding a cure? Or had he simply gone insane?

Episode 1.6 "TS-19" picks up with our survivors finally meeting this Dr. Edwin Jenner. The CDC initially seems like a paradise. It's safely underground, and is stocked with plenty of supplies, power, hot water, and even wine. For the moment, it's as if civilization has been restored. Our characters sink gratefully into this comfort. Carol exclaims, "It's a miracle, isn't it?" Even Rick is duped: "We don't have to be afraid anymore. We're safe here."

As always, the series quickly rips that safety away. We learn several important things over the course of the episode, namely that Dr. Jenner has not been able to do any good; his attempts at researching the walkers have failed completely. Disgusted with his failures, he's decided to kill everyone in the CDC. So, when Dr. Jenner tells Rick, "It'll all be okay," the double-meaning of that phrase—safety as death—emerges as the crux of the episode. The unravelling of safety is the most profound narrative pattern of *The Walking Dead*: the constant attempts to find security (Truth), only to have that safety ripped away over and over again. From Atlanta to Hershel's farm to the Prison to Terminus, our survivors can find no resting place.

To expand on this, Dr. Jenner shows the survivor his research, including brain scans of an infected subject, the Test Subject 19 of the episode's title. Pointing to an enormous television screen, Dr. Jenner displays the "ripples of light" (electrical impulses) in the brain that make us "human." Dr. Jenner then shows the subject dying, neatly represented by black lines moving through the brain. After that, we get an illustration of how one is "resurrected" into a walker, this time with ominous red lights flooding the screen. None of this brain mumbo-jumbo is present in the comic series. The television series is baiting an explanation, but the characters know better than to believe the lie:

ANDREA: You have no idea what it is, do you?

DR. JENNER: It could be microbial, viral, parasitic, fungal.

JACQUI: Or the wrath of God?

DR. JENNER: There is that.

ANDREA: Somebody must know something.

That line of Andrea's—that there must be an answer out there, and, more than that, that somebody must have it—is our philosophical quandary. What if no one knows? What if no one can know?

Rick himself picks up this line of questioning, calling out this lack of Truth: "But you don't know? How can you not know?" No one in *The Walking Dead* knows or can know. This is a show that moves us beyond a simple idea of "knowing." Instead of One Truth to be disseminated, there are simply multiple ways of thinking about the walkers—as a scientific phenomenon, as a curse, as the wrath of God—with no process that can resolve that multiplicity into the crisp, scientific singularity that people like Dr. Jenner want.

The Stakes of Belief

The breakdown of Dr. Jenner's scientific worldview results in the breakdown of his desire to live. Without his "Truth," he turns to suicide. Rick rejects this myopic reaction, and this is a huge step forward for Rick and the series. Liberated from the chimera of the ONE, he leads our characters forth on a new quest for survival, unburdened by the illusions of government rescue. If we push this reading of *The Walking Dead* to the next level, we can see Rick's quest for survival as a metaphor for all human survival, walker apocalypse or not. While our lives are in no way as dramatic as Rick's, many of the same questions—what does life mean? what does death mean? is there a Truth to be found?—are still the questions of our time. As such, the show says more about our human desire to reduce the complexity of reality down to easily understandable pieces than it ever has about walkers.

Back in 1.6 "TS-19," Dr. Jenner reveals that the CDC is almost out of emergency fuel. When the fuel runs out, the CDC will automatically decontaminate, destroying everything. While remarkably convenient from a plot perspective (what are the chances they'd show up with only a day's fuel left?), the symbolic interpretation is both obvious and profound: the scientific attempt to understand the world is destroying itself. Dr. Jenner is not killed by the walkers, but rather by his need to understand the walkers. That same plot point recurs again and again throughout the television show, as characters find themselves hopelessly drawn to finding the Truth (or cure) of the walkers: Hershel keeping the dead in his barn, the Governor keeping Penny in chains, Abraham's quest to reach Washington, DC.

On screen, Dr. Jenner and the survivors have an extended argument about the walkers being "our extinction event." Again, this is a core philosophy of *The Walking Dead*. The series offers its audiences enough hope that survival—or even a cure is possible—while at the same time keeping the world dangerous enough that we have to acknowledge that, in the long run, neither a cure nor Truth is achievable. The search for Truth is not merely abstract, but intensely personal—we learn that Subject 19 is Dr. Jenner's wife—and ultimately ineffective. In a dramatic race against the clock, Rick and his band have to break out of the CDC, the very place they were trying to get into a mere episode ago. They escape, and find themselves back in the world with no resolution reached.

Eventually, the characters simply move on. That's what happens in *The Walking Dead*: no real resolution is possible. Everything simply continues, in multiple branching paths, without destination. Or, in other words, *The Walking Dead* is just like life. The failure of the CDC represents the failure of single-minded thinking, of Freud's desire to find castration everywhere, in the survivor's desire to find the ONE true safety. In its place, we are left with unknowability and multiplicity: multiple interpretations instead of one truth, thousands of walkers instead of one cure.

Another Doctor, Another Liar

It might be tempting to write off the CDC arc as being unimportant to *The Walking Dead* as a whole. It was part of the unpolished first season, and the show has definitely evolved in terms of its tone and content since then. This makes Dr. Eugene Porter all the more important. With this character, *The Walking Dead* once again plays with our expectations, offering us the promise of finding the Truth of the walkers only to snatch any meaning away from us. Dr. Eugene Porter first appears in 4.10 "Inmates," where he, Abraham, and Rosita rescue Glenn and Tara from a group of walkers. This group is heading towards Washington, DC, claiming that Eugene is a scientist who has vital information on curing the walker plague.

Eugene's possible cure offers new hope at a pivotal moment in the series. The prison has just been destroyed by the Governor, scattering Rick and his friends. While Glenn is desperate to find his wife Maggie, our survivors lack long-term goals. This is exactly what Dr. Eugene Porter and Abraham can offer the group: a new quest, a new unifying order. As Abraham explains to Glenn in 4.11 "Claimed":

> **ABRAHAM:** I'm gonna have to insist that you hold the hell up. All right, believe it or not, the fate of the entire damn human race might depend on it.
>
> **GLENN:** What the hell are you talking about? Who is this guy?
>
> **ABRAHAM:** I'm Sergeant Abraham Ford. And these are my companions Rosita Espinosa and Dr. Eugene Porter. We're on a mission to get Eugene to Washington, DC. Eugene's a scientist and he knows exactly what caused this mess.

Tricked as he was by our earlier Dr. Jenner, Glenn responds with suspicion, and asks what Dr. Porter knows. Eugene gruffly replies that his knowledge is "classified," as if Glenn could share the information with—what? Spies? Walkers?

We're thus launched into a plot arc that lasts for the next ten episodes, as *The Walking Dead* once again teases us with a desire for simple, unified knowledge. Dr. Eugene Porter, with his scraggly mullet and clipped way of speaking, hardly looks like a competent scientist. He isn't even a decent survivor. When he tries to protect the group from some walkers, he shoots the gas tank of their own truck, leaving them stranded. Still, and despite all these red flags, we *want* to believe. The series is taunting us once again, hinting that there is a secret knowledge we might be able to acquire, a key to the walkers that will save us all. Abraham has bought into the lie completely, and we see, over the course of the next few episodes, how Glenn—and eventually Maggie—fall under Eugene's spell. This siren-call of knowing, of finally having "Truth," is so appealing that Abraham, Glenn, and even us viewers will choose it over the unappealing multiplicity of reality.

Shouldn't we have learned our lesson from Dr. Jenner? Just like the CDC, Dr. Porter's promise of unity, Truth, and meaning betrays us. After stretching Dr. Porter's story out over nearly ten episodes, *The Walking Dead* finally shows its cards in 5.5 "Self Help." During that episode, Eugene reveals his inability to make it on his own, telling Tara that, "I know empirically and definitively I cannot survive on my own. I cannot." That pseudo-scientific language ("empirically") hints at the symbolism of this plot arc: science, instead of leading us to Truth, can only lead to survival. That's all that is left in this walker world, and all that can be left.

Eugene has lied to give himself some sort of value. Since he is inept, the only thing he has to offer a group of survivors is a false hope of "Truth." Even that false hope, though, cannot survive in the face of the walker pack. As more and more people have believed and died for Eugene's lie, it begins to collapse under its own weight. The worst possible thing is happening: success. By "Self Help," it looks like the survivors will actually make it to the Capitol. What will Dr. Porter do then? In *The Walking Dead* universe, achieving your goals is just as terrifying as not reaching them.

At the end of this episode, Abraham, Glenn, Eugene and the others are pushing towards Washington, DC, when they encounter an enormous group of walkers. Despite the risk, Abraham decides they have to keep going. This reality is too much for Eugene, so he starts screaming over and over, "I'm not a scientist, I'm not a scientist!" Our survivors are stunned by this revelation. Once he regains his senses, Abraham reacts with extreme violence, nearly beating Eugene to death. For the whole of his next episode, Abraham kneels on the road, his purpose in life lost. Without the lie to drive them forward, the survivors now have to face the reality of simply surviving. One Truth, one purpose, has given way to the multiple and unknowable chaos of existence.

By repeating this "bait-and-switch" plot twice, *The Walking Dead* reinforces its intent of not providing us viewers with answers or resolution. How many times does the show have to fake us out before we wise up? The survivors are not going to find the Truth about the walkers because that truth doesn't matter. Time and time again, *The Walking Dead* is showing us how the desire for Truth, for certainty, distorts reality. People are so eager—so desperate—to believe Dr. Eugene Porter's lie that they choose it over the real world. How do they end up? Dead, dead, and more dead.

Multiplicity and the Walker Curse

So we come back to our most basic question: what is the cause of the walkers in *The Walking Dead*? Classical philosophy would lock us into a "one cause for one effect" explanation. Multiplicity might give us "multiple causes for multiple effects," with an inability to pinpoint one as being the "true" or "absolute" cause. Let me give you a list of possible causes for the walkers that'll likely make you groan:

1. Robert Kirkman and the various artists of *The Walking Dead* comic: they invented and drew the walkers, after all.

2. The crew of the TV show: they slather the make-up on, and without that, you'd just have normal people lurching around.

3. The producers of the TV show: it takes lots of money to get those walkers on screen and into your house.

4. The viewer: without us to watch and believe the illusion, those walkers wouldn't exist.

As television viewers, we hold all these multiple causes in our head at once. This multiplicity doesn't hurt us; it doesn't kill us. We know there isn't one "Truth" to the walkers because it takes many things to make those walkers.

Deleuze and Guattari would have us embrace those multiple layers of meaning, not run away from them, or, even worse, subsume them into a false idea of unity. As a television show demonstrates for us, this desire for unity, for singular explanation, is powerful. The survivors let themselves be fooled again and again, and they're always at risk when they grasp at those unifying straws. When the survivors try to discover the cause, whether with Dr. Jenner or Dr. Porter, they are let down, and end up either dead or back in the inescapable multiplicity of their lives. There is no Truth to be found—at least so far—in the landscape of the series.

How is *The Walking Dead* going to end? How can it end? I like to imagine some scared TV executive crying out: "But where do the walkers come from! You have to explain them!" That's not the point of *The Walking Dead*.

I'd like to hope that *The Walking Dead* is brave enough to never give us an explanation. They can learn from history: *Lost* was never the same show after it explained what was going on. We won't know until the series ends, and it's exactly this state, of being suspended between multiple interpretations, between not knowing absolutely, that Deleuze and Guattari want to celebrate as being ultimately more humane and more human than the ONE. As philosophers that celebrate the many, they would find much to admire in how *The Walking Dead* is pushing us towards multiplicity.

17
What if Our Reality Is One Big Hallucination?

ROBERT ARP

The Walking Dead's third season has Rick experiencing haunting hallucinations of his dead wife, Lori. He hears her voice for the first time in 3.6 "Hounded," sees her for the first time on a catwalk of the prison in 3.9 "The Suicide Kings," and again not only sees her in her wedding dress standing over her own grave, but also actually is touched by her and follows her around the outskirts of the prison in 3.10 "Home."

Seeing Things

Deriving from the Latin *hallucinates* meaning "deceive," "wander in the mind," "ramble in thought," or "dream." The US National Institutes of Health sponsors a website called MedlinePlus, and there *hallucination* is defined as "a sensation of something while awake that appears to be real, but instead has been created by the mind." Common hallucinations include:

- Hearing sounds such as music, footsteps, or voices when no one has spoken—which are the most common type of hallucination, actually—as when Rick hears the voices of Amy, Jim, Jacqui, and Lori on the phone in "Hounded." Oftentimes, the voices are critical, but also can be complimentary or even command the person to do something, as when criminals plead insanity and claim, "I was hearing voices that told me to commit the crime."

- Seeing objects, people, or other things that aren't really there, as when Rick has his numerous visions of Lori, or when Michonne confesses to Rick that she, too, has seen things that aren't there, such as her boyfriend Mike when he was alive.

- Feeling bodily sensations, as when Rick thinks that Lori is touching him on the face or kisses her in "Home."

Dude, What Did I Just Take?

There are many causes of hallucinations. Dementia, psychiatric disorders, and drugs like LSD, peyote, PCP, and opioids can cause hallucinations as well. My wife is a survivor of cancer of the esophagus—you *definitely* don't want that kind of cancer—and had to have her esophagus removed back in 2000. After the surgery, they gave her lots of morphine (an opioid), and that caused her to hallucinate and think she was having visitors in her hospital room when there weren't any. I left to grab lunch one day, and when I came back she asked me to come over to the bed so she could touch me: "I want to make sure it's really you standing there," she said, telling me that she thought friends had just come to visit when they hadn't, and we immediately notified the nurse so she could lower my wife's morphine dosage.

The Cause of Rick's Hallucinations

Post-traumatic stress and psychotic depression can cause hallucinations, too. MedlinePlus notes: "In some cases, hallucinations may be normal. For example, hearing the voice of, or briefly seeing, a loved one who has recently died can be a part of the grieving process." That's exactly what happened to Rick.

In the spring of 2013 there was a live event recorded for the Paley Center for Media that was hosted by Chris Hardwick and featured interviews several actors on the show, including Andrew Lincoln (Rick Grimes). Several topics were discussed, including whether Rick is going crazy from his hallucinations. In preparation for the episodes where he has to play someone seeing things, Lincoln says that he started doing some research into folks who have hallucinated after the loss of a loved one:

"When people lose someone they love, the brain plays tricks with them, placing that person they lost in the spaces where they used to be." Maybe Rick tries to keep Lori present because the notion of losing her completely may be too upsetting or frightening to him. He wasn't prepared for her sudden death (but who is?), and he may find the images to be comforting or soothing. In the graphic novel, we see Rick maintain phone "conversations" with Lori for a much longer time, perhaps even knowing that her voice is a product of his own mind.

Real Hallucinations

How do we know when someone is having a hallucination such that we can distinguish a perception with no external stimulus (the hallucinogenic perception) from one with an external stimulus? One way is from the first-person perspective or point of view of the person who has the hallucination. Rick himself seems to be able to distinguish a perception that's all in his mind from one that actually corresponds to something out there in the world. This itself requires that Rick not only 1. understands that his mind is powerful enough to fabricate or make up perceptions, as one does when fantasizing or daydreaming, but also that he 2. has numerous perceptions that regularly match up with reality in a coherent fashion, which he obviously does.

When Rick lops a walker's head off with a machete, the head and body don't magically reattach themselves—the head falls to the ground, the body falls to the ground, and the two parts remain motionless. And Rick experiences other events taking place around him that regularly follow laws of cause and effect and other natural (and logical) laws in *The Walking Dead* universe, one of these being that when someone's brain is destroyed—whether it be a human or a walker—they cease to move and are "gone" altogether.

So, when something irregular happens like hearing Lori's voice or seeing her walking around when she shouldn't be doing those things, Rick himself can recognize the dissonance, incongruity, and "This ain't supposed to happen out there in the world" aspect of these experiences and chalk them up as them as products of his own powerful mind (hallucinations) which can fabricate reality at times. In "Home" Rick acknowledges the possibility that he's hallucinating, and that if the voices and images of Lori are all in his head, then he must be crazy. In 3.6 "Hounded" Rick realizes that the phone was never connected when he was speaking to Lori and, again, this incongruity gets him to thinking that he may be hallucinating.

Another way to know when someone is hallucinating is from the third-person perspective or point of view of the people who are observing the person having the hallucination. This is the obvious way that psychologists, scientists, doctors have defined and described hallucinating, by observing people having them over and over and over again. In 3.10 "Home" Michonne watches Rick interacting with a non-existent Lori outside the fence, and all she can see is Rick stroking the air in front of his face. We the viewers see this, too, and this is the kind of third-person perspective we use to verify the fact that Rick is hallucinating. Since a third party doesn't confirm the observation made by that person, the person's observation is suspect. In fact, the greater the number of third parties who can verify that the external stimulus is really there, the greater the confidence someone can have in the reliability of their own perceptions.

In the episode 3.12 "Clear" Rick seems to be able to do a bit of first-person and third-person reflection on his own hallucinations when he encounters Morgan, someone we haven't seen since the first episode. Morgan is alone and has created a bunker of sorts surrounded by armaments and booby traps. He's protected his territory but also seems to have "barricaded" himself in this isolated, desperate world. He doesn't recognize Rick, has scribbled incomprehensible notes to himself on the walls with chalk, and mutters incoherently about being "clear." Rick sees how Morgan is unraveling by living this solitary existence, and you get the sense that Rick appreciates the value of social interaction not only for emotional stability, but also for the third-person perspective that can check whether he or anyone else is hallucinating or not, given the hell on earth people are experiencing in this post-zombie-apocalyptic world. In fact, in the Paley Center for Media interview I mentioned above, Robert Kirkman creator of the comic series and one of the executive producer of the show, confirms that in this episode, seeing Morgan may set Rick on the path to psychological healing.

My Own Trip

Although I've never tripped, been stoned, wasted, or used any illicit drugs ever (I swear!), I had a bizarre reaction to an opioid painkiller called Demerol (pethidine) when I was in the hospital once, and I thought someone had stacked pebbles on the bedside stand next to me that I had to eat. From my hallucinogenic perspective, the pebbles were *there*, waiting to be eaten. I called the nurse in to ask her if she saw the pebbles, too, and after laughing a bit, she told me I was "seeing things" that weren't there, probably from the painkiller. It was actually Jello on my bedside stand!

Rick's hallucinations, as well as my wife's and my own, get me to thinking about the difference between what I perceive to be the case and what really is the case concerning myself, the world around me, and reality in general. But what makes up a person's "reality?" Is reality just my own collection of perceptions and ideas only, or is there a world outside of me? Also, if there is my world of perceptions and a world outside of me, then how, if at all, can I get beyond these perceptions to know if they match up, or correspond with, reality? Further, assuming that there's a reality beyond my perceptions, I want to be secure in my knowledge of that reality. I want to *know that* my perception of a pebble is in fact a pebble, or that my experience of Jello *really is* Jello. And my wife, Rick, and others want to know if the people around them are really there or not.

The Three P's

It seems obvious that other people, prisons, shotguns, cities, TV shows, TV stations, even mathematical relations like the Pythagorean theorem, exist "out there" beyond our perceptions of them. Walkers are fictions of the mind, but people dressed up to look like them in *The Walking Dead* are real, as are the scripts written about them by the writers of the show. Most of us take it for granted that there's a world of things existing outside of our minds, regardless of whether we're perceiving them or not. Also, we think that these things would continue to exist whether or not they were perceived by us, even if we ceased to exist.

However, take a moment to think about what you are aware of when you perceive other people, prisons, shotguns, and the like. For example, right now I am sitting at my computer typing this chapter in a Starbucks. I see the computer screen in front of me with these words on it, I smell coffee, I hear the music and the chatter of others, I feel the tips of my fingers strike the keys of the keypad, and the hardwood floor under my feet. And I can close my eyes and form an image or idea of the screen, the words, keypad, and floor. Notice that we can talk about three different types of things in this example:

1. **The Perceiver**: there is me, the *perceiver* who has the perceptions and ideas.

2. **The Perception**: there are *my perceptions* of the screen, words, keypad, and floor that take the forms of the sensations of sight, sound, and feeling, as well as images, ideas, and thoughts.

3. **The Perceived**: there are the *external objects of my perception*, the actual computer and keypad sitting on the table in front of me, the Starbucks windows, the hardwood floor.

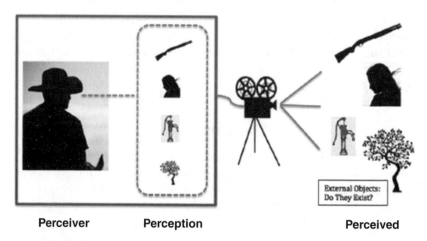

| Perceiver | Perception | Perceived |

FIGURE 1: Rick Grimes the Perceiver, His Perceptions, and His Perceived World

Look at Figure 1. There is Rick Grimes, who is the perceiver. There are his perceptions, which include his sensations, thoughts, and ideas about shotguns, people, water pumps, trees, and other things. Finally, there are the external objects of his perceptions, which include *actual* shotguns, people, water pumps, trees, and other things out there in the world to which his perceptions refer or which they are supposed to represent. This is a common-sense picture of how almost everyone in the world thinks about these things, including scientists and religious folks.

But now, certain questions arise given that there is me, my perceptions, and the external objects of my perception. Can I really get beyond my own perceptions so as to have access to the screen, keypad, floor, Starbucks, and people *themselves* as they really are? Maybe all that I can perceive are my own perceptions? How can I be sure that the external objects of my perception are really there, or that how they present themselves to me in my perceptions match up with or correspond with how they really are? After all, I can't step outside of my own perceptions and look at myself in relationship to external objects to see if, in fact, my perceptions correspond with these external objects. Am I "locked inside" of my own world of sense perceptions? If so, how do I know that there is even any world out there beyond my perceptions?

An Empty World

These questions and their surrounding issues have caused some thinkers to hold philosophical positions known as *epistemological idealism* and *metaphysical antirealism*. An epistemological idealist thinks that our perceptions or ideas (thus, *idea*lism) are the only source of knowledge. (I'm talking about *epistemological* idealism, which has nothing to do with the common understanding of 'idealism' as referring to people committed to ideals.) Epistemological idealism can have the consequence that I can never tell if my perceptions correspond with the external objects of my perception, as if the perceiver is forever barred from access to the objects of perception.

A metaphysical antirealist (of the hard-core variety) thinks that there is no real world outside of our perceptions or ideas. Idealism and antirealism can be made consistent with one another, and so fit together nicely. "After all," reasons the idealist, "all I can ever know are my own perceptions of things as they appear to me." In other words, my own perceptions make up or constitute *all of what I can know*. And "after all," reasons the antirealist, "if all I can ever know are my own perceptions of things as they appear to me, and I can't get outside of myself to see if my perceptions match up with any reality, then my perceptions must be the *sum total* of my reality." In other words, my own perceptions make up or constitute *all of reality*.

Let's Get Real

Now, epistemological idealism and metaphysical antirealism can be contrasted with *epistemological realism* and *metaphysical realism*. According to an epistemological realist, even though a person has perceptions there must be a world outside that our perceptions represent because, otherwise, we wouldn't have certain perceptions in the first place. Despite the fact that the mind can be very creative in making up all kinds of ideas and thoughts in imagination and prose, there seem to be certain perceptions and ideas that couldn't have been generated by the perceiver. In other words, there must be some things "out there" that directly cause the representation of our perceptions "in here."

For example, we can see how someone like Robert Kirkman, Tony Moore, and Charlie Adlard can imagine all kinds of walkers and other imagined characters in *The Walking Dead* stories. People have been speaking about, then writing about, fantastic beings and worlds for as long as they have been able to tell stories. However, how can the mind generate the idea of a fossilized fern, or the Pythagorean theorem solely from its repertoire of perceptions and ideas? These things seem to have been *discoveries*, not invented constructions of the mind. It's hard to imagine that these things—although they are understood, articulated, and explained by minds—were invented *solely* by minds.

This is where epistemological realism and metaphysical realism fit together nicely. If you believe that there's a world of things "out there" that really do exist and would continue to exist whether or not you or anyone perceive them, then you are a metaphysical realist. Consider that according to the theory of evolution, there was a time when human beings, complete with perceptions, didn't exist. "Are we to think," asks the realist, "that prior to the evolution of the human mind, there was nothing occurring out there in the world?" What are we to make of the fossilized fern? Was there no evolution occurring prior to our perceiving or thinking about the fern or any other fossil? This seems absurd, according to the realist. Didn't the fern exist and fossilize at some point prior to the existence of human minds and their perceptions? And wouldn't the fern still have existed and still have fossilized, even if humans with minds to perceive things never existed?

Dead Trees Falling

Also, consider this *Walking Dead* twist on an old proverbial question: "If a dead tree falls over in a forest, and no one is around to hear the dead tree fall—including Merle and Daryl—does it make a sound?" Sound requires a thing *to make* a noise as well as a thing *to hear* the noise. According to a realist, the tree's crashing to the ground of the forest would produce sound waves whether there was anyone (like Merle or Daryl) or any other observer, perhaps a walker, around to perceive or pick up the sound waves, or not. From one point of view, the tree hitting the ground would not make a sound if no one or no thing with the capacity to hear were present. But the dead tree hitting the ground still would produce sound waves that could be picked up by a person or thing with a capacity for hearing sounds. On the other hand, the antirealist would have us believe that there wouldn't even be sound waves that are produced from the crashing of the tree if there were no perceivers in existence.

Further, realists believe that Pythagoras *discovered* and *formulated* the theorem that $a^2 + b^2 = c^2$ for a right triangle, rather than *wholly invented* it. They also believe that the theorem would be what it is and exist as what it is regardless of whether it was ever known by any mind. In fact, the realist believes that right now, out there in reality, there are all kinds of things waiting to be discovered by the human mind and its perceptions. "The solar system that is twenty million light years from ours in the universe does exist," claims the realist— we just haven't been able to discover it, and we may never be able to. Despite the fact that the mind can be quite creative in its imaginations, and despite the fact that there can be many different ways of perceiving, there is still some reality out there beyond the mind and its perceptions. To think that "reality" is constituted by the mind and its perceptions, as the antirealist does, seems false, according to the realist.

Mistakes Do Happen

Most people are epistemological and metaphysical realists. Despite the fact that the mind is full of all kinds of perceptions that could be categorized as having been imagined, we seem to take it for granted that our perceptions do, at times, accurately represent external objects. The same goes for the characters in *The Walking Dead*. *That* the stories in *The Walking Dead* contain instances of hallucinations, as well as delusions, illusions, and dream sequences indicate that the characters in the show, as well as the writers of the show, advocate straightforward epistemological and metaphysical realism.

While trying to survive in their post-zombie-apocalyptic world, Rick and others have moments when they can be mistaken about whether their perceptions represent external objects in their world accurately, but they believe that their perceptions still can accurately represent external objects (insofar as there really are denizens and objects of *The Walking Dead* universe). In fact, it's arguable that because Rick, Michonne, and others are aware of, and concerned with, the confusion, hallucinations, and crazy logic they perceive in themselves and others indicates that they think there is an accurate representation to be found in external objects. The confusion, hallucinations, and crazy logic arise from a discrepancy in the relationship between their perceptions and the external objects of their perception existing in *The Walking Dead* world.

Now, we have to be careful here. I am maintaining that Rick and others *think* or *believe* that there's a real world out there to be discovered, and they think that it can be accurately represented in their perceptions. Whether there is, in fact, an actual world out there is another question. Obviously, *The Walking Dead* universe is not real! But it seems that folks in that universe, like most of us, take it for granted and just assume that there's a real world beyond our perceptions, combining their epistemological realism with their metaphysical realism. It seems that they think that it's possible for perceptions to represent external objects of perception accurately, and this is so because they believe that there is, in fact, a real world of external objects that exists whether perceived or not. When Rick is deceived by a person or thing presenting him or her or itself as someone/something other than who/what they are, they believe there is some real person or thing, out there, doing the deceiving.

In the history of Western philosophy George Berkeley seriously entertains the idea that we may be trapped inside of our perceptual reality, with no access to the external world.

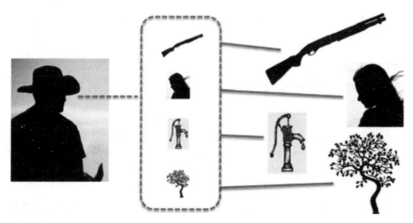

FIGURE 2: Rick Grimes Stuck in His Own Mind

Berkeley's view is illustrated in Figure 2. Think of Rick as being locked inside the room of his own mind, kind of like someone trapped inside of a movie theater. Now imagine that there's a movie screen inside the theater, representing his or anyone's perceptions, that's connected to a movie camera on the outside of the theater that views the outside world. The camera represents a person's five senses. A perceiver, like Rick, only has access to his own perceptions on the movie screen of his mind. He could never get outside of the room of his own mind to see if his perceptions match up with some external world, let alone whether such a world even exists!

Now it may seem absurd that nothing exists outside of your mind since obviously something is causing the perceptions on the movie screen. But consider this: you can never be one hundred percent sure that what your experiencing "out there" matches up with what's "in here" which, if you think long enough about it, can be quite frustrating and freaky, too. You can't ask someone else to verify things for you because they're outside of you, too, so you wouldn't know if what they're saying to you is exactly what you're hearing. Told you it was frustrating and freaky!

Now I'm Gonna Blow Your Friggin' Mind

But it gets worse. You would think that *something* exists out-side of your mind that causes your perceptions, even if you don't know what the heck they are exactly. However, think about someone who hallucinates again. The mind is such a powerful thing that it can make up all kinds of things that aren't there, right? Well, what if reality for you is one big hal-lucination? Again, you can't ask someone else if you're halluci-nating because *they* could just be another one of your hallucinations, in which case you'd be simply fooling yourself into thinking that there was something "out there" when there wasn't.

I said I was gonna blow your friggin' mind, but actually there's no way for you to tell if it's really me blowing your mind—it may just be *you* blowing *your own* mind because I may be just a figment of your own mind! Recall the hard-core metaphysical antirealist who thinks that there's no real world outside of our perceptions or ideas. There is much in common with this philosophical view and the belief that reality for you is one big 'ole hallucination.

There isn't space here to get into how philosophers and other thinkers have tried to show that reality is or isn't one big hallucination, but people doing work in epistemology and something called *global skepticism* are concerned with this stuff. However, I'll leave you with this final thought. Even if it were true that reality is one big hallucination for us all, we sure do seem to act as if it's not. I'm not willing to walk off a cliff to test whether I'm merely *hallucinating* that my body goes splat on the ground below, are you?

WALKER BITE

Are You Being Saved?

MELISSA VOSEN CALLENS

In 5.4 "Slabtown," viewers finally find out what happens to Beth after she's separated from Daryl in Season Four.

Beth wakes up in a bright, clean hospital room at Grady Memorial Hospital in post-apocalyptic Atlanta, Georgia, and for a brief moment, it appears as though she is safe. As the episode unfolds, however, viewers learn that this is far from the case. The people in charge of the hospital are forcing patients to stay against their will in order to pay off their accumulated medical expenses. After their care, patients, like Beth, are physically fine, but financially and emotionally crippled, much like patients in the real world who have suffered a life-threatening accident or illness and the subsequent medical debt that follows.

Noah, for example, has been a patient at Grady Memorial for over a year; after his physical injuries healed, he was forced to work in the laundry room, cleaning scrubs and pressing police officers' uniforms. Even after a year, Noah, wanting desperately to leave, is still nowhere near paying off his insurmountable medical debt, in addition to his accumulating room and board charges. The healthcare system in which Noah is entrenched has strong parallels to the American healthcare system.

Unfortunately for Noah, and sadly, for many in the real world, it is a continuous cycle of debt. In one exchange between Beth and Lieutenant Lerner, the woman in charge of Grady Hospital's operations, Beth explains that she does not want much to eat because she wants to pay off her debt faster.

Lerner, however, argues that she needs to eat because if she does not eat, she won't be strong enough to work and might even need more care. Throughout the episode, Beth is frequently told she should be thankful she was rescued and in a secure facility. At one point, Beth exhaustedly proclaims, "I never asked for your help." Lt. Lerner simply replies, "No, but you needed it."

Lerner, however, is right. Most of us in an emergency, do not ask for help. Our family and friends do. In some cases, strangers do. When an ambulance is called, where one is taken, and the care provided, is most often done without any discussion of price. Unlike any other service we purchase, we rarely know what medical services cost before we use them, particularly the life-saving ones. We're merely billed after treatment, and while we may be happy to be alive, we are likely sick with debt. While most of us believe our lives are priceless, in reality, every life-saving measure has a price tag. In many cases, multiple price tags per measure.

The American healthcare system has been criticized for these inflated costs, resulting in mounds of patient debt and thus basically enslaving patients to the system. It's a vicious cycle of care and debt, as patients are forced to go back to the same facilities that bankrupt or nearly-bankrupt them in order to obtain much needed care, and in some cases, life-saving care. Many continue to work, well beyond retirement, in order to pay off medical bills or pay rising insurance premiums (much in the way Noah is forced to continue to work). To combat rising costs and the numbers of uninsured people in the United States, the Affordable Care Act, was passed. Just as our system needed some type of medical reform, the healthcare system, after the apocalyptic-collapse of society, needed reform in *The Walking Dead*. Enter Lt. Lerner.

In this episode, Dr. Edwards is the only actual doctor left. Most times, his decisions regarding patient care are not his, but rather Lerner's. Edwards explains to Beth that initially his group was unable to help survivors because of the lack of resources, but after scavenging and establishing their little community, they now are able to help some. He explains that they can't guarantee free care or help everyone who needs it. Because of their limited resources and their own growing needs, they decided that after helping people, they would require them to work off their debt to make the reform viable.

This constant evaluation and revaluation of resources seems to indirectly pose the question, "What is someone's life worth?" When initially proposed, one criticism of the Affordable Care Act was that some bureaucrats ("death panels") would somehow limit resources, choosing whom to save and whom to deny access to care. Despite the fact that medical professionals denied there would be any death panels, the fear still remains for some. In Lerner's system, a further enslaving system rather than a freeing one, she is the bureaucrat, the non-medical professional who makes medical decisions.

Edwards and Lerner, at least initially, believe their system is for the greater good. Lerner repeatedly tells Beth, "Try to look at the good we're doing." She believes she's keeping the community safe until all returns to normal. Unfortunately for Beth, Noah, and the others, her system looks very similar to the one we are currently trying to escape—one in which people are physically saved, but emotionally and financially exploited. This episode asks again and again, "Are we being saved in order to be enslaved?

18
Gruesome Walkers

WAYNE YUEN

Everyone knows that walkers are a little gruesome. From bicycle girl in the first episode of the series, to the "skin off his back" walker which attacks Tara outside of Alexandria (5.12 "Remember"), part of the fun is that the walkers are gross! But you probably didn't know that the walkers are gruesome in a completely different way as well. The walkers represent a challenge, not only to our survivors, but to knowledge itself, and it all goes back to the Scottish philosopher David Hume.

David Hume was a skeptic when it came to knowledge. Since Plato, philosophers have believed that there are three conditions that need to be met in order to have knowledge. The first condition is that we need to believe it. It doesn't make much sense to say that someone knows something, but doesn't believe it. Carol might have a crush on Daryl (my wife tells me that everyone has a crush on Daryl). But Daryl wouldn't have knowledge of this crush if he didn't believe that Carol liked him. So, this first condition, believing something, is pretty important to saying that you *know* something.

However, there are lots of things that we believe that we wouldn't call knowledge. If I believed that Carol and Daryl *are* in a romantic relationship, I wouldn't have knowledge because it isn't true. As much fun as it would be to imagine a "Darol" or "Caryl" relationship it just isn't true. This relationship is doomed to failure simply because their names don't make a good mash-up. Its phonetically always just one of their names! So the second condition that needs to be met is that the belief we have needs to be true.

Defining what "true" is turns out to be pretty difficult, but for simplicity let's just say that something is true so long as it corresponds to some state of affairs in the world. We might have to accept that Carol and Daryl don't exist in our world, but do exist in *The Walking Dead* worlds. We'll just be a little loose here by what we mean by 'world'. Sometimes we're talking only about the real world, sometimes we're talking about the TV world of *The Walking Dead*, oftentimes we're talking about both worlds.

True belief isn't quite enough for knowledge, though. When the group takes shelter from a storm in a barn (5.10 "Them") they don't *know* that it will be a safe place for them to take shelter in. It turns out that it was, in fact, a safe place to take shelter in. So even if they believed that it was a safe place and that it turned out to be true that it was a safe place, they didn't *know* it was a safe place. What is missing from the definition of knowledge is justification, some good reasons for believing that the belief we hold is true, otherwise it would turn out that guesses or predictions would count as knowledge. This is the third condition that needs to be met in order for someone to have knowledge. David Hume is a skeptic because he doesn't believe that we can ever get adequate justification for something to be knowledge.

Hume believed that there was a problem in all of our justifications for knowledge; a problem that has been labeled the problem of induction. In its most simple form, the problem states that our generalized or universal beliefs can't be justified from our past experiences. I'd like to believe that the dead cannot rise and start attacking us. I believe this, in part, because I've never seen it happen, nor have heard of anything like that happening in the past. Does this give *justification* for believing that walkers will never come? This is the position that Rick and all of our survivors in *The Walking Dead* are in, pre-apocalypse, but as it turns out for them they were wrong. Hume argues that the reason this is not sufficient justification for knowledge is because the idea that the past is some kind of reliable guide to future events rests on another principle: That the universe is uniform in its behavior in all places and all times. That the way the universe behaves here now and in the past, is going to be how it will behave in the future. Hume calls this the principle of uniformity of nature.

If we know that the principle of uniformity of nature is true, then we could in fact be justified in making universal, or predictive statements about the world. The past gives me good justification for how things will be everywhere, or in the future. But here is where Hume finds a problem, it doesn't seem like we can in fact justify uniformity of nature. The principle of uniformity of nature is itself a kind of knowledge, which needs to satisfy the conditions of knowledge as well. We all want to believe the principle of uniformity of nature, and it might even be true. But do we have good reasons to believe it? Hume points out that we can't justify the principle of uniformity of nature like we could justify math, with pure logic, since it's a fact about the world. I couldn't prove facts about the world with logic any more than I can prove that my shirt is green with pure logic. Facts about the world can only be proven by some kind of observation or experience of the world.

So all we need to do is use an observation about the world, to justify that the world is uniform in all times and places. All of my observations reinforce this idea that the world is uniform, so is this really a problem? Well, in fact yes. Remember what we were using the principle of uniformity of nature to justify? We were using it to justify that our observations of the past can be generalized about the world, or have predictive powers about how the world will be.

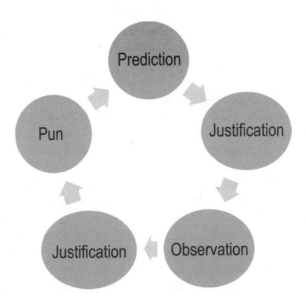

So let's follow this chain of reasoning. I want to justify my predictive statements about the world. I'm going to use observations to justify them. But the problem of induction prevents me from doing that unless I know that the principle of uniformity of nature (PUN in the diagram) is true. But it needs justification, and the principle is essentially a prediction about the universe. This will be justified through my observations, which is precisely what justifies my predictive statements about the world . . . which is also undermined by the problem of induction. There is no escaping this circular reasoning, we can't seem to justify our generalizations about the world or predictive statements about the future. Since we can't get justification, we're only left with "true belief" which we've already seen isn't knowledge. This is why Hume is a skeptic.

Woodbury, Terminus, Grady Memorial Hospital . . . Lesson learned?

In the second half of Season Five, our survivors meet Aaron and Eric who lead them to a seemingly safe place: Alexandria. But Rick is suspicious of Aaron and Alexandria, with good reason. Rick's experiences at Woodbury, Terminus, and what he knows of what happened at Grady, leads him to believe that people who have built a small community often have some sinister or exploitive motives when it comes to outsiders. However, this is the problem of induction all over again. Rick is using his past experiences to justify that citizens of Alexandria's motives must also be exploitive or sinister as well. He likes Alexandria, but isn't comfortable there. "We'll just take this place," he says coldly in 5.12 "Remember" because he remembers all too well what has happened to him and his extended family in the past. Is Hume saying that Rick is making a mistake here? Certainly, Michonne who advocates that they trust Aaron and give Alexandria a shot thinks that he is.

It turns out that Hume doesn't think it's a mistake that Rick is making here. Hume thinks that human beings are psychologically built so that they *must* use induction. We just intuitively find that using our past experiences to justify our generalizations about the world and predictive statements about the future to be plausible. We can't help it! So Hume is a philosophical skeptic, but practically or psychologically, we'll keep believing that we know things even if we're not justified in believing things. Hume is acknowledging that humans simply don't make decisions or live their lives in accordance with what is perfectly rational; we can't live in a perfectly rational way. He famously writes in his *Enquiry concerning Human Understanding*, "Be a philosopher; but, amidst all your philosophy, be still a man." Rick can't fight his impulse not to trust Alexandria or Deanna because of his past experiences. It's a really *useful* way of reasoning, even if it isn't *knowledge* that he's operating on.

Despite the fact that it's really useful to believe this, the problem of induction will lead us to make mistakes about what we take to be true. We live in the real world and we'd like to believe that we don't have to ever worry about walkers overrunning civilization. This might in fact really be a useful thing to believe, but it doesn't mean that it's true. Michonne might be a little too optimistic about Alexandria and we might be a little too optimistic in our belief about the zombie apocalypse.

Another philosopher, Bertrand Russell, expressed the problem of induction in a way that might be relevant to us when considering the zombie apocalypse. Imagine that you're a chicken. Every day, a man in overalls, carrying a bucket, brings you food at about the same time. Day after day, this happens for your entire life. You start to get excited when you see the man. You might run up and greet the man, hoping to get a little more food than the other chickens. You do this because you've formed the belief that whenever you see the man in the overalls with the bucket, you will be fed. This belief has been true in the past and that is justification enough for you to believe it. Or maybe our chicken brain can't help but believe it, like Hume suggests.

So you run towards the man in the overalls with the bucket to get that extra bit of food. But today the man bends down, grabs you by the neck and with a swift twist snaps your neck. Your body goes limp and you wonder, "What happened?!" Similarly, tomorrow morning, when you wake up and get out of bed, you might expect that when you open the door to your home, you'll find your neighbors getting ready to commute to work, people jogging or walking their dogs, and children or young adults walking off to school. Instead you find a walker, who sinks its teeth into your neck. The simple *possibility* of walkers forces us to rethink what we think we know about tomorrow, much like how the possibility of what the farmer could do to the chicken should make her rethink about what will happen to her when she sees him next.

What Color Was That Walker?

Hume's psychological explanation of how we use induction the way we do might work well in most cases, but strangely, we're not always compelled by past events to form generalizations. I'm much more likely to believe that braining a walker will make it stop attacking me, after seeing it succeed several times, than to believe that kitchens with "fredag" signs in them also contain large cans of chocolate pudding, even if I saw several kitchens with "fredag" signs and chocolate pudding in those kitchens. If psychology is driving us to form generalizations, we should be forming generalizations here. Sometimes we do, and call them superstitions, other times we simply fail to do so. Hume's psychological model isn't quite enough to explain it all.

Nelson Goodman introduces a variation on the problem of induction that puts knowledge that isn't generalized or predictive into doubt as well. Goodman imagines that when I'm looking at my green shirt, that I could in fact be making a mistake in calling it a green shirt. I believe it to be green right now and in fact it is green right now. This appears to be true belief, that is justified by immediate sense experience, but Goodman imagines that in fact it is not true that the color of the shirt is green, even if it is green *right now*. The color I'm looking at is the color "grue." Goodman imagines the color grue to be a color that appears to be green right now, but at some moment in time in the future the green shirt will instantaneously become blue. Grue colored objects would be identical to green objects today, but say at the stroke of midnight Pacific Time on March 3rd 2050 all grue colored objects would transform to be blue. There would still be green objects (as opposed to grue objects), but telling them apart from grue objects before this date and time would be impossible. The question is, would our experiences, current or past, ever give us justification for saying that some object that I'm looking at is green or grue?

Goodman's grue-colored object forces us to re-evaluate why we might make a generalization in the case of braining a walker and not in the case of kitchens with chocolate pudding. In fact, *The Walking Dead* is based around an event almost identical to the grue case. For (arguably) the entire history of man, dead humans did not stand up and attack the living. Then one day, Rick Grimes wakes up from a stay at the hospital and the world is just different . . . more *grue*some. Let's try to be precise here: grue colored objects were always grue colored objects; we just needed to wait around long enough to see them change. It could be the case that dead humans were always going to just one day get up, by the laws of nature, we just haven't quite gotten to that point in time yet. This isn't entirely implausible. Take cicadas as an example. Some cicadas have an incredibly long life cycle of seventeen years where they live underground for most of it. Now perhaps you've lived sixteen entire years in an area and you've never seen a cicada. Does this experience give you justification to believe that cicadas don't live in this area? Could it be that walkers simply have an incredibly long life cycle as well? Trying to comfort ourselves by saying that walkers aren't real in *our* world isn't even enough to undermine the argument, because we don't know if they are just waiting for the right time like the cicadas.

The problem of induction also has serious ramifications for science. So far, the only real scientist that we've met is Dr. Jenner. Dr. Jenner had multiple "test subjects" that he conducted experiments on to try to uncover the nature of why the dead were walking. As a good scientist, I imagine that Dr. Jenner would be formulating a hypothesis to explain why the dead were walking, create an experiment to test the hypothesis, make observations from the experiment and use these observations to help confirm or disprove his hypothesis. But if the problem of induction is introduced into this process, then we can't use the experiment to produce knowledge. The experiment could be repeated nineteen times, with the same result, but that wouldn't mean that the next time we did the experiment we should expect the same result. In some sense, the problem of induction turns everything into a gamble. If I were to play roulette one hundred times and bet on 24 every time, and observed a particular result, that I lost every time, would that justify the belief that the ball never lands on 24? If the problem of induction is correct, then it would appear that science is completely undermined in its project to understand the world.

Popper Goes Philosophy

Many scientists, including some very notable ones, have stated that philosophy is a waste of time, dead, inconsequential, unimportant, and so forth. I'm looking at you Stephen Hawking. I've also got my eye on you Neil deGrasse Tyson. I'll use Carl's eye to maintain vigilance on Richard Feynman too.

Often they accuse philosophers of not understanding the problems that they're dealing with, but quite the contrary, philosophers really are very much aware of what scientists are doing. Most philosophers support and defend scientists and the work that they are doing. So of course philosophers are going to want to save science from huge problems like the problem of induction. Karl Popper most notably tries to defend science by reframing science. Most people would characterize science the way I described Dr. Jenner doing it, by describing the scientific method being utilized to discoverer or justify truth. But this characterization of science is susceptible to the problem of induction. If you consider each day you live as an experiment testing your hypotheses about the world, then all of your conclusions about the world are put into doubt by the problem of induction. To dodge this problem Popper argues that what science is doing is looking to *disprove* theories, rather than to prove them.

The problem of induction seems to undermine justification of knowledge; I can't ever *know* anything with certainty. Popper proposes that instead of thinking of science as an endeavor to know something, science is really a way of examining the many theories and eliminating most of them from consideration.

To see what Popper's getting at, let's imagine that Jenner is conducting his experiments and he has a hypothesis that a bacterial infection is causing the dead to walk. He conducts an experiment where he bathes a dead body in antibiotics and waits. In a few minutes the body reanimates. So we can eliminate bacteria being the cause of the dead walking. Eighteen hypotheses later, Jenner has the idea that it's a viral agent that is causing the dead to walk. He administers a universal antiviral drug (of course the CDC has one of those!) and the dead doesn't walk!

So, has Jenner proved that the dead walk because of a virus? According to Popper, no! What Jenner has done is simply failed to eliminate this theory from consideration, while some alternative theories have been eliminated. As science does the business of science, it will continue to eliminate theories from consideration until it is left with a set of theories that are not eliminated. These may or may not be true, but at least they haven't been shown to be false.

Part of the reason why the problem of induction is so powerful is because it is incredibly hard to prove a universal truth. Math and pure logic might be able to make universal truths, but how would I justify a universal truth like "All walkers have brains"? The simple, albeit impractical, answer would be to examine all the walkers that are in the world. Since this is so impractical, it's not something that can ever be proved or justified. Popper's reformulation of science side-steps this problem. I can have a theory that states that "all walkers have brains" and continually test this theory by cutting open walker after walker, to see if they have brains, in an attempt to falsify the theory.

We see something like this at the end of Season Two. Rick and the group are under the impression that people turn into walkers because they are either bitten or scratched by a walker, spreading some sort of infection that turns them. Rick is told by Jenner, at the end of Season One, that this isn't true. They are all infected already and they will all inevitably turn. Rick doesn't share this with the group, because he isn't sure that it's true. Rick has two theories now, the "walkers make walkers" theory and the "everyone makes walkers" theory. All of his observations so far fail to eliminate either theory from contention, until he kills Shane with a knife to the heart. When Shane reanimates after Rick breaks his heart (All's fair in love and war, right?), Rick's forced to eliminate the "walkers make walkers" theory. Does this mean that the "everyone makes walkers" theory is the right theory? We don't have any justification for it, so we can't say that we *know* it.

Instead of *justification* for a theory, Popper says that theories can be *corroborated*. Corroborated theories have been tested and have not been falsified. The more corroborated a theory, the higher the probability of the truth of the theory, but we would never know with certainty. In light of the problem of induction, this is the best that science can hope to achieve.

Popper was particularly concerned with what people were accepting as science. Astrology, psychic phenomenon, paranormal research, and the like, were not scientific, even if they were being studied with methodology that looked scientific on the surface. Popper was particularly concerned with Freudian psychology, which primarily revolved around the idea that our behaviors were the result of largely unconscious psycho-sexual desires or beliefs. Popper wanted to reject Freudian psychology as science because it made no claims that could in principle be proved false. A Freudian psychoanalyst would simply tell a compelling story that supported what the psychoanalyst believed, and since we could never really access the unconscious to prove or disprove what the psychoanalyst believed, we could never *in principle* test whether the theory was false. Falsifiability is the metric between science and *not*-science for Popper.

Where does this leave us? Rick is justified, to some extent, that they should exercise caution when entering Alexandria, but he can't be certain that Alexandria is dangerous. Certainty doesn't come easy after the apocalypse. On the other hand, we need to be a little more cautious about what we think we know about the future, or even the present. We might be worrying about global warming now, but it just could be that walkers are around the corner instead. Are walkers probable? No, since they aren't a highly corroborated theory, but we certainly can't eliminate them from possibility either. What this teaches us is that we need to be more careful about what we say we *know* because, despite what we *believe*, our *justifications* for the things we say we know always seems to fall short. Stumbling is a *very* bad thing in the apocalypse, even if what we're stumbling over is a belief about what we know.

References

Aquinas, Thomas. *The Summa Theologica*. Translated by the
   Fathers of the English Dominican Province.
   <dhspriory.org/Thomas/summa>.
Aristotle. 1999. *Nicomachean Ethics*. Hackett.
Barnes, Jonathan. 2001. *Aristotle: A Very Short Introduction*. Oxford
   University Press.
Bostrom, Nick. 2003. Are You Living in a Computer Simulation?
   Philosophical Quarterly 53:211.
Bryant, Richard A., et al. 2014. Treating Prolonged Grief Disorder: A
   Randomized Clinical Trial. *JAMA Psychiatry* 71:12.
Chalmers, David J. 2005. The Matrix as Metaphysics. In Grau 2005.
Cohen, Marshall, ed. 1961. *The Philosophy of John Stuart Mill*.
   Random House.
Colebrook, Claire. 2004. *Irony*. Routledge.
Deleuze, Gilles, and Felix Guattari. 1987. *A Thousand Plateaus:
   Capitalism and Schizophrenia*. University of Minnesota Press.
Epicurus. 2014. *Principal Doctrines and Letter to Menoeceus*.
   CreateSpace.
Fogel, Stefanie. 2012. Playing the Hero: Why We Make Good Moral
   Choices in Video Games. *Gamesbeat*.
Gilligan, Carol. 1982. *In a Different Voice: Sex Differences in the
   Expression of Moral Judgment*. Harvard University Press.
Grau, Christopher, ed. 2005. *Philosophers Explore the Matrix*. Oxford
   University Press.
Greene, Richard, and K. Silem Mohammad. 2010. *Zombies,
   Vampires, and Philosophy: New Life for the Undead*. Open Court.
Hare, R.M. 1981. *Moral Thinking: Its Levels, Method, and Point*.
   Oxford University Press.
Kant, Immanuel. 1993. *Grounding for the Metaphysuics of Morals/A
   Supposed Right to Lie because of Philanthropic Concerns*.
   Hackett.

Laplace, Pierre-Simon. 1951. *A Philosophical Essay on Probabilities*. Dover.

Machiavelli, Niccolò. 2011. *The Prince*. Penguin

Maslow, Abraham H. 1943. A Theory of Human Motivation. *Psychological Review 50*.

McMahan, Jeff. 2009. *Killing in War*. Oxford University Press.

John Stuart Mill, 1961. Utilitarianism, in Cohen 1961.

Nietzsche, Friedrich. 1961. *Thus Spoke Zarathustra*. Penguin.

————. 1974. *The Gay Science: With a Prelude in Rhymes and an Appendix of Songs*. Vintage.

————. 2000. *Basic Writings of Nietzsche*. Vintage.

Plantinga, Alvin. 1991. Reason and Belief in God. In Plantinga and Wolterstorff 1991.

Plantinga, Alvin, and Nicholas Wolterstorff, eds. 1991. *Faith and Rationality: Reason and Belief in God*. University of Notre Dame Press.

Rasmusen, Eric. 2006. *Games and Information: An Introduction to Game Theory*. Fourth edition. Wiley-Blackwell.

Regan, Tom. 2004. *The Case for Animal Rights*. Second edition. University of California Press.

Sartre, Jean-Paul. 2000. *Essays in Existentialism*. Citadel.

Slavin, Robert E. 2006. *Educational Psychology: Theory and Practice*. Eighth edition. Allyn and Bacon.

Walzer, Michael. 2015 [1977]. *Just and Unjust Wars: A Moral Argument with Historical Illustrations*. Basic Books.

Yuen, Wayne, ed. 2012. *The Walking Dead and Philosophy: Zombie Apocalypse Now*. Open Court.

We're Friends with the Chick with the Sword and the Kid in the Hat

ROBERT ARP does intelligence work for the US Army. He has authored, co-authored, edited, and co-edited many volumes on both academic and popular philosophy, including *The Devil and Philosophy: The Nature of His Game* (2014), *1001 Ideas that Changed the Way We Think* (2013), and *What's Good on TV? Teaching Ethics through Television* (2011). See his website at: <robertarp.com>. He thinks that Abraham is wise to comment that "Every direction is a question."

DAVE BEISECKER is chair of the department of philosophy at the University of Nevada, Las Vegas. In addition to work on American Philosophy and the Philosophy of Mind and Language, he has contributed chapters to *The Walking Dead and Philosophy: Zombie Apocalypse Now* (2012) and *We Are All Infected: Essays on AMC's Walking Dead and the Fate of the Human* (2014). Living far from the glittering lights of the Las Vegas Strip, he has already selected his companion for when it all falls apart. She is brindled and has a tail.

COLE BOWMAN is a writer and independent scholar living in Portland. She has contributed to other popular philosophy collections, including *Dracula and Philosophy: Dying to Know* and *More Doctor Who and Philosophy: Regeneration Time*. She spends most of her time arguing over fictional universes and carefully selecting members for her apocalypse team.

HEATHER L. CASTRO is a PhD candidate in Art History at Temple University, where she is writing her dissertation on the traumatic grotesque as seen in contemporary art and zombie films. Her MA degree is from the University of Louisville, where she explored an art-based theory of the grotesque. Her research concentrates on examining the connections between fine art and popular culture to further understand the visual expression of social fear and anxiety. She accepts that we can't beat the apocalypse; she's joining the herd.

ANGEL M. COOPER is an adjunct professor at Bridgewater State University. She received her M.A. in philosophy at Kent State University. Her research interests include existentialism, Friedrich Nietzsche, ethics, and philosophy of popular culture. She recently wrote a chapter for *More Doctor Who and Philosophy: Regeneration Time* (2015) and a scholarly paper on video games and virtue ethics. For her birthday, she got herself a katana . . . just in case.

STEVEN B. COWAN teaches philosophy and religion at Lincoln Memorial University in Harrogate, Tennessee. He is co-author of *The Love of Wisdom: A Christian Introduction to Philosophy* (2009), and co-editor and contributor to *Idealism and Christian Philosophy* (2016). His primary interests are in the metaphysics of free will, the nature and extent of divine providence, and Berkeleyan idealism. He lives with his family in a home on top of a high sloping hill in rural Virginia from which he can easily spot any approaching walkers. He is also keenly aware of the likelihood that being a philosopher will be of little use in the zombie apocalypse—which motivates him to do a lot of target practice with his 9mm pistol.

MICHAEL DA SILVA is pursuing a doctorate in law at the University of Toronto. He likes foot long cheese dogs, the San Francisco Giants and Toronto Blue Jays, and professional wrestling (ideally all at once). He worries that the loss of these items would constitute an apocalyptic scenario.

ROBERT A. DELFINO is associate professor of philosophy at St. John's University, New York. He received his PhD from SUNY Buffalo, where he specialized in metaphysics and medieval philosophy. His current research interests include metaphysics, ethics, and the relationship between science, philosophy, and religion. He is working on a book about what zombies lack—the human soul; and in preparation for the zombie apocalypse he is considering getting a tattoo of Aquinas holding a shotgun with the words Faith, Reason, and Guns inscribed below it.

WILLIAM J. DEVLIN is associate professor at Bridgewater State University and Summer Lecturer at the University of Wyoming. He is the co-editor of *The Philosophy of David Lynch* (2011), and has published articles and book chapters in philosophy of film and philosophy of popular culture concerning such topics as time-travel, ethics, Nietzsche, and selfhood. Bill is published in edited volumes such as *The Philosophy of Steven Soderbergh* (2011), *The Philosophy of the Western* (2010), *The Philosophy of Science Fiction Film* (2008), and *Lost and Philosophy* (2008). He also publishes in the field of philosophy of science and is co-editor of the volume, *Kuhn's Structure of Scientific Revolutions: 50 Years On* (2015). Though Bill loves writing on philosophy, he has decided to trade this life to 'run' for Governor of Woodbury.

SABATINO DiBERNARDO is an Associate Lecturer in Religion, Philosophy, and Humanities at the University of Central Florida and the Director of the Religion and Cultural Studies Program. His research areas are irony studies, poststructuralism, deconstruction, and skepticism. His most recent chapter publications are included in *This Is the Sound of Irony: Music, Politics and Popular Culture* (2015) and *Music at the Extremes: Essays on Sounds Outside the Mainstream* (2015). Given his desire to provide the undead with a better quality of unlife, he speculates that music therapy might soothe the zombie beast; or, since they're attracted to noise, recruiting a few musically inclined undead to start an undeath metal band would rock! Possible band names: The Ungrateful Dead, The Wröcking Dead, or Roamer Mortis. If these experiments fail, his Fender Stratocaster may be weaponized to deliver serious blunt force trauma to a zombie head.

RICHARD GREENE is professor of philosophy at Weber State University. He's also served as Executive Chair of the Intercollegiate Ethics Bowl. He's co-edited a number of books on pop culture and philosophy including *The Sopranos and Philosophy: I Kill Therefore I Am* (2004), *Dexter and Philosophy: Mind over Spatter* (2011), *Boardwalk Empire and Philosophy: Bootleg This Book* (2013), *Girls and Philosophy: This Book Isn't a Metaphor for Anything* (2014), and *The Princess Bride and Philosophy: Inconceivable!* (2016). Richard personally knows many zombies and as long as they come to class, do the assigned readings, and raise their hands when they ask questions, he has no problem with them.

GORDON HAWKES is a graduate student in philosophy at the University of Calgary, Alberta. To him, studying philosophy is a lot like surviving in the world of *The Walking Dead*: you can only do it well with the help of others, your wardrobe becomes less of a priority, you become cautious about judging based on first appearances, and you're constantly attacking dead people.

BRANDON KEMPNER is a professor of American literature at New Mexico Highlands University. Previous chapters of his have appeared in *The Walking Dead and Philosophy: Zombie Apocalypse Now* (2012), *Neil Gaiman and Philosophy: Gods Gone Wild!* (2012), and *Jurassic Park and Philosophy: The Truth Is Terrifying* (2014). Safe in the mountains, he's waiting for the zombie apocalypse to devastate America so that he can emerge, triumphant, as a Governor-style dictator.

LEA R. LESINSKI is an honors student at St. John's University, New York. She is part of the five year Bachelors/Masters program and is double majoring in psychology and criminal justice, with a minor in philosophy. Her senior thesis in psychology was going to be on zombie behavior until the Institutional Review Board noted that zombies cannot give their informed consent. Subsequently, however, half of the IRB were eaten by zombies and she was given authorization to study the former IRB members, who are now zombies, for her Master's thesis. So, it all worked out in the end!

GREG LITTMANN is a pile of entrails on the sidewalk. He was torn apart by walkers on the campus of SIUE, where he was formerly associate professor of philosophy, publishing in metaphysics, philosophy of logic, and philosophy of professional philosophy. He has written numerous chapters for books relating philosophy to popular culture, including volumes on *Boardwalk Empire, Breaking Bad, Doctor Who, Game of Thrones, House of Cards,* and *Sons of Anarchy.* He almost made it to his car, but for a split second he got distracted by a thought about Aristotle and the dead students were upon him, ripping the flesh from his bones with their teeth. He wasn't even tasty.

MARTY McKENDRY is a lawyer and policy advisor to a Member of Parliament. He eats subs almost every day, generally while listening to the Grateful Dead in his underwear. He hopes Jerry Garcia will still be able to jam if he rises.

RICK MORRIS is a graduate student and occasional instructor in philosophy at the University of California at Davis, where he currently focuses on the philosophy of biology and on various debates in ethics. As a marine veteran, he's unreasonably confident in his ability to survive the world of the Walking Dead and will probably be eaten first.

MELISSA VOSEN CALLENS is an assistant professor of instructional design at North Dakota State University in Fargo, North Dakota. She has contributed to numerous publications including *100 Entertainers Who Changed America: An Encyclopedia of Pop Culture Luminaries*

(2013) and *A Sense of Community: Essays on the Television Series and Its Fandom* (2014). She begrudgingly shares a birthday with Merle, secretly wishing she shared one with Daryl. In preparing for the apocalypse, she avoids places with people and has learned to bake without gluten.

SETH M. WALKER teaches courses in religious studies, philosophy, and humanities at the University of Central Florida. He's also one of the founding editors of *Nomos Journal*, an online magazine engaging the intersection between religion and popular culture. Seth has contributed chapters to *Jurassic Park and Philosophy: The Truth Is Terrifying* (2014) and *Orange Is the New Black and Philosophy: Last Exit from Litchfield* (2015). He hopes to never have to choose between an undead-infested existence and a hasty thermobaric suicide, but keeps both a polished crossbow and an old military grenade handy just in case.

WAYNE YUEN is the editor of *The Walking Dead and Philosophy: Zombie Apocalypse Now* (2012), and co-editor of *Neil Gaiman and Philosophy: Gods Gone Wild!* (2012), and has contributed chapters to several other volumes in the Popular Culture and Philosophy series. He is a professor of philosophy at Ohlone College in Fremont, California, and received his MA at San Jose State University. He avoids places with flowers, and has learned how to bake his own cookies.

Index

DOCTOR WHO

POLICE PUBLIC BOX

POLICE TELEPHONE
FREE
FOR USE OF
PUBLIC

ADVICE AND ASSISTANCE
OBTAINABLE IMMEDIATELY

OFFICERS AND CARS
RESPOND TO
URGENT CALLS

PULL TO OPEN

AND PHILOSOPHY
BIGGER ON THE INSIDE

EDITED BY COURTLAND LEWIS AND PAULA SMITHKA